MAXIMUM IMPACT
SHORT-TERM MISSION

The God-commanded, Repetitive Deployment of
Swift, Temporary, Non-professional Missionaries

by

ROGER PETERSON
GORDON AESCHLIMAN
R. WAYNE SNEED

edited by

KIM HURST

STEM*Press* (a division of STEM Int'l, Inc.)
Minneapolis, Minnesota U.S.A.

MAXIMUM IMPACT SHORT-TERM MISSION
The God-commanded, Repetitive Deployment of Swift, Temporary, Non-professional Missionaries

Packaged by Pine Hill Graphics, Eugene, Oregon.
Cover design by Alpha Advertising.

Interior design: STEM*Press*, Minneapolis, Minnesota.

Printing and binding: Bethany Press International, Minneapolis, Minnesota.

Funding for research, writing, publishing, and printing was provided, in part, by grants from the PF Foundation, Des Moines, Iowa.

Published by:
STEM*Press* (a division of STEM Int'l, Inc.)
P.O. Box 386001
Minneapolis, Minnesota 55438-6001
U.S.A.
1-877-STEM-min
www.STEMmin.com
MISTMbook@STEMmin.org

ISBN 0-9711258-1-3
Printed in the United States of America.

CONTENTS

Addenda

List of Tables

List of Illustrations

PREFACE

TO DATE, ONLY COMPARATIVELY SMALL AMOUNTS OF published literature are available on short-term mission, given the purported size of the movement which we currently estimate annually at more than 1,000,000 from a globally-sent perspective (cf. Chapter 11). What presently exists are less than a dozen pieces all written from a Western, 'developed nations' perspective (i.e., most authors are either U.S. or U.K. citizens). Although we applaud the authors and publishers for their excellent entry-level efforts, we find three primary concerns not fully addressed in these previous writings:

1. *Anecdotal, non-integrated experience*

   Most of the previously-published short-term mission literature are introductory, anecdotal pieces written from a personal (and there-fore somewhat limited), non-integrated experiential basis. Until now, no piece currently exists to help the church and the broader mission community form a comprehensive, integrated understanding of the various types and kinds of short-term mission, or of how and why—or even if—God is behind this flurry of activity.

2. *Means focus and self focus*

   Earlier writings have generally focused primarily on the *means* of doing short-term mission (i.e., the pragmatic how-best-to steps), as opposed to the *ends* (i.e., the bigger picture of everyone's agenda involved, God's Kingdom purpose, the values and philosophies that undergird its decision making). The focus has also been primarily on

self (meaning the responsibilities for what we call the 'sending entity' and 'goer-guests'). Little recognition has been given to other
members of the participant trilogy (cf. Chapter 6)—members who
cannot be excluded in any short-term mission. At times the imbedded tone within some of the earlier writings seems to have come
from an untested assumption that 'we're the top dog,' and 'we have
all the answers.' This long-standing presupposition has been modeled not only by the West's traditional long-term career mission community, but by virtually every sphere of influence within the Western
societies where these books have been conceived and written.

3. *Absence of accurate industry terminology*
    Linguists and anthropologists remind us that a given word does not
    carry a precise, universal meaning among people and cultures.
    People simply affix whatever meaning they want. Entry-level writings
    within any industry can't possibly tackle such issues of terminology—
    but now with a million or more short-termers, we believe it's time to
    help their sending entities and field facilitators clarify some impor-
    tant understandings. For example, even within the traditional career
    mission community, the word 'sender' is confusing. Sometimes it
    means what we're identifying as 'sending supporters;' at other times
    it means the 'sending entity.' These two meanings are very distinct
    from each other, with very unique responsibilities within any short-
    term mission.

By God's grace we trust this book has begun to address these issues,
thereby helping the mission community advance their short-term mission
efforts to an even more mature, more strategic level for the sake of the
Kingdom of God.

Target Audience

ALTHOUGH the average short-termer (what we call the 'goer-guest') may
find this book helpful, we haven't written it for you. We're instead aiming
this book toward Western-related *short-term mission practitioners*.

Short-term mission practitioners are the sending-side and receiving-side
mission leaders within the structure Jesus set up after departing from Mount
Olivet 2,000 years ago (the church, or *ECCLESIARUM*). This includes pastors, min-

isters, lay leaders, field facilitators (expatriate missionaries, local national pastors, other local national leaders), and all others who have been given missionary responsibility as deontic (institutionally-appointed) *leader* at any level within the church and church-related structures which do Christian mission. We intend this to include the following six broad segments of church missionary leadership:

1. Christian Church Pastors, Ministers, Priests, and Other Church-appointed Leaders

This category may include the senior pastor, associate pastor, other paid staff members, mission pastor, mission committee chair, or volunteer lay leaders who have accepted specific responsibility (or those who reluctantly have it by default) from a given church body for that church's mission/evangelism/outreach program. This would entail no less than one person per church (currently there are about 350,000 Protestant churches in the United States alone).

2. Parachurch Mission Agency Leadership (Denominational and Nondenominational)

Specifically this includes three broad leadership levels within parachurch agencies: (1) the Board, CEO, Presidential, and Vice-Presidential levels of leadership (persons charged with the theory, philosophy of ministry, and *ends* results for their agency); (2) agency department heads charged with *pre-field* responsibility for the agency's short-term mission program (the *planning* people within an agency); and (3) the agency's field personnel—both national and expatriate missionary staff—responsible for the agency's *on-field* short-term mission program (the *program delivery* sector of an agency). This three-level composite of *parachurch mission agency leadership* must be viewed collectively within one of two broader classifications: (1) traditional mission agencies which may or may not have retooled their respective strategies to now include some form of short-term mission; and (2) the newer nontraditional agencies or other informal groups which focus primarily, if not exclusively, on nothing but short-term mission as their 'how-best-to' strategy for fulfilling the Great Commission.

3. Christian Schools' Mission Leadership

Many Christian high schools, colleges, and seminaries are directly sending students on some form of cross-cultural ministry outreach, often issuing school credit for this programmed activity. Therefore this book is also aimed at certain leadership levels within any educational institution—those persons to whom have been given direct responsibility for managing the institution's short-term mission sending program.

4.   Christian Mission Educators
This book is also intended for formal classroom use. It's for the professional Christian educators who have been given responsibility to train students in Christian mission, who need a solid textbook on *short-term* mission.

5.   Short-Term Mission 'Team Leaders'
Although there are differing structures of short-term mission methodology, this book is aimed at what we call the 'goer-guest leaders' where short-term mission is being done within a group, team-type of setting.

6.   Short-Term Mission Field Facilitator Leadership
Field facilitators are explained on page 160 (Chapter 6—The Participant Trilogy). Briefly, field facilitators are the on-field, on-site point people who manage the receiving-side of any short-term mission endeavor.

We've laid out this book to help readers at all experiential levels of mission delve quickly into chapters and sub-sections of perceived personal need, while easily identifying and skipping sections of little perceived personal worth. For example, those who already have a relatively good understanding of *Christian Mission* can essentially skip the entire first half of Chapter 2 (Arriving at a Definition, part I) which provides a Biblical and ecclesiastical definition of the word *mission*.

Whatever your current assessment of the contemporary short-term mission movement, we pray God will use this book to further develop your heart and mind for the express purpose of *His* Kingdom. "May Your Kingdom come, and may Your will be done throughout Your church worldwide, O Lord!"

Roger Peterson, Gordon Aeschliman, R. Wayne Sneed
January 2003

INTRODUCTION

There's a Catch to It

by JOHN M. DRESCHER

NOW IT CAME TO PASS THAT A CERTAIN GROUP CALLED THEM-selves "Fishermen." And, lo, there were many fish in the waters all around. In fact, the area was surrounded by streams and lakes filled with hungry fish.

Week after week and month after month, these fishermen met to talk about their call to fish, the abundance of fish, and how they might go about fishing. They carefully defined what fishing means, defended fishing as an occupation, and declared fishing to be a primary task of fishermen.

Continually they searched for new methods of fishing. Further they said, "The fishing industry exists by fishing as fire exists by burning." They loved slogans such as "Fishing is the task of every fisherman," and "Every fisherman is a fisher." They sponsored special meetings called "Fishermen's Campaigns" and "The Month for Fishermen to Fish." They sponsored costly nationwide and worldwide congresses to discuss and promote fishing as well as hear about all the new fishing equipment, fish calls, and bait.

These fishermen also built large, beautiful buildings called "Fishing Headquarters." They organized a board of men who had the great vision and courage to speak about fishing, to define fishing, and to promote catching fish of different colors in far-away streams.

The board also hired staffs and appointed committees to define fishing, to defend fishing, and to decide what new streams should be considered.

Large, elaborate and expensive training centers were erected to teach fishermen how to fish. Over the years courses were offered on the needs of fish, the nature of fish, where to find fish, the psychological reactions of fish, and how to approach and feed fish. Those who taught had doctorates in fishology. After tedious training, many were graduated, given fishing licenses, and sent to do full-time fishing—some to distant waters.

Many spent much study and travel to learn the history of fishing and see faraway places where the Founding Fathers had great catches in centuries past. They lauded the faithful fishermen of years before.

Further, the fishermen built large printing houses to publish fishing guides. Presses were kept busy day and night, producing materials solely devoted to fishing methods, equipment, and programs for meetings to talk about fishing. Offices were set up to schedule special speakers on the subject of fishing.

Many who felt called to be fishermen responded. They were commissioned and sent to fish. But, like the fishermen back home, they engaged in all kinds of other occupations. They built power plants to pump water for fish and tractors to plow new waterways. They traveled here and there to look at fish hatcheries, fish slaughter houses, and fishing boats. Some said they wanted to be part of the fishing party, but felt called to furnish fishing equipment.

Others felt their job was to relate to the fish, so they would know the difference between good and bad fishermen. Others felt that simply letting the fish know they were nice, land-loving neighbors was enough. A few felt that swimming lessons for the fish and better fish food would help. Some spoke of purifying the water, moving fish to other waters, or getting rid of their natural enemies.

After one stirring meeting on "The Necessity for Fishing," a young fellow left to go fishing. The next day he reported catching two outstanding fish. He was honored for his excellent catch and scheduled in big meetings to tell how he did it. So, to have time for sharing his experience with other fishermen, he quit fishing. He was also placed on the Fishermen's General Board as a person with considerable experience.

Almost no one on the Board ever fished. So those they sent out to fish did exactly as those who sent them. They formed groups and held meetings to talk about the great need for fishing. They prayed much that many fish might be caught. They analyzed the fish and discussed what is necessary to catch them. They waxed eloquent on how others fished wrongly and bemoaned the fact that fish were not processed properly when they were caught. But one thing they did not do. They did not fish.

However, they were still called fishermen by those who sent them. They wrote glowing letters back to the board and home fishing clubs about all the fishing potential. A little criticism came sometimes that no fish were caught. But because those who criticized didn't catch fish either, the criticism was not taken too seriously.

Now it's true many of the fishermen sacrificed and put up with all kinds of difficulties. Some lived near the water and bore the smell of dead fish every day. They received the ridicule of some who made fun of their fishermen's clubs and the fact that they never fished. They wondered about those who felt it was of little use to attend the weekly meetings to talk about fishing. After all, were they not obeying the Master who said, "Follow me and I will make you fishers of men?"

Imagine how hurt some were when it was suggested that those who don't catch fish are really not fishermen. Yet it did sound correct. Is a person a fisherman if year after year he never catches a fish? Is one following if he isn't fishing?

Reprinted from *OMS Outreach* (No. 7/1979) by permission of OMS International, and by the author John M. Drescher.

GOD'S FOOLS

A Biblical Model of Mission: Real People Called by God to do God's Work in a Real World

COULD SHORT-TERM MISSION BE A VALID CONTEMPORARY expression of a strategy God had in mind when Jesus reiterated[1] the Father's mission[2] 2,000 years ago? Do parts of God's church labor in vain trying to complete this glorious task, simply because we fail to contextualize and understand our times?[3] Will factions of the church continue to assign the task merely to full-time professionals, whose numbers unfortunately are diminishing with each ensuing year?

Is the church really doing MISSIO DEI (God's mission) God's way?

God's plan of mission cannot be viewed as an utopian, unattainable work of fiction, nor can it be viewed as an option slated only for the professional segment of Christianity. It is instead a doable task, but only when our human-designed initiatives intentionally incorporate the *entire* Body of Christ as active, front line agents of the Holy Spirit. Few methodologies, other than short-term mission, can so quickly unleash the world-wide, Kingdom-focused *DUNAMIS* needed to help complete the job.

Although a far cry from being issue-free in implementation, we believe the basic nature of short-term mission to align with crucial Biblical ideals often overlooked by some professionals. Fully in line with our definition (cf. Chapter 3), the basic nature of short-term mission:

- allows *swift*, immediate response by any believer—regardless of age, culture, or experience—to the action explicitly demanded by the Gospel;
- allows *temporary* engagement by Christian people not called, or not yet called, into full-time professional ministry (realistically, that's the overwhelming majority of the church);
- allows lay *non-professionals* (again, that's the overwhelming majority of the church) opportunity to perform what God commands of all disciples—regardless of age, gender, race, culture, training, social status, economic status, or experience;
- provides *repetitive deployment* opportunities to lay non-professionals over and over again—an ongoing, constant flow of people back to same on-field locations as well as new locations; and
- is a Biblically-solid, theologically-correct response to God (i.e., *God-commanded*) as we'll present within this Chapter and Chapter 10.

But that's not all. The basic nature of this wildly-escalating, mistake-laden, often times out-of-control movement called short-term mission has immense potential to readily and actively involve a much larger percentage of the entire church body—the complete 'trilogy' of mission participants (senders, goer-guests, and host receivers—cf. Chapter 6).

Yet let's be clear: we're not suggesting the *ECCLESIARUM* (the church) toss out other mission strategies, like the night janitor flings out the kitchen garbage. Every time-honed, prayer-conceived strategy has its place. Unfortunately for the average church member, some of those strategies work only within tightly knit professional circles, where entrance requirements seem to grow less amiable with each oncoming year.

Real Fools: God's Historical Norm

MUCH LIKE HIS WORD,[4] God's *plan* produces life and breath—at least to the extent we engage our lives in accord with that plan. Throughout

Biblical history God has called living, breathing people to immerse them-selves in that plan (*MISSIO HOMINUM*—God's mission for *humankind*), or according to Paul Pierson's interpretation, "to be the light to the unbelieving nations of the world."[5] In New Testament parlance, Pierson states the church—the Body of Christ—"has been called, chosen, and ordained of God to go into all of the world with the Good News of Jesus Christ"[6] (*MISSIO ECCLE-SIATO*—God's mission for the *church*).

This same scholar astutely concludes "God does not work through a vac-uum; He works through real people."[7] Missionary trainer David Harley agrees: "God has not chosen to use angels for the task of world evangelisation. He uses weak, inadequate, sinful human beings."[8] In his first letter to the church at Corinth, the Apostle Paul unequivocally blurts this same startling, yet Biblically normative, truth: "God chose what is foolish in the world ... God chose what is weak in the world ... God chose what is low and despised in the world ..." (I Corinthians 1:27). Startling, yes. But true nonetheless.

Here's where traditional mission structure (within both church and para-church) can encounter organizational heartburn—a stomach-churning, ever-since-the-fall paradox with which its present-day professional circles at times refuse to seek resolve. Real people chosen by God are almost always per-ceived as weak and foolish when screened and analyzed through the routine prepatorial and procedural practices of the world.

What organization would ever want weak, foolish people on their payroll?

JESUS RECRUITS REAL FOOLS

Yet even our Lord understood God's mission to unfold through average, real, fools. As Jesus launched His earthly ministry, His first recorded sermon (Matthew 5:3–7:27) began with a list of non-professional, *real* people including the poor in spirit, those who mourn, the meek, those hungering and thirsting for righteousness, the merciful, the pure in heart, the peacemakers, those who are reviled and persecuted for His sake (Matthew 5:3–11). In that sermon Jesus simultaneously blessed each 'category' one-by-one (i.e., "Blessed are ..."). Unfortunately it seems we often forget to include verses 13–16 within the Teacher's opening Beatitudes, which explain *why* those real people are being blessed. The reason?—without any shred of doubt is *MISSIO DEI*.

The beauty of Matthew's passage is that it so closely parallels a similar Old Testament principle of mission (we're blessed to be a blessing).[9] According to Matthew, Jesus reminds the "great crowd"[10] (of *real* people, as we have already established) that they are blessed, and as a result are now "the salt of the earth," and again, "the light of the world" (Matthew 5:13,14). In other words, the Bless-*or* (God the Son) has a reason for endowing blessing upon a bless-*ee* (in this case, real people)—the reason being so the bless-*ee* might *become a blessing* (in this metaphorical elucidation, as salt and light) to the unbelieving world.

Real Fools Have Already Been Called

Important to note is the original Greek verb tense Matthew used in verses 13 and 14 (present indicative). In other words, average, real, foolish people *are already* the salt and light of the earthly Kingdom of God—whether or not we want to be is of no accord. Further, the verb tense used is not a verb of action, but a verb of being; this only serves to emphatically emphasize the believer *is already* the salt and light of the world—regardless whether the believer understands it or not or likes it or not.

But perhaps the greater significance derived from Matthew's original text lies in the structure both sentences use to start verses 13 and 14. Jesus' statements about *already being* "the salt of the earth" and *already being* "the light of the world" both begin with the use of the personal pronoun ("Ye are . . ."). Lutheran pastor and theologian Todd Wallace observes "this is not technically necessary because the person is implied within the verb form. When a personal pronoun is used to begin a statement of being it is always for the purpose of intensifying the point being made. Literally, in English we would render it as *"You, yes YOU* are [already] the salt of the earth . . .".[11]

MISSIO ECCLESIATO must conform to *MISSIO DEI*. Any man-made plan of mission which sidesteps real, average believers who *are already* appointed as God's salt and light, overtly circumvents the design of God. Therefore it behooves us to ask the obvious question: are we structuring our Great Commission efforts to purposely include the foolish, the weak, the low, and the despised (i.e., the *real* people) in our churches? If not—then according to God's Word—we are refusing to conduct *MISSIO DEI* God's way.

APOSTOLIC RECRUITERS OF FOOLS

Not only is Saul-turned-Paul recognized as the first missionary of the early Christian church, but he is esteemed by many as the greatest missionary ever. This 'greatest missionary ever' accepted the Great Commission mandate as his personal agenda[12] (to name Christ where He has not been named); furthermore, he viewed the mandate as applicable to the *entire* Body of Christ,[13] not just a few selected professionals.

Within this entire Body, Paul understood many whom God called would not be wise according to worldly standards. He understood not many would be powerful, not many would be of noble birth. More importantly he understood God would choose "what is foolish in the world ... so that no human being might boast in the presence of God" (cf. I Corinthians 1:26–31). When a person succeeds in any task, but does not demand credit, the world deems him a fool—precisely the person God beckons on board.

Perhaps our argument can be fortified by a Pauline colleague (a *real* man: a loudmouth, foolish fisherman). In his First Epistle, Peter wrote to the Jewish exiles in Pontus, Galatia, Cappadocia, Asia, and Bythynia (I Peter 1:1) and contextualized an earlier writing of Moses:[14] "But you are a royal priesthood, a holy nation, God's own people, that you may declare the wonderful deeds of Him who called you out of darkness into His marvelous light" (I Peter 2:9).

The Royal Priesthood:
ALL Have Been Called to Declare God's Deeds
Although Peter originally penned that piece to the dispersed Jews and not to the Gentile world, colleague Paul reminds us in no uncertain terms that those words are meant for the *entire ECCLESIARUM*: "and if [we] are Christ's, then [we] are Abraham's offspring, heirs according to promise"[15] (Galatians 3:29/RSV). In other words, Peter's proclamation really states that saved membership of the *entire* church body world-wide—each one of us!—are a royal priesthood. We have *all* been called to declare God's wonderful deeds—not just Jewish brethren, not just ecclesiastical professionals—but *each one of us*. Therefore any Great Commission plan which falls short of potentially including the *entire* Body risks 'missing the mark' (*HAMARTIA*, or sin) set by God.

"Average" People vs. the Professionally Trained
Since Peter's and Paul's writings concur with both the aforementioned scholar and the missionary trainer (God works through *real* people), and their collective teachings comply with those of Christ, the church really could have a problem on its hands, a wrenching dichotomy its professional circles often find discomforting to accept. For upon faithful execution of God's plan—making disciples of Jesus from all nations—depends the salvation of the world. Surely such magnanimous a task requires only the best the church has to offer, and not our average, real people who are, well, you know, average. This

non-Biblical line of inductive thinking sucks us even deeper into the missio-logical muck: surely, then, we must *always* train ourselves in hermeneutics, mission history, church history, church planting, church growth, Greek 101, apologetics, 3-point preaching, folk religions, Islam, Hinduism, Confucianism, community development, urban mission, unreached peoples, language acquisition, evangelism, sociology, cultural anthropology—not to mention a plethora of other '-ologies'—*before* attacking God's gargantuan task!

What if St. Francis or William Carey or Gladys Aylward had followed this line of thought?

REAL CONTEMPORARY FOOLS

Francis, Carey, and Aylward are merely three of many possible post-Biblical examples today considered as historic heroes of the world Christian movement. Yet in their day, respective professional contemporaries labeled them fools. (Note: although these three are normally viewed as long-term career missionaries, it's supportive to note both Francis and Aylward—just like the Apostle Paul—continually utilized similar short-term mission methodologies [swift, temporary, and repetitive deployment], unrelentlessly moving about without planting themselves in one particular geographical locale. Even so, the purpose of this section is meant to illustrate their respective identities as 'real fools'—not whether they were short-term or long-term career folks).

Francis of Assisi[16] (1182–1226)

Francis of Assisi walked away from his family's wealth (only a fool would do such a thing—right?). The great mission historian Kenneth Scott Latourette provides historical information to help us understand why Francis would do such a thing: "He had little formal education ... At first he was a play-boy, a boon companion of the [happy-go-lucky] young scions of the local aristocracy, and a leader among them in their revelries." In late adolescence Francis began growing in his faith and "began giving himself to the service of the poor and in spite of his loathing for their disease, visited lepers and cared for them." Latourette even notes "his fellow-townsmen at first thought him insane."

Eventually his wealthy father could stand the foolish son no longer, and took Francis before the bishop to disinherit him. In a public act most rational people would deem irrationally foolish, Francis "strip[ped] himself of the clothing which he had had from his sire and [stood] naked before the bishop, declar[ing] that henceforth he desired to serve only 'our Father which art in heaven'."

Francis, of course, was the fool God used to establish the Franciscans—one of the three greatest missionary orders of the Catholic church (the other two being Dominicans and Jesuits). The Franciscans were modeled after Francis (note his swift, temporary, repetitive deployment short-term methodologies) who

> "was enthusiastically missionary in purpose and practice. He himself traversed much of Italy, preaching ... He went to Spain to open a way to Morocco ... to reach Moslems who had recently been defeated by a coalition of Christian princes ... in 1219 he went to Egypt ... [and from there] he won some who helped to spread the Franciscan movement to Northern Europe. He also presented the faith to the Sultan ... He returned to Italy (1220) by way of Palestine and Syria. Not content with himself going on missions he sent out his friars to various parts of Europe and to Morocco."

Through Francis' life of witness and influence a second and third order of Franciscans sprang up. The second, the Poor Clares, was an order for women (education- and mission-focused), and the third, the Order of Penitents, an order for lay men and lay women—unprecedented opportunities for more real fools to yoke with *MISSIO DEI* in Europe during the early thirteenth century.

William Carey[17] (1761–1834)

Carey, posthumously honored as the Father of Modern Missions, was a humble English village cobbler originally birthed into an obscure Baptist family, and "described as having the appearance and manners of a peasant. He was short in stature and usually poorly dressed ... He wore a wig because an illness had left him bald. The wig was ill-fitting and stiff." Author Basil Miller further notes "there was little in Carey's background to indicate the greatness that was to stem from his life." By even the most generous of standards, William Carey could easily have been described as just an average, foolish-looking little fellow.

Many of Carey's own colleagues also thought him a fool. During one meeting when Carey suggested they discuss whether the Great Commission was binding in their generation, the meeting's chairman exclaimed, "Young man, sit down! You are an enthusiast. When God pleases to convert the heathen He'll do it without consulting you or me ...". Historically we now see the true fool in that meeting—yet at the time the fool was perceived to be the little cobbler.

Miller continues:

> "There was no promise of genius in his youth ... from a poor English lad with little education, he became a noted Sanskrit scholar and changed the outlook of an empire. As incredible as it seems, though practically untutored, Carey gave the Bible to more of the earth's inhabitants than any other man ... His career points to the fact that God in the life of a man can achieve the impossible."

Yes, Baptist missionary William Carey was a fool—the kind of fool in whom God took pleasure, and through whom He launched the modern world-wide Protestant mission endeavor.

Gladys Aylward[18] (1902–1970)

Gladys was born into a 'common' London working-class family. Commenting on this lower socio-economic status, Trinity Evangelical Divinity Professor Ruth Tucker notes:

> "it was among that segment of society that she seemed doomed to carry out her existence. She entered the work force at the age of fourteen ... [as] a parlor maid, a genteel term for a house servant ... a job that trapped some single women for the whole of their lives. The days were routine and dull, and the occasional nights off were cut short by an early curfew. Only in her fantasies did she break out of her drab existence. Here she moved in fast circles—drinking, smoking, dancing, gambling, and attending theaters."

Saved in her mid-20s following a confrontation from a stranger concerning her relationship to Christ, Aylward's life began to change—including dreams "about serving the Lord as a foreign missionary." Those dreams brought her to China Inland Mission (CIM) in 1929 where "she was not invited to continue her training after her probationary term was over"—perhaps her contemporaries still thought her a fool?

Her next foolish step occurred three years later. As a young single woman thumbed-down by CIM, she nonetheless purchased rail passage through Europe, Russia, and Siberia into China. Even while journeying she may have appeared rather the fool to other passengers: "bundled up in an orange frock worn over a coat, Gladys was a curious looking traveler, resembling a gypsy more than a missionary." Yet when she finally arrived and began traveling around China (note her repetitive deployment short-term methodology) "her ministry blossomed. Wherever she went people came out to see her and to listen to her Bible stories ... her prestige grew ... During the years [she traveled] from village to village, she made friends and converts ...". Later, for the whopping sum of ninepence she purchased a tiny abandoned child, and eventually adopted nearly one hundred other children and spent her energies protecting them from the ravishes of the Chinese-Japanese war.

With publicity efforts of this and other missionary work by her mother and the media, Gladys Aylward rose to become an internationally known celebrity. She was in demand around the world at large churches and with such dignitaries as Queen Elizabeth.

In times past royalty may have summoned the court jester; this time it got blessed with a fool.

A BRIEF BIBLICAL REVIEW OF REAL FOOLS

Subsequent to the fall (Genesis 3:1–14), the Biblical account contains a long list of real people who may have been perceived by their contemporaries as foolish, weak, low, or despised in the ways of the world (i.e., they were *real* people), and therefore unqualified by professional standards to readily participate in *MISSIO DEI*:

- *Noah* was a lewd drunkard (Genesis 9:21);
- *Abraham* came from the pagan background of Ur (Genesis 11:28–31);
- *Moses* was a murderer (Exodus 2:11–12) and a man of "slow speech" (Exodus 4:10);
- *Rahab* was a prostitute (Joshua 2:1);
- *Hosea* married one (Hosea 1:2–3);
- *Samuel, Jehoash,* and *Josiah* were pre-pubescent boys (I Samuel 3:1–4; II Kings 11:21; and II Kings 22:1);
- *David* was not the eldest son (I Samuel 16:11–13); he was an adulterer and murderer (I Samuel 11:2–17), and later led a public parade wearing nothing except his underwear (cf. II Samuel 6:12–20);
- *Ruth*'s racial line was not of the chosen Israelites (Ruth 1:4);
- *Nehemiah* was an exiled servant (Nehemiah 1:2 and 2:2);
- *Esther* was an orphan and merely one of who-knows-how-many women in a king's harem (Esther 2:2–3,7–8);

- *Esther* and *Deborah* were women (cf. Esther 2–9; and Judges 4:4) in male-led patriarchal societies;
- *Gideon* apparently was a common farmer (Judges 6:11);
- *Jephthah* was the son of a harlot (Judges 11:1);
- *Samson* probably looked wild and unkempt (Judges 16:17);
- *Saul, Isaiah,* and *Micah* publicly exposed their nude bodies (I Samuel 19:24; Isaiah 20:2; and Micah 1:8);
- *Jeremiah* was so despised his "kindred betrayed him and the people of his native town threatened his life …;"[19]
- *Jonah* was overtly disobedient to God (Jonah 1:1–3);
- *Sarah* and *Elizabeth* were both barren and too old to conceive—and therefore considered 'useless' women in their societies (Genesis 17:17 and Luke 1:7);
- *Zechariah* doubted God (Luke 1:20);
- the *Virgin Mary* became pregnant out of wedlock (Matthew 1:18–23);
- *John the Baptist* ate, dressed, and lived like a wild man (Mark 1:6);
- *Saul of Tarsus* breathed "threats and murder against the disciples of the Lord" (Acts 9:1);
- *Timothy* was an 'unqualified' youth (I Timothy 4:12);
- *Aquila, Priscilla,* and *Lydia* were common tradespeople (Acts 18:2–3 and Acts 16:14); and
- *Philemon* owned a slave (Philemon 15–16).

A Dozen Other Fools

Several of the 12 disciples chosen by Jesus (Mark 3:13–19A) exhibited personal traits and characteristics that made them as 'real' as anyone else at the time:

- *Simon Peter* and *Andrew* were common fishermen (Mark 1:16);
- *Peter* was a liar (Luke 22:56–60);
- *Peter* and *Judas* were at times possessed by Satan (Matthew 16:23; and Luke 22:3 and John 6:70–71);
- *Levi* (Matthew) was a [hated] tax collector (Mark 2:14);
- *James* and *John* were manipulative and selfish (Mark 10:35);
- *John* and *Peter* were uneducated and common (Acts 4:13); and
- *Thomas* was a doubter (John 20:24–27).

Clearly God chooses *real* people—those who appear foolish in the world—in order to wisely accomplish His plan of mission. As He reminded the prophet Samuel who hastily assumed Jesse's eldest would be anointed King in place of Saul, "Do not look on his appearance or on the height of his stature ... for the LORD sees not as a man sees; man looks on the outward appearance, but the LORD looks on the heart" (I Samuel 16:7).[20]

Contesting the Old Paradigm

D URING early years of the Jewish Diaspora the prophet Isaiah pro-claimed, "Thus says the LORD ... 'Remember not the former things, nor consider the things of old. Behold, I am doing a new thing; now it springs forth, do you not perceive it'?" (Isaiah 43:14,18–19/RSV). Could one interpre-tation of that *new thing* be short-term mission? Or has the concept of short-term mission always been around—but blocked from view because profes-sional mission structure occludes its reality?

In one of the earliest academic studies on the topic of short-term mission (1976), a Dallas Seminary student noted professional Christianity's "almost obsessive attempt" to semantically constrain its reality:

> "Some boards have created several categories to account for the many different ways, and varying lengths of time one can minister with them in an almost obsessive attempt to maintain the special status of what for years has been defined as the 'real missionaries.' Such des-ignations have tended to make the Great Commission unapplicable [*sic*] to the whole body of Christ and, in effect, declare it to be the task of a holy few, whose right to the title *missionary* was usually inti-mately linked with the degree of their loyalty to an organization or time spent in a particular geographical area ... such designations are obviously artificial ...".[21]

This perceptive student viewed professional, traditional structure as the culprit preventing real people from engaging in mission. He chided such structure—whether intentional or unintentional—as 'not Biblical:'

> "Yet quite subtly and unintentionally the missionary mandate that was committed by our Lord Jesus Christ Himself to the universal church ... has been slowly, but surely, taken away. It has been taken away by the *organizational* church and by the many and varied 'parachurch'

structures and organizations, including mission boards, institutes, and agencies ... To the degree, however, that they have intentionally, or unintentionally, monopolized the missionary mandate by declaring the average member of the body of Christ ineligible, unqualified, and unworthy of the term missionary, they are to be faulted, for such is not the Biblical concept of missions."[22]

ACADEMIC ANARCHY:
ALTERING THE ORIGINAL INTENT

Some missiology giants—those respected elders upon whose tantalizing quotes the ECCLESIARUM sometimes builds its missiological foundations—press for a more academic, learned approach to MISSIO DEI. An Uppsala University missions professor and former bishop in Bukoba, Tanzania, argues that "knowledge of the social and religious milieu in which the service of Christ is to be fulfilled is an absolute necessity ... to bear witness to Him requires close knowledge of the situation of those religions."[23]

In no way do we abdicate responsibility to acquire 'close knowledge' of the milieu encompassing any impending mission, whether long-term or short-term. Our concern is that some professional circles have altered—ever so slightly—the former Bishop's logic, demanding its missionary force acquire 'close knowledge' *prior* to engaging in mission. Demanding 'close knowledge' be acquired *only before* engaging in mission is not the DE FACTO mandate of the Bible—regardless of human logic used to sway our rationale. Adoption of such thinking often results in non-compliance with God's mandate, especially for the average, real fool who never quite measures up to professional intellect.

Real Fools Don't Always Acquire
Sufficient 'Close Knowledge' Before Going

Consider Jonah's two-day short-term mission to Nineveh (Jonah 2:3–4,10), or Philip's one-day short-term mission with the Ethiopian eunuch (Acts 8:26–40). Did either have sufficient 'close knowledge' of their impending cross-cultural situation? Yet both men achieved success (cf. Chapter 10). What about 19-year old Bruce Olson—had he acquired sufficient 'close knowledge' of either the Yukos or Motilones (two South American Indian tribes) before engaging in mission?[24] Although he clearly prepared himself as much as possible before going, Olson's *primary* 'close knowledge' acquisition occurred *as he was going* and in the very midst of doing *MISSIO DEI*—specifically while on the field searching for, and eventually finding and living with, an utterly unreached people group called the Motilone Indians.

Real Fools Often Acquire
Sufficient 'Close Knowledge' "As They Are Going..."

Of the seven so-called New Testament Great Commission texts (cf. endnote #1), perhaps Matthew's ascension version is quoted most often: "Go therefore and make disciples of all nations ..." (Matthew 28:19/RSV). Matthew's primary verb emphasis is 'disciple' (i.e., 'to make disciples' from the original "disciple ye all the nations"[25]) with the secondary emphasis on 'going.' Yet of more importance than which verb has primary dominance, is the original Greek tense Matthew used for the secondary verb (translated in the KJV, RSV, NIV, and most other translations as) 'go.' The word is not a simple command in the imperative form (like commanding Fido to "Sit!" or "Fetch!"), but a participle in the present active indicative form; its status is much more accurately translated as, 'as you are going,' or 'as you go along in life.' In other words, Christ (to Whom has been given all authority in heaven and on earth) is commanding God's people (the *real* people, the foolish in the world) to 'make disciples as a normal part of our daily life, and do so wherever it is we are going.' Our personal involvement in *MISSIO DEI* is really much less complicated than some professionals have led us to believe.

When we give too much emphasis to pre-field academic preparation, we begin factoring out the Holy Spirit. The more a missionary relies on academic head knowledge, the less opportunity the unexplainable wind of the Holy Spirit has to work.[26] Certainly this is one reason Jesus told us not to worry about what to say (because the Holy Spirit *wants* to speak through us).[27] *MISSIO HOMINUM* will achieve success with *MISSIO DEI* only to the extent it relies *more* on the Holy Spirit than it does its acquired pre-field academic head knowledge (even though adequate preparation—which is much more than just head knowledge alone—is always important). That's why God chooses fools. Church mission structures (*MISSIO ECCLESIATO*) should purpose to do the same.

Academic Rationale vs.
the Holy Spirit and God's Word

Fortunately not all missiology giants succumb to the professional approach to mission. A former Fuller Theological Seminary School of World Mission professor seems fully cognitive of the malicious use of human philosophy used to rationalize certain methodologies. Arthur Glasser cites Max Warren's warning that the Holy Spirit's operations are "incalculable [and] uncontrollable as the wind ... unless the missionary movement can be responsive to the unpredictability of the Holy Spirit, it will soon cease to be a movement."[28] He also notes a Charles Bennett observation which reminds the church of its responsibility to weigh academic reason against the reality of God's Word: "in our study of missionary methods ... we sometimes 'discover' laws and principles in the Scriptures where none, in fact exist ...".[29] May God forgive the professional church for 'discovering' those groomed, orderly missiological 'laws' which bridle God's fools from full participation in *MISSIO DEI*!

In his retirement years after having strategized, taught, and authored extensively on Christian mission, missiology giant Herb Kane comes to this radical conclusion:

> "We may be entering a new era when missionary work will not be left to professional missionaries, but will be the common task of the rank and file of church members in the course of their daily occupations.

> "... [L]ay persons in all walks of life are making an unprecedented attempt to get involved in world evangelization ... This trend should by all means be encouraged. Not only young people but also middle-aged people and senior citizens should be encouraged to get involved in various kinds of Christian service at home and overseas ... there is no reason for anyone to hesitate to spend a summer overseas."[30]

And as former Wheaton College campus pastor Dennis Massaro asserts, "The short-term mission movement is rooted in the Scriptures [as we'll further explain in Chapter 10] and will continue to be a driving force for the advancement of the global cause of Jesus Christ."[31]

Summary

IN ITS well-intentioned efforts to tackle the Great Commission task, the church has often birthed structures *limiting* involvement rather than facilitating involvement. Yet the Great Commission applies to all disciples everywhere. Our Biblical mandate, with roots reaching several millennia into Old Testament history, must be repackaged today into a facilitating structure which purposely releases the church's average man and woman, the church's average boy and girl—the laity, the non-professionals, the real people, the people who appear foolish, the people who appear weak, the people who appear low, the people who appear despised in the world. That package looks, tastes, and smells quite like what the church already calls 'short-term mission.'

For every additional hour required of preparation, for every additional characteristic demanded of our recruits, there will be thousands—perhaps millions?—who remain sidelined as too average, too real, too foolish to that particular expression of *missio Dei*. In our feeble attempts to birth a missionary without spot or blemish, the world continues going to hell without Jesus Christ.

The more we understand about the size, shape, and weight of this new package, how to "judge with right judgement" (John 7:24) its pros and cons within a comprehensive integrated framework of the big-picture analysis, and how to best synthesize it into other expressions of *missio Dei*, the better our chances of "equipping ... the saints for the work of ministry" (Ephesians 4:12/NKJV). Then we come closer to the standard God has set—mobilizing the *entire* Body of Christ into the world that God so loves.

Endnotes
Chapter 1

1. *(p. 15)* The seven so-called Great Commission texts (all of which were spoken directly by Jesus Himself) implied throughout this book are deemed to be: (1) Matthew 24:14; (2) Matthew 28:19–20; (3) Mark 13:10; (4) Mark 16:15–16; (5) Luke 24:47; (6) John 20:21; and (7) Acts 1:8. Of these, #1 and #3 are the two pre-resurrection prophetic versions, while the remaining five are the post-resurrection versions.

2. *(p. 15)* The 'Father's Mission' (or 'mission') is discussed in more detail in Chapter 2 (cf. Genesis 12:1–3; Isaiah 49:6; Matthew 28:19–20; *et al*).

3. *(p. 15)* Cf. I Chronicles 12:32 and Esther 1:13.

4. *(p. 16)* Among the most significant parallel attributes, God's Word produces life and health, it is God-breathed, and is living and active (cf. Proverbs 4:20–22; II Timothy 3:16; and Hebrews 4:12).

5. *(p. 17)* **Paul E. Pierson**, *Historical Development of the Christian Movement* (Pasadena CA: Fuller School of World Mission, In-Service Program MH520, Audio Tape #1). Dr. Pierson was Dean of Fuller Theological Seminary's School of World Mission from 1980 until 1992.

6. *(p. 17)* *Ibid.*

7. *(p. 17)* *Ibid.*

8. *(p. 17)* **C. David Harley**, *Preparing to Serve—Training for Cross-Cultural Mission* (Pasadena CA: William Carey Library, 1995), p. 67.

9. *(p. 17)* In Matthew chapter 5, we believe one of the intents of Jesus' sermon's opening remarks was to restate part "B" (Genesis 12:3) of the original Abrahamic covenant (cf. Genesis 12:1–3; Genesis 18:18; Genesis 22:18; Genesis 26:4; Genesis 28:14; Acts 3:25; and Galatians 3:8), which provides understanding why God blesses a people—so that the blessed person(s) may in turn bless other persons, specifically with the greatest blessing of all, the glorious Good News of God. [For more in-depth discussion of part "B" of the Abrahamic covenant, consult the JOHN R. W. STOTT article, "The Living God is a Missionary God," found in: **Ralph D. Winter and Steven C. Hawthorne, eds.**, *Perspectives on the World Christian Movement* (Pasadena CA: William Carey Library, 1999), pp. 3–9.]

10. *(p. 17)* Matthew 4:25. Although Matthew 5:1 initially may seem to suggest Jesus delivered the entire Sermon on the Mount only to the (twelve) disciples, the entire Sermon (Matthew 5:3–7:27) must be viewed within the context of preceding and subsequent verses, vv. 4:25 and 7:28, where Matthew leaves no doubt Jesus was speaking to the entire crowd, and not merely the (twelve) disciples.

11. *(p. 18)* Personal theological response, by request, from Rev. Todd Wallace to Roger Peterson dated May 1998.

12. *(p. 18)* Cf. Acts 9:15; Acts 13:2; Acts 20:16–21; Acts 21:13; Acts 22:21; Acts 26:14–19; Romans 1:1–5; Romans 1:13–14; Romans 15:18–21; *et al.*

13. *(p. 19)* No Scripture reference *directly* proof-texts this claim. However when we consider Paul dispensed the "whole counsel of God" (Acts 20:27), and viewed his own job description as "further[ing] the faith of God's elect and their knowledge of the truth" (Titus 1:1), and that he "fought the good fight...[and]...finished the race" (II Timothy 4:7), wouldn't we conclude the 'whole counsel' and 'furthering the knowledge of the truth'—completed within the context of the 'finished race'—to include applicability of the Great Commission? Secondly, Paul saw the *entire* church as recipients of God's truth, not just a few selected professionals (cf. Acts 20:20). Thirdly, Paul always had other people with him on his missionary journeys—many of whom Scripture does not name (they must have been just average, foolish people). Therefore we conclude Paul did indeed view the Great Commission mandate as applicable to the entire Body.

14. *(p. 19)* Exodus 19:6.

15. *(p. 19)* Cf. Romans 4:16–17; Romans 9:6–8; Romans 10:12–13; I Corinthians 12:13; Galatians 3:7–9; Galatians 3:28; and Colossians 3:9–11. Although the Galatians 3:28 Scripture is specifically a salvation issue (salvation as a result of justification by faith), its phrase "neither Jew nor Greek" further illustrates that all nationalities who belong to Christ—not merely the Messianic Jews—are Abraham's offspring, and therefore rightful heirs to all Scriptural promises made to Abraham and his cultural lineage. Further understanding is provided by Anglican theologian John R.W. Stott, who reminds us Paul leaves no doubt that
> "the true beneficiaries of God's promises...are believers in Christ of whatever race. In Romans 4 he points out that Abraham not only received justification by faith but also received this blessing *before he had been circumcised*. Therefore Abraham is the father of all those who, whether circumcised or uncircumcised (that is, Jews or Gentiles), 'follow the example of [his] faith' (Romans 4:9–12). If we 'share the faith of Abraham,' then 'he is the father of us all, as it is written, "I have made you the father of many nations"' (vv. 16–17). Thus neither physical descent from Abraham, nor physical circumcision as a Jew, makes a person a true child of Abraham, but rather faith. Abraham's real descendants are believers in Jesus Christ, whether racially they happen to be Jews or Gentiles" [JOHN R. W. STOTT, "The Living God is a Missionary God," found in: **Ralph D. Winter and Steven C. Hawthorne, eds.**, *Perspectives on the World Christian Movement* (Pasadena CA: William Carey Library, 1999), p. 7].

16. *(p. 20)* All quoted material on Francis of Assisi is taken directly from: **Kenneth Scott Latourette**, *A History of Christianity—Volume I: Beginnings to A.D. 1500* (New York NY: Harper San Francisco, 1975), pp. 429–432.

17. *(p. 21)* All quoted material on William Carey is taken directly from: **Basil Miller**, *William Carey—The Father of Modern Missions* (Minneapolis MN: Bethany House Publishers, 1980), pp. 1–35.

18. *(p. 22)* All quoted material on Gladys Aylward is taken directly from: **Ruth A. Tucker**, *From Jerusalem to Irian Jaya* (Grand Rapids MI: Academie Books, 1983), pp. 249–254.

19. *(p. 24)* **Clarence H. Benson**, *Old Testament Survey—Poetry and Prophecy* (Wheaton IL: Evangelical Teacher Training Association, 1972), p. 49–50.

20. *(p. 25)* Cf. I Samuel 2:3; I Kings 8:39; I Chronicles 28:9; and Luke 16:15.

21. *(p. 25)* **Donald Kitchen**, *The Impact and Effectiveness of Short-Term Missionaries* (Dallas TX: Dallas Theological Seminary Department of World Missions, 1976), p. 6.

22. *(p. 26)* *Ibid.*, pp. 12–13.

23. *(p. 26)* **Brengt Sundkler**, *The World of Mission* (Grand Rapids MI: Wm. B. Eerdmans Publishing Company, 1965), p. 47.

24. *(p. 26)* Cf. **Bruce E. Olson**, *Bruchko* (Altamonte Springs FL: Creation House, 1989).

25. *(p. 27)* *The Zondervan Parallel New Testament in Greek and English* (Grand Rapids MI: The Zondervan Corporation, 1981), Matthew 28:19, p. 101.

26. *(p. 27)* Cf. John 3:8.

27. *(p. 27)* Cf. Matthew 10:19–20; Mark 13:11; Luke 12:11–12; Luke 21:14–15; John 14:26; and I John 2:27. Although the first three of these first five references were spoken within the context of not worrying about what to speak or say when "being delivered up to councils...and beaten in synagogues...and dragged before governors and kings for [Jesus'] sake," the collective understanding of all six references seems clearly to imply the disciple of Christ can trust the Holy Spirit for the right words at the right time.

28. *(p. 28)* **Arthur F. Glasser**, *The Kingdom and Mission* (Pasadena CA: Fuller Theological Seminary School of World Mission, 1989), p. 266.

29. *(p. 28)* *Ibid.*, p. 267.

30. *(p. 28)* **Herbert J. Kane**, *Wanted: World Christians* (Grand Rapids MI: Baker Book House, 1986), pp. 208–209.

31. *(p. 28)* DENNIS MASSARO, "Short-Term Missions" entry contained in: **A. Scott Moreau, ed.,** *Evangelical Dictionary of World Missions* (Grand Rapids MI: Baker Books, 2000), p. 874.

(pp. 16–28) This book, originally conceived by Gordon Aeschliman and Roger Peterson, was in the making for a period of 9 years. Chapter 1 was completed by Roger Peterson several years prior to this book's publication, and in 1999 approximately 12 paragraphs contained within pages 16–28 of Chapter 1 were excerpted from this unfinished work. They were transferred to another work published by the same publisher, STEM*Press.* [Cf. **Daniel P. McDonough and Roger P. Peterson**, *Can Short-Term Mission Really Create Long-Term Missionaries?* (Minneapolis MN: STEM Ministries, 1999), pp. 26–28.]

DEFINING 'MISSION'

SINCE 'SHORT-TERM' ACTS AS A MODIFIER TO THE NOUN 'mission,' we first need to understand the nature of Christian mission itself, before ever thinking we can understand or explain what its modifier 'short-term' may mean. In this chapter we'll provide a theological/Biblical basis of *MISSIO DEI*, and also bring in a contemporary human perspective derived from our viewpoints and the viewpoints of the three major theological traditions.

In 1975 Anglican theologian John R.W. Stott encouraged what we trust is a basal norm for every person who names Jesus Christ as Lord, regardless of ecclesiastical affiliation: "All of us should be able to agree that mission arises primarily out of the nature not of the church but of God Himself. The living God of the Bible is a sending God."[1]

Stott goes on to theologically support this position, providing what he calls 'the essential Biblical background to any understanding of mission:'

"So He sent forth Abraham, commanding him to go from his country and kindred into the great unknown, and promising to bless him and to bless the world through him if he obeyed (Genesis 12:1–3). Next, He sent Joseph into Egypt, overruling even his brothers' cruelty, in order to preserve a Godly remnant on earth during the famine (Genesis 45:4–8). Then He sent Moses to His oppressed people in Egypt, with good news of liberation, saying to him: 'Come, I will send you to Pharaoh that you may bring forth my people . . . out of Egypt' (Exodus 3:10). After the Exodus and the settlement He sent a continuous succession of prophets with words of warning and of promise to His people. As He said through Jeremiah: 'From the day that your fathers came out of the land of Egypt to this day, I have persistently sent all my servants the prophets to them, day after day, yet they did not listen to me . . .' (Jeremiah 7:25,26; cf. II Chronicles 36:15,16). After the Babylonian captivity He graciously sent them back to the land, and sent more messengers with them and to them to help them rebuild the temple, the city and the national life. Then at last 'when the time had fully come, God sent forth His Son;' and after that the Father and the Son sent forth the Spirit on the Day of Pentecost (Galatians 4:4–6; John 14:26; 15:26; 16:7; Acts 2:33).

"All this is the essential Biblical background to any understanding of mission. The primal mission is God's, for it is He Who sent His prophets, His Son, His Spirit. Of these missions the mission of the Son is central, for it is the culmination of the ministry of the prophets, and it embraced within itself as its climax the sending of the Spirit. And now the Son sends [us] as He Himself was sent."[2]

Now let's expand on Stott's summary a bit by considering for the next few moments one of Gordon Aeschliman's earlier writings describing Christian mission, extracted from *The Hidden Half*, Chapter Six, "A Blessing to All Nations:"[3]

❖   ❖   ❖

RIGHT AT THE BEGINNING OF SCRIPTURE, SHORTLY AFTER THE ACCOUNTS OF THE FALL, the flood and the tower of Babel, God visited a man called Abram. He gave Abram a strange command and some amazing promises.

> "Leave your country, your people and your father's household and go to the land I will show you. I will make you into a great nation and I will bless you; I will make your name great and you will be a blessing. I will bless those who bless you, and whoever curses you I will curse; and all peoples on earth will be blessed through you" (Genesis 12:1-3).

Many Christians through the years have had a great deal of respect for Israel, and rightly so—being made into a great nation by God, from the beginning of history, is no small thing. But all too often we miss the whole point of God's singling out Israel. The key to Israel's role in the Old Testament world is given at the end of verse three: "... and all peoples on earth will be blessed through you."

God chose Israel as a channel of his blessing. In his desire to reach the whole world with his love, God chose Israel, blessed it, and made it a standard of righteousness to show the other nations that the Lord is the only true God.

Much like Mary, the mother of Jesus, Israel simply acted as a channel through which the Messiah, the Savior, was presented to the nations. Israel wasn't great because of the number of people or the wars it won or the cities it built—Israel was great because God called the nation to demonstrate his character and love to the nations around it.

From Genesis to Revelation, God's strategy for winning the nations shows up again and again. In the Old Testament, God chose to bring his salvation to the nations primarily through Israel. In the New Testament, he works through a "new Israel"—the Church. After the death and resurrection of Christ, Christians are God's channels of blessing to the nations.

Spread It Around!

There were many ways that God worked through Israel. Israel demonstrated its special relationship with God in its political structure and relations with other nations. Israel was the only nation ever called to represent God as a political body. The law given to Moses ordered every facet of life.

Israel's king was God. The other nations had their kings and gods, too. When Israel went to war, the battle was between the God of Israel and the ruler of the other nation. And if Israel won the battle, it proved that its God was superior.

When Israel was meticulously obedient to God, not one of its soldiers would be wounded. Thousands of the enemy's men would die or surrender, but there was not a soldier scathed from the army of the Hebrew God! The other nations took note!

But whenever Israel sinned or chose to do things its way, it suffered injuries and even defeat. It was obvious to the other nations, who was behind Israel's victories.

Israel was to demonstrate the love of God as well as his power by showing hospitality and kindness to strangers and outcasts. Throughout Scripture, God emphasized his concern for these people.

> "Do not mistreat an alien or oppress him" (Exodus 22:21).
> "The alien living among you must be treated as one of your native-born. Love him as yourself, for you were aliens in Egypt. I am the Lord your God" (Leviticus 19:34).
> "Cursed is the man who withholds justice from the alien, the father-less or the widow" (Deuteronomy 27:19).

Other nations would be attracted to this strange Hebrew God who demanded that kindness be shown to the alien. As they lived out God's love and justice and power, Israel would reveal the name of their God to the nations around them.

"What's in a name?" you might ask. Well, let's see what God says about his name:

> "I will cause all my goodness to pass in front of you, and I will proclaim my name, the Lord, in your presence. ... And he passed in front of Moses, proclaiming, "The Lord, the Lord, the compassionate and gracious God, slow to anger, abounding in love and faithfulness, maintaining love to thousands, and forgiving wickedness, rebellion and sin. Yet he does not leave the guilty unpunished..." (Exodus 33:19; 34:6–7).

These were the Lord's words to Moses on Mount Sinai. This God was totally unlike the gods of the other nations. Israel was to present that Name to the nations. The goodness of God was "good news" for the nations.

A Blessing to the Nations

Even Abram, the one God gave the promise to, had to be reminded again and again that God really would make him into a great nation and bless the world through him. God brought him through years of testing to prepare him to be that blessing.

Abram's first struggles of faith came as he grew older and didn't yet have a son. How could he ever be the father of a great nation?

The Lord came and repeated his promise. He didn't immediately give Abram a son, but instead demonstrated the seriousness of his promise. He had Abram get a heifer, a goat, a ram, a pigeon and a dove. Abram cut the animals in half and separated the carcasses. A blazing torch appeared and passed between the halves.

This was a customary way of making very serious promises. It meant, "May what happened to these animals happen to me if I don't keep my word." And God repeated his promise that Abram's descendants would possess the land.

A few years later, when Abram was 99 and still without an heir, God prepared him further for the great role he would play in blessing the nations (Genesis 17:5).

Even before the birth of Isaac, Abraham got a taste of what Israel's role before God would be. God told him that Sodom and Gomorrah were about to be judged for their sin, and he gave Abraham a chance to intercede for those cities. Scripture makes it clear that this too was part of God's long-range plan for Abraham and his descendants.

> "Shall I hide from Abraham what I am about to do? Abraham will surely become a great and powerful nation, and all nations on earth will be blessed through him" (Genesis 18:17–18).

There was one more test in store for Abraham—one more opportunity to make sure he understood God's purposes. God told Abraham to take his son Isaac up the mountain and offer him as a burnt sacrifice.

You might expect Abraham to shout: "Give me a break, will you?" But by this time he fully trusted that God would make him a channel of blessing to the nations—even if he didn't understand how. So he went up the mountain, built the altar, arranged the wood and was about to plunge the knife into his son's chest when God stopped him. The Lord couldn't conceal his joy from Abraham:

> "I swear by myself... through your offspring all nations on earth will
> be blessed, because you have obeyed me" (Genesis 22:16,18).

The Old Testament Thread

The promise was repeated not only to Isaac and Jacob, but over and over to Israel throughout the Old Testament.

The Psalms expressed the heights of Israel's worship, and they are full of references to the nations worshiping God, too.

> "Among the gods there is none like you, O Lord ... All the nations
> you have made will come and worship before you, O Lord; And they
> will bring glory to your name" (Psalm 86:8–9).
> "All the ends of the earth will remember and turn to the LORD, and all the
> families of the nations will bow down before him ..." (Psalm 22:27).
> "Shout with joy to God, all the earth! Sing to the glory of His name ...
> So great is your power that your enemies cringe before you. All the
> earth bows down to you ... they sing praise to you..." (Psalm 66:1–4).

The following blessing might sound familiar to you from church, but look at the whole Psalm.

> "May God be gracious to us and bless us and make his face shine upon
> us; may your ways be known on earth, your salvation among all
> nations. May the peoples praise you, O God; may all the peoples
> praise you. May the nations be glad and sing for joy, for you rule the
> peoples justly and guide the nations of the earth. May the peoples
> praise you, O God; may all the peoples praise you. Then the land will
> yield its harvest, and God, our God, will bless us. God will bless us,
> and all the ends of the earth will fear him" (Psalm 67).

The prophets called Israel to remember its purpose as a nation. And when Israel's disobedience got in the way of the nations' knowing God, the prophets made it clear that God would bless the nations as he had promised.

Therefore, say to the house of Israel, "This is what the Sovereign Lord says: It is not for your sake, O house of Israel, that I am going to do these things, but for the sake of my holy name, which you have profaned among the nations where you have gone. And I will show the holiness of my great name, which has been profaned among the nations, the name you have profaned among them. Then the nations will know that I am the LORD," declares the Sovereign LORD, "when I show myself holy through you before their eyes" (Ezekiel 36:22–23).

Revival in Israel was to extend to the nations:

"I will cleanse [Israel] from all the sin which they have committed against me and will forgive all their sins of rebellion against me. Then this city will bring me renown, joy, praise and honor before all the nations on earth that hear of all the good things I do for it; and they will be in awe and tremble at the abundant prosperity and peace I will provide for it" (Jeremiah 33:8–9).

The Messiah was promised, not only as Israel's King, but as the Savior and King of the nations.

"Here is my servant, whom I uphold, my chosen one in whom I delight; I will put my spirit on him and he will bring justice to the nations. He will not falter or be discouraged, till he establishes justice on earth. In his law the islands will put their hope" (Isaiah 42:1,4).

"In my vision at night I looked, and there before me was one like a son of man, coming with the clouds of heaven. He approached the Ancient of Days and was led into his presence. He was given authority, glory and sovereign power; all peoples, nations and men of every language worshiped him. His dominion is an everlasting dominion that will not pass away and his kingdom is one that will never be destroyed" (Daniel 7:13–14).

Back to the Temple

Remember how Jesus cleared out the temple because of the abuse of the Gentile courtyard?

When Solomon dedicated the temple he prayed a long prayer. His prayer dealt with two areas: how the temple would be a source of cleansing and healing for individuals and how it would be a blessing to the nations. In fact, the former is a means of ensuring the latter.

"As for the foreigner who does not belong to your people Israel but has come from a distant land because of your name—for men will hear of your great name and your mighty hand and your outstretched arm—when he comes and prays toward this temple, then hear from heaven, your dwelling place, and do whatever the foreigner asks of you so that all the peoples of the earth may know your name and fear you ... and may know that this house I have built bears your name. And may these words of mine which I have prayed before the Lord, be near to the Lord our God day and night, that he may uphold the cause of his servant and the cause of his people Israel according to each day's need, so that all of the peoples of the earth may know that the Lord is God and that there is no other" (I Kings 8:41–43, 59–60).

Loving Other Nations

The Old Testament is full of stories of individuals who demonstrated the love of God by touching the lives of people from other nations. Here are just a few:

- Abraham intercedes for Sodom and Gomorrah (Genesis 18);
- Joseph saves thousands of Egyptians and other surrounding nations from starvation (Genesis 41);
- Joshua spares Rahab and her Canaanite family (Joshua 2, 6:22–23);
- Naomi is a blessing to Ruth, a Moabite (Ruth);
- Solomon shares his wisdom with Sheba, an Arabian (I Kings 10);
- Elisha heals Naaman, a Syrian soldier (2 Kings 5); and
- Daniel witnesses to the kings of Babylon and Persia (Daniel).

But the sad fact remains that the net actions of the nation of Israel were a big negative. People who reached out to other nations were the exception rather than the rule. Old Jonah was typical of Israel's attitude.

Israel never forgot that they were a chosen people—unfortunately, they forgot what they were chosen to do. The call to bless the nations runs all through Scripture, yet the Jews kept missing it. Perhaps it was this tragic failure of his people that Jesus wept over as he looked out over Jerusalem.

Fortunately, God's faithfulness does not depend on ours. Even Jonah remembered the words God used to describe his name to Moses on Mount Sinai: "Compassionate and gracious, slow to anger, abounding in loving kindness and truth" (Jonah 4:2). In the New Testament, God turned the Old Testament's story of failure around.

❖   ❖   ❖

OUR CURRENT
UNDERSTANDING OF CHRISTIAN 'MISSION'

The etymology of the English word 'mission' dates 1606 A.D. from Latin words such as *MISSIO* (a letting go, sending away, or a release from captivity, setting at liberty, liberation) or *MITTERE* from their Latin root *MITTO* (to cause to go, let go, send, to send off, despatch, or to send word, announce, tell, report anything to anyone). The word has evolved today to its commonly-accepted English definition meaning "a ministry commissioned by a religious organization to propagate its faith or carry on humanitarian work [or] assignment ... or work in a field of missionary enterprise."[4,5]

The Greek *APOSTOLOS* (messenger, ambassador, envoy, or an apostle) can also contain within itself the definition of 'mission' when used in Literary Greek. In New Testament Greek, its root *APOSTELLO* literally means "to send forth ... to send on service, or with a commission." Closely-related Biblical Greek words include *PEMPO* (to send, send forth), *EXAPOSTELLO* (to send forth, to send away), *EKPEMPO* (to send forth, being sent forth, sent away), and *APOLUO* (to set free, to let go—not commissioning, but letting go).[6,7]

As shown above in both its Latin and Greek semantic origins, the word 'mission' contains a wonderfully rich and prominent sense of *sending*, or of *being sent*—specifically *sending a messenger to announce and effect "liberty!"* To Christians, then, 'mission' always entails *sending messengers to announce with word and demonstrate with deed the Good News that sets anybody free from anything that binds them.*

So much for that brief chronicle on the origins of the word mission. If we agree the basal definition of Christian mission is *to send*, the next logical step to help us better understand Christian mission is to apply the journalistic questions:

- *Who* (whom) do we send?
- *What* do we send?
- *Where* do we send?
- *When* do we send?
- *Why* do we send?
- *How* do we send?

Who (Whom) Do We Send?

We send missionaries!—people intentionally sent into another culture to be active Gospel messengers in both word and deed.

Who, then, is qualified to be a missionary? This book argues that the Bible tells us any believer—no, *every* believer!—is called as a missionary, regardless of age, gender, culture, race, experience, training, social status, or economic status. Yet since most believers may not be called as full-time paid professional missionaries, the vehicle of short-term mission allows remaining believers—the part-time unpaid non-professionals (common sense tells us that's the overwhelming majority of the church worldwide)—opportunity to respond to the missionary action explicitly demanded by the Gospel.

What Do We Send?

Based upon the simple etymological study of the word 'mission' presented above, *what* we send is first and foremost an announcement, a proclamation of news. But as viewed throughout all of Scripture, we understand that such news is not just any old announcement *per se*, but rather some form or another of what we now call God's 'Good News!' The Old Testament proclamations and announcements of Good News prophetically pointed to a Messiah and the cross. Now in our New Testament post-resurrection times, the proclamations and announcements of Good News are some level or another of conveying that Jesus Christ is the foretold Messiah for every tribe, tongue, and nation, that He is the sinless Son of God, that He was crucified on a cross and shed his blood to pay the penalty for our sins, that He rose from the grave, and that if we truly repent, know, and believe (nothing more is required!),[8] we have eternal life. However, mere *verbal* proclamation of this Good News is in and of itself not complete, as we'll soon discuss below.

Scripture, when studied as a whole and understood within its entire context, clearly shows that God's Good News is only complete when it is proclaimed in *both* word and deed. The Apostle James has two perspectives on this. First, he tells us that *hearing and receiving the Word* is not complete unless we act, unless we do, unless we perform deeds correlated to that Word (James 1:22–35). Secondly, he tells us in no uncertain terms *our faith* without works, without deeds, isn't real and is in fact actually dead (James 2:14–26). These are hard words, yes—so hard in fact, that the great Protestant reformation leader Martin Luther didn't believe the Book of James belonged in the Canonical Scriptures!

But most persuasive to this understanding that proclamation of Good News means *both* word and deed, is Jesus' own declaration of His job description shortly after the official launch of His earthly ministry:

"The Spirit of the Lord is upon me,
because He has anointed me to preach
Good News to the poor.
He has sent me to proclaim release to the captives
and recovering of sight to the blind,
to set at liberty those who are oppressed,
to proclaim the acceptable year of the Lord" (Luke 4:18–19/RSV).

Compare Luke's version above, with the text Jesus was quoting (and prophetically fulfilling) from Isaiah below:

"The Spirit of the Lord God is upon me,
because the Lord has anointed me
to bring good tidings to the afflicted;
He has sent me to bind up the brokenhearted,
to proclaim liberty to the captives,
and the opening of the prison to those who are bound;
to proclaim the year of the Lord's favor,
and the day of vengeance of our God;
to comfort all who mourn" (Isaiah 61:1–2/RSV).

Now let's examine the crucial action verbs of Jesus' job description in both passages as they pertain to our argument that the proclaimed Good News means *both* word and deed. Notice the wonderful, inseparable blending of Good News *oral*-proclamation verbs (preach, proclaim) with Good News *deed*-proclamation verbs (bring, bind, set, comfort):

Isaiah 61:1–2	*Oral-proclamation*	*Deed-proclamation*
• to bring		✓
• to bind		✓
• to proclaim (twice)	✓✓	
• to comfort		✓

Luke 4:18–19		
• to preach	✓	
• to proclaim	✓	
• to set at liberty		✓
• to proclaim	✓	

The proclamation, the announcing, the preaching of the Gospel is paramount with respect to the original understanding of both words 'send' and 'mission'—but Scripturally, our understanding lags incomplete unless performed as *both* word and deed.

Now the big question becomes, "What, then, are the deeds we need to *deed*-proclaim?" As we'll point out later in this same chapter, Emilio Castro contends, "We are free to engage in all kinds of human activities [i.e., *deed*-proclamations] provided that those human activities become entry points to the Kingdom, and from there we point in the direction of Jesus" (cf. endnote #24).

Finally, please note that throughout this book we refer to the aggregate *oral*-proclamations and *deed*-proclamations (i.e., the object of *what* we send) interchangeably as one or more of the following italicized phrases:

- *activity* (cf. Chapter 3, variable #2);
- *goer-guests' giving/sowing* portion of the 'Two-way On-field Serendipity' (cf. Chapter 7); or
- *target tasks, intended tasks, intended activity,* or *ministry activity*

Where Do We Send?

Based on what we've seen so far in the section above, it should be clear that there are no geographical, no geopolitical, no cultural, no ethnic, no nothing!—no borders, limits, or boundaries whatsoever in terms of *where* we should send.

Yet when we examine the context of the Biblical texts where many of the *sending* words appear, it often is a sending *away* from one's culture, *away* from one's home, and *into another* culture or another people group or another nation. From our sender's perspective, this *other* culture (people or nation) is in essence an 'intended receptor' (cf. Chapter 6)—the human beings or other aspects of God's creation, or of human creation, which are the intended recipients of the missionary's *activity* (i.e., Good News words and Good News deeds). Here are a few selected examples:

Genesis 12:1–3

God sent Abram (Abraham) *away* from his country, his people, and his father's household, and *into another* land (the name or location of which God did not reveal at the time He sent Abram).

INTENDED RECEPTORS: "all peoples on earth."

Genesis 37:12–50:21

God sent Joseph (via the cruel jealously of his brothers) *away* from his family and his home in Canaan, and *into* Egypt not only to preserve his own family during seven years of severe famine in response to the "I will bless you ..." promise He made to Abraham, but also to be an influential witness of Godly integrity to the Egyptian peoples as well.

INTENDED RECEPTORS: the hungry peoples of ungodly Egypt and Canaan.

Numbers 13:16–31

God sent 12 spies (via Moses—cf. Numbers 13:1–2, 16–17) *away* from Israel encamped at Kadesh in the dry Desert of Paran, and *into* the fruitful hill country of Canaan—where the Anak giants and the Hittites, Jebusites, Canaanites, and the Amorites lived.

INTENDED RECEPTORS: the peoples and lands of Canaan.

Nehemiah 1–2

God sent Nehemiah (via prayer—cf. Nehemiah 1:4–11, 2:4) *away* from his daily job and lifestyle in Susa of Persia, and *into another* type of work and lifestyle in Jerusalem of Judah.

INTENDED RECEPTORS: the non-Diaspora Jews of Jerusalem.

Jonah 1:1–3:3

God sent the Northern Kingdom Prophet Jonah *away* from his Jewish brethren in Judah, and *into* the Gentile city of Nineveh.

INTENDED RECEPTORS: the Ninevites.

Matthew 28:18–20

Jesus sent his Jewish disciples *away* from Israel, and *into all other* nations of the world.

INTENDED RECEPTORS: all ethnic people groups.

John 4:34–20:21

More than 20 times in the Gospel of John, Jesus refers to Himself as the "sent of God" (e.g., in the RSV: "Him who sent Me"—John 4:34, "the Father who sent Me"—John 6:44, "He sent Me"—John 8:42, "Thou didst send Me"—John 11:42, "Jesus Christ Whom Thou hast sent"—John 17:3, *et al.*). God sent Jesus *away* from the glorious splendor and sinless perfection of Heaven and of the Father of Lights, and *into* a sinful, selfish, flesh-and-bones material world.

INTENDED RECEPTORS: the lost sheep of Israel (Matthew 15:24); and the entire world of people for whom Jesus died, from all cultures, times, and generations (John 3:16).

Acts 9:1–30

The Lord announces he will be sending Saul (Paul) *away* from the Jewish believers in Jerusalem and Damascus (the Lord also announces He will be changing Saul's job description!), and *into* the Gentiles (cf. also Acts 22:21, 26:17–18), their kings and other Jewish people—which resulted in seven[9] separate short-term mission endeavors to such locations as Judea, Phoenicia, Syria, Cilicia, Crete, Pamphylia, Lycia, Lycaonia, Lydia, Macedonia, Achaia (i.e., Asia Minor—or what is present-day Israel, Lebanon, Syria, Turkey, and Greece).

INTENDED RECEPTORS: cf. endnote #9.

Acts 10:1–48

The Lord sent Peter (via a heavenly vision) *away* from the Jews and Samaritans in Joppa where he had just raised Dorcas (Tabitha) from the dead, and *to* a God-fearing Italian family and their friends in Caesarea.

INTENDED RECEPTORS: an Italian family and their friends in Caesarea.

Acts 13:2–3

The Holy Spirit sent Paul and Barnabas (during a time of worship and fasting with other prophets and teachers) *away* from Antioch and *into* *other* cities and nations—the places or locations of which the Holy Spirit had not yet revealed.

INTENDED RECEPTORS: cf. endnote #9.

Yet our *where* discussion would be far from complete if we failed to aim at what currently may be the most crucial 'where' target of all—the marginalized, hidden, unreached peoples of the world (the wild, unsettled frontier of today's Christian mission work). Since Paul made it his "ambition to preach the gospel, not where Christ has already been named ..." (Romans 15:20), our *where* mission efforts should employ that same challenge as much as possible—searching out the villages, the cities, the mountains, the valleys, the islands, the ethnic groups, the nations, the peoples who have little, if in fact any, Gospel witness among themselves. Many of these peoples live in what missiologists often call the poverty-stricken '10/40 Window' nations of northern Africa and in Southern and Central Asia (the African and Asian nations located between 10° North latitude and 40° North latitude). Most of this vast region has but one missionary per 1,000,000 people, with very few indigenous believers capable of reaching their own people. The nations and peoples living inside this 'window' present one of the most challenging tasks for missionaries to live, serve, and share the Gospel. Cultural, physical, and emotional burn-out rates are among the world's highest. Yet this is the most unreached part of the world where Christ is virtually unknown.

The Acts 1:8 'Where' Model

We don't mean to gloss over the necessity of the Holy Spirit for true power in becoming effective messengers for Christ, but the *where* focus of the Acts 1:8 model is actually 1:8B which reads in the NIV: "and you will be my witnesses in Jerusalem, and in all Judea and Samaria, and to the ends of the earth." To illustrate in bullet-point format, Jesus is telling us that through the power of the Holy Spirit, we'll be His witnesses:

- in *Jerusalem*,
- **and** in all *Judea and Samaria*,
- **and** to the *ends of the earth*.

This is, of course, what actually began to take place in the remainder of the book of Acts:

Jerusalem (Acts 2–7)

Immediately at Pentecost with the *DUNAMIS* of the Holy Spirit, Jesus' disciples began to boldly declare (i.e., the Good News *oral*-proclamation we call evangelism) in Jerusalem "the wonders of God in our own tongues!" (Acts 2:11B). Various forms of Good News *oral*-proclamation and *deed*-proclamation continued to take place in Chapters 2–7, just like Jesus said it would.

Judea and Samaria (Acts 8–12)[10]

In Acts 8 following the stoning death of Stephen, the church is persecuted and scattered: "On that day a great persecution broke out against the church at Jerusalem, and all except the apostles were scattered throughout Judea and

Samaria" (Acts 8:1). Two observations bear comment at this point. First, the connecting word (the conjunction) 'and' which we've set in bold type in the bullet-list above, and again in this paragraph: disciples and followers of Jesus "will be [His] witness" not just in one place vs. the other, but in all three (in *Jerusalem*, **and** in all *Judea and Samaria*, **and** to the *ends of the earth*). Second, only the apostles stayed back in Jerusalem for the time being—everyone else was "scattered throughout Judea and Samaria." Notice, the 'professional' witnesses stayed behind, while the 'non-professional' witnesses went out (scattered, perhaps unintentionally or even against their will—but they were sent throughout Judea and Samaria nonetheless).

Ends of the Earth (Acts 13–27)
Most missiologists and theologians view Acts 13 as the official Biblical launch of the missionary movement, and it's easy to see why: "While [the prophets and teachers at the church in Antioch] were worshiping the Lord and fasting, the Holy Spirit said, 'Set apart for me Barnabas and Saul for the work to which I have called them'" (Acts 13:2/RSV). Later on (at the launching point of his seventh short-term mission outreach—cf. endnote #9) when Paul was making his defense in Jerusalem, Paul explained his aforementioned Acts 13:2 instructions to the commander of the Roman troops: "Then the Lord said to me, 'Go; I will send you far away to the Gentiles'" (Acts 22:21). "Far away to the Gentiles" is clearly the same thing as the Acts 1:8 *"ends of the earth."*

Summary and Application of the Acts 1:8 'Where' Model
Jesus prophetically announced that His Spirit-empowered disciples would be witnesses in three identifiable "where" regions. We believe this still holds true for all Spirit-empowered believers today—that we are charged, and indeed "shall be" (Acts 1:8/RSV) His witness in three similar present-day "where" regions of the world God so loves.

Speaking to the July 1974 International Congress on World Evangelization in Lausanne, Switzerland, former missionary to the Mayan Indians (Guatemala) and U.S. Center for World Mission founder Ralph Winter challenged conference participants that the Acts 1:8 "where" model should not be viewed as geographical distances, but rather as cultural distances:

"Jesus ... distinguishes between different parts of [the] world and
does so according to the relative distance of those people from his

hearers ... It seems likely He is taking into account cultural distance as the primary factor."[11]

Winter went on to recommend what he termed E-1, E-2, and E-3 evangelism strategies based on his understanding of this Scripture. Roughly speaking, the strategies are as follows:

- *Jerusalem* (E-1 evangelism) represents each believer's own neighborhood, own community, own city, amongst whom exists the same language and same culture. It represents every person's near neighbors where the only real boundary for effective evangelism is the distance or frontier which exists between the church and the world.
- *Samaria* (E-2 evangelism) is necessary whenever any believer from any part of the world has to cross a second boundary or frontier "consituted by significant (but not monumental) differences of language and culture."[12] Referring to the Samaritan woman at the well in John 4, Winter also notes "that although it was easy for Jesus and His disciples to make themselves understood to the Samaritans, the Jew and the Samaritan were divided from each other by a frontier consisting of dialectal distinctions and some other very significant cultural differences."[13]
- *Ends of the Earth* (E-3 evangelism) involves an even greater cultural distance. "The people needing to be reached in this third sphere live, work, talk, and think in languages and cultural patterns utterly different from those native to the evangelist."[14]

In summary of *where* we send, we send:
- *away* from the home culture, and
- *into another* culture—the 'intended receptors' of which are usually a "Judea and Samaria," or an "ends of the earth" requiring an E-2 or E-3 form of oral-proclamation and deed-proclamation.

When Do We Send?

We send *now*!—not tomorrow, not later, but now. In no way do we abdicate the need for trained and prepared missionaries. In no way do we endorse culturally-insensitive, personal-agenda, what's-in-it-for-me? witnesses. In no way can we support those who go without being passionately propelled by God's AGAPE love for people lost and unsaved. But the oh!-so-easy-to-understand Biblical evidence woven throughout all of Scripture, is that there is an urgency to send now, a need to go as soon as possible, to be about the work of *MISSIO DEI* without delay. God did not say, "Build seminaries and write books" (cf. Introduction). Instead He commanded "Go!" What we argued in Chapter 1 bears repeating here again:

"For every additional hour required of preparation, for every additional characteristic demanded of our recruits, there will be thousands [of potential missionaries]—perhaps millions?—who remain sidelined ... In our feeble attempts to birth a missionary without spot or blemish, the world continues going to hell without Jesus Christ" (cf. "Summary" section of Chapter 1).

In fact the only 'delay' *requirement* of Scripture is that the messengers being sent (i.e., the missionaries) "stay ... until you are clothed with power from on high" (Luke 24:49), and "wait for the promise of the Father" (Acts 1:4). The Holy Spirit is the only non-negotiable *must* for determining *when* the missionary can be sent.

Why Do We Send?
This chapter is our attempt to answer *why* we send. You're reading it right now.

How Do We Send?
In the next chapter (Chapter 3) and continuing through Chapter 11, is our attempt to help you better understand *how* we might send the majority of potential missionaries (i.e., the unpaid, non-professional 'real people,' 'real fools,' the Royal Priesthood—the majority of the *ECCLESIARUM* world-wide).

OUR SUMMARY OF CHRISTIAN 'MISSION'
Based on the Biblical and etymological evidence we presented above, we now define Christian 'mission' as an ACTIVE VERB as follows:

Sending messengers (missionaries) away from their 'normal' home culture as soon as possible, and into another culture and people (intended receptors), for the express purpose of proclaiming with word and deed (the intended activity) the Good News that sets any person free from anything that binds them.

A simplified version would read (likewise an ACTIVE VERB):

Sending active Gospel messengers into another culture.

A 'missionary,' then, would be:

A person sent into another culture to be an active Gospel messenger in both word and deed.

THREE MAJOR THEOLOGICAL VIEWPOINTS OF CHRISTIAN 'MISSION'

We recognize a healthy human perspective to encompass wide and varied understandings of what Christian 'mission' means. Although we approach mission from an evangelical/activist position, we feel strongly that God continually reveals snippets of *MISSIO DEI* throughout the doctrinally diverse Body of Christ. Within this wonderful God-given vicissitude there is a remarkable unity of what 'mission' means. This section will explore some of those fascinating pieces categorized by the three major theological traditions: *1. Evangelical* (including Pentecostal); *2. Mainline Ecumenical;* and *3. Roman Catholic* (including Orthodox).

1. An Evangelical Definition of 'Mission'

Emerging from Puritanism, Pietism, Moravianism, Methodism, and other 18th- and 19th-century 'awakening' post-Reformation movements, evangelicalism's identifying features are usually seen as: conservative theology; infallibility and absolute authority of the Scriptures; confidence in the power of the Gospel; decision theology (and subsequent baptism by full immersion of adult professing believers); a strong emphasis on spontaneous prayer, evangelism, and mission; active participation in varieties of informal worship; present day validity of all spiritual gifts[15] within the Pentecostal/charismatic branches of evangelicalism (and within the neo-Pentecostal offshoots of mainline ecumenical and Catholic traditions); active involvement of lay membership; leadership developed more through giftedness and anointing then by academic preparation. Sometimes Evangelicals hold a cautious view of mainline Ecumenicals, and may view Catholic and Orthodox peoples as entirely unsaved.

Examples of Evangelicals could include: Assembly of God, Baptist, Christian Missionary and Alliance, Church of God, Covenant, Evangelical Free, Mennonite, and scores of smaller denominations, independents, fundamental Bible churches, Pentecostal bodies, and other non-affiliated Christian churches.

We'll begin the evangelical understanding of 'mission' by looking at the definition provided by Charles Van Engen:

"Mission is the intentional crossing of barriers from church to non-church, faith to non-faith, to proclaim the coming of the Kingdom of God in word and deed through the Church's participation in God's mission of reconciling people to God, to themselves, to each other, and to the world, and gathering them into the Church through faith in Jesus Christ with a view to the transformation of the world as a sign of the coming of the Kingdom of God in Jesus Christ."[16]

Although Van Engen's exhaustive 84-word definition may require some rumination, he provides an easier-to-digest review of David Bosch's 24-word definition: "... geographic expansion, verbal proclamation, planting of the church, the totality of the task which God has sent His church to do in the world."[17]

Urban missiologist Ray Bakke tweaks Bosch's 'geographical' definition somewhat, suggesting "missions can be divided into two categories. First, there is the traditional mission to people who are geographically distant from us. The second category of missions is to people culturally distant from a church, but living under the shadow of its spire."[18]

Gathering at the U.S. Center for World Mission in Pasadena, California, for the Second Student Mission Mobilizer's Consultation (SMMC II) in early 1994, Korean student mission mobilizers elevated not only mission's preeminent purpose for the church, but included the bottom line action required of mission—the *obligatory response* (shown in italics below):

"We believe that mission is not just a passing trend or substitute for other Christian ministries but is rather the all encompassing purpose of God for the world from the very first chapter of Genesis. Consequently, *every believer must find his or her strategic role in world mission...*"[19] (italics ours).

John Piper—the sagacious theologian, author, and senior pastor of a large inner-city, mission-minded church—offers a *goal* of mission, helping shed even more light on the evangelical definition of 'mission:'

"The ultimate goal of God in all of history is to uphold and display His glory for the enjoyment of the redeemed from every tribe and tongue and people and nation. His goal is the gladness of His people because God is most glorified in us when we are most satisfied in Him ... the goal of missions therefore is the gladness of the peoples in the greatness of God."[20]

Herbert Kane sees the very nature of Jehovah God as a 'missionary God' and adamantly re-roots any misunderstanding of mission far beyond the New Testament's Great Commission:

"The missionary obligation of the church would have been just as imperative if Jesus had not spoken [the Great Commission]. The missionary mandate antedates the Incarnation and is rooted in the very character of God. Indeed, if Jehovah were not a missionary God, there would have been no Incarnation."[21]

Within this past century the general evangelical mission thrust has birthed several umbrella movements, for the purpose of uniting the broader world-wide body of evangelicals as tethered muscle for mission. Some of those 20th Century, still-influential umbrella structures include:

1917—*Interdenominational Foreign Mission Association* (IFMA)

1945—*Evangelical Fellowship of Mission Agencies* (EFMA)

1946—*Urbana* tri-annual student mission conferences launched in Toronto, sponsored by InterVarsity Christian Fellowship (IVCF)

1947—*International Fellowship of Evangelical Students* (IFES) working to strengthen existing national evangelical student groups in more than 140 nations (as of early 2003)

1951—*World Evangelical Alliance* (WEA; formerly W. E. Fellowship)

1973—*Advancing Churches in Missions Commitment* (ACMC; formerly Association of Church Missions Committees)

1974—*Lausanne Committee for World Evangelization* (LCWE), from momentum of the Lausanne Movement (initial leadership from Dr. Billy Graham) and two earlier events: (1) the Berlin Congress on World Evangelization (1966), and (2) the Wheaton Congress on the Church's Worldwide Mission (1966) jointly sponsored by the IFMA/EFMA

1976—*United States Center for World Mission* (USCWM), with a primary focus on frontier, unreached peoples

1981—*Fellowship of Short-Term Mission Leaders* (FSTML)

1989—*AD 2000 Movement* (birthed at Lausanne II in Manila), with a primary focus on 10/40 Window nations

From one of these groups emerged what is perhaps current evangelicalism's most widely accepted document, the Lausanne Covenant. The Covenant has become the ongoing basis for cooperation in mission among Evangelicals throughout much of the world. Its 15 Affirmations include, in part: the missionary purpose of the Triune God; the divine inspiration and authority of the Scriptures; the uniqueness of Christ (specifically in terms of eternal salvation); the primacy of evangelism; the urgency of the world-wide evangelistic task; the Biblical necessity of socio-political involvement and responsibility; the reality of constant spiritual warfare with the powers of evil; persecution; and the power of the Holy Spirit. In its Affirmation #6 (The Church & Evangelism), the Covenant states:

> "We affirm that Christ sends His redeemed people into the world (John 17:18; 20:21; Matthew 28:19,20) as the Father sent Him, and that this calls for a similar deep and costly penetration of the world. We need to break out of our ecclesiastical ghettos and permeate non-Christian society ... World evangelization requires the whole Church to take the whole Gospel to the whole world (Acts 1:8; 20:27). The Church is at the very centre of God's cosmic purpose (Ephesians 1:9,10; 3:9–11) and is His appointed means of spreading the Gospel ...".[22]

Finally, John Stott offers this simple, all-encompassing definition: "'mission'... is properly a comprehensive word, embracing everything which God sends His people into the world to do. It therefore includes evangelism and social responsibility, since both are authentic expressions of the love which longs to serve man in his need."[23]

2. A Mainline Ecumenical Definition of 'Mission'

Generally the mainline ecumenical (*OIKOUMENE*—the whole inhabited earth) churches are characterized by commitment to historical forms of traditional worship (liturgy, robed ministers, pre-written prayer, formal sanctuaries, etc.); substantive theological dialogue (both within and outside their respective denominations); sacramental theology (including baptism of infants by sprinkling or pouring of water); a liberal view of the Bible; relief and development activities, and advocacy of justice, peace, and human rights as foremost in mission; passive lay involvement; stronger emphasis on academic preparation for leadership development as opposed to giftedness and anointing. Mainline ecumenicals are generally open to dialogue with Catholicism and Orthodoxism, and may view evangelicalism as fundamentalistic and theologically less grounded.

Some of the larger, well-known mainline denominational examples could include: Anglican, Congregational, Episcopalian, Lutheran, Methodist, Presbyterian, and United Church of Christ.

The World Council of Churches (WCC), formed in Amsterdam in 1948 with churches from 47 different nations, is perhaps the primary expression of the mainline ecumenical group of Christians. Its former General Secretary, Emilio Castro, holds a "conviction that the mission of the church is the mission of the Kingdom of God ... [and he is] persuaded that we are sent free to be signs of the Kingdom ...".[24] Expanding on the freedom-in-doing-mission concept, he states "We are free to engage in all kinds of human activities provided that those human activities become entry points to the Kingdom, and from there we point in the direction of Jesus."[25] Applied to the ECCLE-SIARUM the General Secretary believes "The mission of the church is to point to Him through whose life, death, and resurrection has been revealed the fullness of God's forgiving and redeeming love ... [it] means asking Christ what we shall do, and being perpetually prepared to do what He asks of us."[26]

When the WCC met in Nairobi (1975) for their fifth assembly, their official report did not directly define the word 'mission' per se—but clearly the following excerpts could easily provide such understanding:

"... As the royal priesthood, Christians are therefore called to engage in both evangelism and social action. We are commissioned to proclaim the Gospel of Christ to the ends of the earth ...

"The Gospel always includes: the announcement of God's Kingdom and love through Jesus Christ, the offer of grace and forgiveness of sins, the invitation to repentance and faith in Him, the summons to fellowship in God's church, the command to witness to God's saving words and deeds, the responsibility to participate in the struggle for justice and human dignity, the obligation to denounce all that hinders human wholeness, and a commitment to risk life itself.

"Because God so loved the whole world, the Church cannot neglect any part of it—neither those who have heard the saving Name nor the vast majority who have not yet heard it. Our obedience to God and our solidarity with the human family demand that we obey Christ's command to proclaim and demonstrate God's love to every person, of every class and race, on every continent, in every culture, in every setting and historical context."[27]

Sixteen years later (1991) in Canberra, Australia, the WCC's seventh assembly noted that "Each church acting in mission is acting on behalf of the whole Body of Christ ... Always we need to remember our original understanding of mission, which is preaching, teaching, and healing ... Jesus Christ through the action of the Holy Spirit is God's saving presence for *all*."[28]

3. Recent Roman Catholic Definitions of 'Mission'

Protestants often quickly write off the Roman Catholic Church (KATHOLIKOS means 'universal,' and KYRIAKON means 'belonging to the Lord').[29] But with around 900 million adherents worldwide, we think to ignore some of the excellent Roman Catholic insight on Christian mission would be a mistake.

From a Protestant perspective, a few of the notable distinctions of the Roman Catholic Church include:

> "[Belief] that the Pope is head over the Church in all authority and power, and is infallible when it comes to doctrine ... Roman Catholics believe Salvation is truly in the only true Church, that being the Roman Catholic Church ... Roman Catholics believe Mary was sinless, without sin [and that she] remained a virgin after the birth of Jesus, [and that] Mary is the Mother of God, that prayers and petitions are to be made to her ... [they also] believe the sacraments of the Roman Catholic Church are required for a person to have salvation, to be justified of their sins ... Roman Catholics believe Purgatory is a place in which people have to go to purge out ... certain sins that people have to take care of themselves in order to be saved."[30]

On December 8, 1975, Pope Paul VI issued his Apostolic Exhortation—a papal document carrying a great deal of weight within the Roman Catholic Church—*Evangelii Nuntiandi* (On Evangelization in the Modern World). In it he stated "The command to the Twelve to go out and proclaim the Good News is also valid for all Christians ... Those who have received the Good News and who have been gathered by it into the community of salvation can and must communicate and spread it."[31]

More recently, Pope John Paul II further clarified the Catholic understanding of 'mission' in his Eight Encyclical, *Redemptori Missio*, published in 1990 (although not considered 'infallible,' a papal document of even greater authority than the Apostolic Exhortation). John Paul quoted Acts 4:12 and emphatically proclaimed "This [Scripture] ... has a universal value, since for all people—Jews and Gentiles alike—salvation can only come from Jesus Christ."[32] The Pope continued:

"... there must be no lessening of the impetus to preach the Gospel and to establish new churches among peoples or communities where they do not yet exist, for this is the very first task of the church, which has been sent forth to all peoples and to the very ends of the earth. Without the mission *ad agentes*[33] [to all peoples], the church's very missionary dimension would be deprived of its essential meaning and of the very activity that exemplifies it."[34]

In 1978, the ecumenically-respected theologian and former missionary to India Lesslie Newbigin commented on the opening words of a Vatican II document:

"'Christ is the light of the nations.' With these majestic words the Second Vatican Council began the greatest of its documents, the "Constitution on the Church." Fundamental to everything else that came forth from the council were the reaffirmation of the missionary character of the church, the recognition of the unfinished task which that implies, the confession that the church is a pilgrim people on its way to the ends of the earth and the end of time, and the acknowledgment of the need for a new openness to the world into which the church is sent."[35]

Its sister tradition, the Orthodox Church, embodies a rich, noble legacy of missionary outreach during the first millennium A.D. During the second millennium its missionary activity has fallen largely into inactivity. Yet as recently as 1990, contemporary Orthodox mission considers the "starting point of all missionary activity to be the promise and command of the risen Lord in its Trinitarian perspective: 'As the Father has sent me, even so I send you ... Receive the Holy Spirit' (John 20:21–22)."[36] The Orthodox position goes on to state,

"The church finds its true vocation in God's mission for the salvation of the whole world ... Mission and evangelism are constitutive of the church's being. They are indispensable expressions of its catholicity and they manifest also the church's participation [*MISSIO ECCLESIATO*] in God's mission [*MISSIO DEI*] for the salvation of the entire world"[37] (Latin insertions ours).

Finally, the Roman Catholic church views inter-religious dialogue as an essential element in direct proclamation of the Gospel (i.e., mission). Another church document (Dialogue and Proclamation) issued in 1991 contained a profoundly wise, child-like statement of mission rooted in *love*:

" ... how could they not hope and desire to share with others their joy in knowing and following Jesus Christ, Lord and Savior? ... Insofar as the Church and Christians have a deep love for the Lord Jesus, the desire to share Him with others is motivated not merely by obedience to the Lord's command, but by this love itself."[38]

That's so Biblical, so right-on. After all, "God is love" (I John 4:8), and "the love of Christ controls us" (II Corinthians 5:14). Mission motivated merely by obedience will lack the very *AGAPE* quality of God Himself—the same love God so had that He sent His only son into the *world* (John 3:16). We *must* do mission that way, "because He first loved us" (I John 4:19).

Summary

MISSIO DEI (God's mission) is firmly rooted in the Old Testament. Ever since the Genesis 3 fall and the Genesis 10 post-flood creation of the nations, God has passionately longed to see the highest pinnacle of his creation—human beings—redeemed and in right relationship with Himself. Although the chapter looked at several theological, Biblical, and missiological aspects of 'mission' to broaden and enhance our understanding, we conclude that the simplicity of Christian mission is this: *sending active Gospel messengers into another culture.*

Endnotes
Chapter 2

1. *(p. 36)* **John R. W. Stott**, *Christian Mission in the Modern World* (Downers Grove IL: InterVarsity Press, 1975), p. 21.

2. *(p. 36)* *Ibid.*, pp. 21–22.

3. *(p. 36)* **Sam Wilson and Gordon Aeschliman**, *The Hidden Half* (Monrovia CA: MARC, no publication date listed), pp. 37–45. Scripture quotations in this section were taken from the NIV Bible © 1973, 1978 by the International Bible Society. This entire section is reprinted by permission from the author (Aeschliman) January 2001, and from the publisher (MARC) February 2003.

4. *(p. 43)* *Merriam-Webster's OnLine Dictionary* (http://www.m-w.com/cgi-bin/dictionary).

5. *(p. 43)* *Lewis & Short Latin Dictionary* (http://www.perseus.tufts.edu/cgi-bin/lexindex).

6. *(p. 43)* (http://www.perseus.tufts.edu/cgi-bin/enggreek).

7. *(p. 43)* Vine's Expository Dictionary of New Testament Words (http://www.menfak.no/bible/vines.html).

8. *(p. 44)* cf. Luke 23:40–43, John 3:16, John 17:3, Romans 5:8, I Corinthians 15:3–5, Hebrews 5:9, I John 4:9–10.

9. *(p. 48)* Most missiologists and theologians routinely recognized merely three mission endeavors made by Paul. But by definition of the word 'mission' as we are proposing in this chapter, we must also include Paul's first two mission endeavors following his conversion, the mission endeavor to Jerusalem for the Council meeting, and his final mission endeavor into Rome as well (cf. Chapter 10 for extensive detail on Paul's seven separate short-term mission outreaches). Here are all seven of Paul's mission endeavors in chronological order:

    (1)   *Mission endeavor of Acts 9:8–30*
          from Jerusalem—into Damascus and Arabia—into Jerusalem;

    (2)   *Mission endeavor of Acts 11:25–30; 12:25*
          from Jerusalem/Tarsus—into Antioch—into Jerusalem;

    (3)   *First-"recognized" mission endeavor 46–48 A.D. of Acts 13–14*
          from Antioch—into Salamis, Paphos, Pisidian Antioch, Iconium, Lystra, Derbe, and Perga—to Antioch;

    (4)   *Mission endeavor of Acts 15:2–35*
          from Antioch—into Phoenicia and Samaria—into Jerusalem;

    (5)   *Second-"recognized" mission endeavor 49–52 A.D. of Acts 15:36–18:22*
          from Antioch—into Syria, Cilicia, Phrygia, Galatia, Macedonia, Achaia [Greece], Ephesus, and Jerusalem—to Antioch;

    (6)   *Third-"recognized" mission endeavor 53–57 A.D. of Acts 18:23–21:16*
          from Antioch—into Galatia, Phrygia Ephesus, Macedonia, Greece, Macedonia, Troas, Miletus, Tyre, Ptolemais, Caesarea—to Jerusalem; and

    (7)   *Mission endeavor 59–60 A.D. of Acts 21:17–Acts 28:31*
          from Jerusalem—into Rome (via Jerusalem, Caesarea, Crete, Malta, and Sicily); after arriving in Rome in 60 a.d., Paul remained under guard as a prisoner for at least two years. Then one tradition tells us

Paul was martyred under Nero's persecution in 67 A.D. Another tradition tells us he was released from prison and went to Spain to do more missionary work—and if true, do we consider this to be an extension of his seventh short-term mission, or was this his eighth?

10. *(p. 49)* Cf. Acts 11:19–20 where the "Judea and Samaria" witnessing efforts began to actually extend beyond Samaria (i.e., to the "ends of the earth").

11. *(p. 51)* RALPH D. WINTER, "The New Macedonia: A Revolutionary New Era in Mission Begins," found in: **Ralph D. Winter and Steven C. Hawthorne, eds.**, *Perspectives on the World Christian Movement* (Pasadena CA: William Carey Library, 1999), p. 342.

12. *(p. 51)* *Ibid.*, p. 344.

13. *(p. 51)* *Ibid.*

14. *(p. 51)* *Ibid.*

15. *(p. 53)* Cf. the following five sets of Biblical spiritual gifts:
    (1) *Romans 12:6–8*
        sometimes called 'personality gifts,' these spiritual gifts are widely accepted as present-day valid gifts within most ecclesiastical groups;
    (2) *I Corinthians 12:4–11*
        sometimes called 'manifestational gifts,' these (sometimes controversial) spiritual gifts are generally accepted as present-day valid gifts only within ecclesiastical groups holding Pentecostal/charismatic theologies;
    (3) *I Corinthians 12:28–31*
        sometimes called 'appointed church gifts,' these spiritual gifts include both widely accepted gifts and controversial gifts;
    (4) *Ephesians 4:11–12*
        sometimes called 'equipping gifts' or 'office gifts,' these spiritual gifts are generally accepted within most ecclesiastical groups, however interpretation of what a specific Ephesians 4:11 gift may mean varies between Pentecostal/charismatic theologies and non-Pentecostal/non-charismatic theologies; and
    (5) *I Peter 4:10–11*
        lists just two widely accepted gifts.

    NOTE: Some theologians inductively reason that there are additional spiritual gifts implied by others texts (other than the five texts given above), such as the gift of missionary, or the gift of martyrdom, or various forms of artistic gifts such as music.

16. *(p. 54)* **Charles Van Engen**, *Biblical Theology of Mission* (Pasadena CA: Fuller Theological Seminary School of World Mission, In-Service Program MT520 Syllabus), p. 176.

17. *(p. 54)* *Ibid.*, p. 47.

18. *(p. 54)* **Ray Bakke**, *The Urban Christian* (Downers Grove IL: InterVarsity Press, 1987), p. 45.

19. *(p. 54)* **In-Ho Kim and Chong Kim, eds.**, *Student Mobilization—Korean Case* (Korea:

Mission Korea '96, 1995), p. 5.

20. (p. 55)   **John Piper**, *Let the Nations Be Glad!—The Supremacy of God in Missions* (Grand Rapids MI: Baker Books, 1993), p. 219.

21. (p. 55)   **Herbert J. Kane**, *Wanted: World Christians* (Grand Rapids MI: Baker Book House, 1986), p. 78.

22. (p. 56)   **James A. Scherer and Stephen B. Bevans, eds.**, *New Directions in Mission and Evangelization 1—Basic Statements 1974–1991* (Maryknoll NY: Orbis Books, 1992), p. 256.

23. (p. 56)   **Stott**, p. 35.

24. (p. 57)   **Emilio Castro**, *Sent Free* (Geneva, Switzerland: WCC, 1985), p. ix.

25. (p. 57)   *Ibid.*, p. 43.

26. (p. 57)   *Ibid.*, p. 102.

27. (p. 58)   **Scherer**, pp. 4, 10, 11.

28. (p. 58)   *Ibid.*, p. 87.

29. (p. 58)   Cf. http://www.freecatholic.org/what_do_free_catholics_believe1.htm

30. (p. 58)   Cf. http://www.apologeticsforchristians.homestead.com/RomanCatholicswhatthey believe.html

31. (p. 58)   **Scherer**, p. 92.

32. (p. 59)   *Ibid.*, p. 170.

33. (p. 59)   The phrase *Ad Gentes* (to all peoples) is also the title of a Vatican II decree on the church's missionary activity.

34. (p. 59)   **Scherer**, p. 172.

35. (p. 59)   **Lesslie Newbigin**, *The Open Secret* (Grand Rapids MI: William B Eerdmans, 1978), p. 1.

36. (p. 59)   **Scherer**, p. 243.

37. (p. 60)   *Ibid.*

38. (p. 60)   *Ibid.*, p. 198.

DEFINING 'SHORT-TERM' MISSION

---

1 Time   2 Activity   3 Size   4 Location
5 Participant Demographics
6 Sending Entity   7 Mission Philosophy
8 Leadership & Training Effectiveness

THE MISSION COMMUNITY[1] HAS YET TO AGREE UPON ONE all-encompassing, succinct definition for the label short-term mission. Although we're not sure an all-encompassing, succinct label is possible, let alone advisable, we recognize the absence of such to have already set the stage for confusion and misunderstanding.

Samuel Wilson discusses the vague, ambiguous definition of 'short-termer' in MARC's *13th Edition Mission Handbook*:

"What is a 'short-termer?' Some years ago the question could be answered easily by saying that a short-termer was a missionary who was not planning to make overseas ministries his or her career. However, in recent years this definition has become fuzzy at both ends. On one hand, the concept of a missionary career is changing dramatically. At one time almost all missionaries thought of themselves and their calling as a lifetime career; now many missionaries plan in advance to discontinue or interrupt their missionary career sometime during their lifetime."[2]

This chapter should help eliminate some of that fuzzy confusion. Keep in mind that when we use the phrase 'short-term mission,' the second word of that phrase—'mission'—is purposely used in accordance with the overall understanding of 'mission' we attempted to present in the preceding chapter.

We observe that the phrase 'short-term' has been defined variously by each person or group that does short-term mission. Such varying definitions almost always correlate to specific experiences these people or groups encountered first-hand. As real and valid as personal, first-hand experience is, it is, unfortunately, usually non-integrated and not fully comprehensive with respect to other types of endeavors falling under the same rubric of 'short-term.'

How many types of mission fall under the rubric of 'short-term?' Based on our eight primary defining variables—each of which contains four or more of 69 major sub-categories—we identify 777,600,000 potential variations of short-term mission (cf. last footnote [**] below TABLE #3.1).

Stated once again: our assessment is that various segments of the mission community are each defining 'short-term' primarily by their own personal, non-integrated experience and observation. Such personal experience and observation is often derived within the confines of one or two (perhaps a handful) of limited experiences, and not within the much larger potential of more than 777 million possible variations.

For example, college students—and their circle of influence including teachers, family, and friends—may view 'short-term' as a *six-week summer work project* wedged in between two successive years of school. A traditional mission agency—and readers on its mailing list—may see 'short-term' as a *one year program designed to provide certain help/support services to its full-time career staff.* Another agency may view 'short-term' as a *six-month tool used to recruit full-time missionary staff.* A Bible church in the southwestern United States may regard 'short-term' as a *weekend tract-passing stint* across the Mexican border, while a Caribbean church in Trinidad and Tobago may see 'short-term' as a *two-week steel pan drums music program* to the neighboring islands. Definitions even include a Nairobi career couple's experience of 'short-term' as a *"team [of] peanut butter ... hogging ... complain[ers]."*[3]

Even within newer types of non-traditional mission agencies—agencies whose significant, if not primary, strategy is to recruit, train, and send short-term missionaries—there exists a varied, programmed difference of short-term mission. A typical Youth With a Mission (YWAM) stint is composed of about four months of discipleship training immediately followed by a two-month cross-cultural mission outreach (a 2:1 pre-field vs. on-field ratio[4]). A typical Teen Mission program kicks off with two weeks of early summer boot camp in Florida immediately followed by six weeks of on-field outreach (a 1:3 ratio). The typical program offered by Short-Term Evangelical Mission (STEM) Ministries falls into a 1:14 ratio, with one day of pre-field prep later followed by a two-week overseas mission outreach.

Our point?—one group's interpretation of 'short-term mission' does not readily jive with another's. The result?—fuzzy confusion and frustration for those within the mission community, and utter chaos for those outside who, perhaps, might want to come in.

Characteristics of the Eight Defining Variables of 'Short-Term'

Drawing upon our cumulative experience of more than 85 years within the short-term mission arena,[5] we have identified eight primary characteristics which can help more accurately complete an understanding of the label 'short-term mission.' It's important to note that an aggregate assessment of the following eight variables taken together must be considered when trying to define 'short-term.' Some of the variables, such as *time* or *activity*, tend to carry more weight than other variables. Yet if short-term mission is viewed merely by a single characteristic or two—which all too often it is—any attempt to arrive at a realistic, usable understanding will be about as helpful as the Proverbs 26:3 lame man's legs.

Of the eight defining variables, four are externally visible and readily identifiable to the passive non-participant (i.e., observer) by either personal observation or in answer to easily-asked questions. Two of the eight simultaneously contain both externally visible and internally hidden elements. The final remaining two variables are internally hidden to the passive non-participant,

TABLE #3.1

THE EIGHT DEFINING VARIABLES OF SHORT-TERM MISSION

DEFINING VARIABLE	BRIEF DESCRIPTION OR EXPLANATION OF THE 69 MAJOR STM SUB-CATEGORIES [†]	PASSIVE OBSERVATION
1. **TIME** p. 69	on-field length of goer-guests' outreach 4	external & visible
2. **ACTIVITY** [††] p. 70	goer-guests' on-field "giving/sowing" intended ministry task(s) 16	external & visible
3. **SIZE** p. 75	number of goer-guests.................................... 5	external & visible
4. **LOCATION** p. 79	host site identity: geo-political nation/area; rural or urban; domestic or international......... 5	external & visible
5. **PARTICIPANT DEMOGRAPHICS** p. 81	age; gender; religious identity; cultural identity; and related experience of the: • goer-guest participants............................. 5 • host field facilitator participants [*] .... 5 • host intended receptor participants............ 5	external & visible and internal & hidden
6. **SENDING ENTITY** p. 86	the administrative/management organization: church; parachurch mission agency; institutional non-mission agency; and/or self 4	external & visible and internal & hidden
7. **MISSION PHILOSOPHY** p. 93	mission definition; ministry values; and ministry expectations of the: • sending entity(s).. 3 • goer-guest participants.............................. 3 • host field facilitator participants [*] .... 3 • host intended receptor participants [*] 3	internal & hidden
8. **LEADERSHIP & TRAINING** p. 100	• effectiveness of leadership & training upon goer-guests: pre-field, on-field, & post-field.... 6 • effectiveness of training upon host receivers (the field facilitator participants [*] and the intended receptor participants [*]) 2	internal & hidden

TOTAL POSSIBLE VARIATIONS OF SHORT-TERM MISSION: **777,600,000** [**]

© Roger Peterson and R. Wayne Sneed, 1995. Revised 2002.

[†]   Cf. Addenda "A" and "B" for a related short-term mission Typology/Definition and Relational formats.

[††] Includes only the Goer-Guests' **Giving/Sowing** portion of the Two-way On-field Serendipity (cf. Chapter 7).

[*]   Not applicable in certain short-term mission endeavors.

[**] The total 777,600,000 was derived by simply multiplying together each figure representing the number of sub-categories (4x16x5x...). Mathematically this is incorrect, because the Activity variable alone is not merely one of 16, but rather any combination of 16. The current number of geo-political nations, or the potential number of ages of participants also far exceed their respective sub-category figures used as multipliers. The actual total (if it could be calculated) would substantially exceed 777 million.

and don't normally surface as defining variables unless probed with a series of tougher diagnostic questions. TABLE #3.1 provides a brief overview of all eight defining variables of short-term mission.

1. TIME

The very nature of the hyphenated compound phrase 'short-term' implies the element of *time*. Time, the on-field length of the short-term mission outreach, is perhaps the most crucial of the eight defining variables of short-term mission. Time is crucial in the sense that it—more than any of the other variables—flags an immediate observable difference between short-term mission and traditional long-term career mission.

The generally accepted time period associated with short-term mission has been *on-field time of four years or less*. We likewise accept this, but readily point out subsequent acceptance mandates inclusion of not just the traditional one or two year stint (i.e., what we call an *extended* short-term), but mission lasting just a few months (a *seasonal* short-term), only a couple of weeks (a *standard* short-term), or merely a day (a *mini* short-term).

Yet this time variable must be probed even deeper. For example, the dynamics of preparing for a two-week *standard* short-term mission differ vast-

---

TABLE #3.2

1. TIME
THE TIME SUB-CATEGORIES OF SHORT-TERM MISSION

	SUB-CATEGORY OF TIME	IDENTIFYING LABEL
1) short-term measured by:	**Days**	*MINI* short-term
2) short-term measured by:	**Weeks**	*STANDARD* short-term
3) short-term measured by:	**Months** *(often associated with a season like summer, winter interim, or the 9-month school year)*	*SEASONAL* short-term
4) short-term measured by:	**Years**	*EXTENDED* short-term

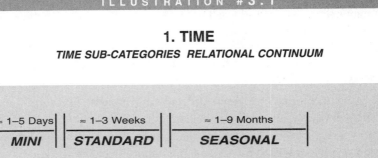

ILLUSTRATION #3.1

1. TIME
TIME SUB-CATEGORIES RELATIONAL CONTINUUM

ly from preparing for a two-year *extended* short-term mission. In reality, preparing for a two-year extended short-term mission may more closely resemble preparation for a long-term career missionary's initial five-year assignment.

Therefore we recognize within the overall defining variable of time its four natural sub-categories. Each of the four sub-categories has its own unique set of pre-field, on-field, and post-field dynamics (cf. Chapter 5—The Process Trilogy) that set it apart from the other three. It's all still 'short-term' by definition—yet comparatively different as 80 degree summer rain from freezing winter snow. The naturally-occurring four major sub-categories of short-term mission *time* are illustrated in TABLE #3.2, along with our identifying labels to help differentiate between the sub-categories.

Also shown is ILLUSTRATION #3.1, a modified relational continuum contrasting the differences between, and showing the overlap in, the four sub-categories of the short-term mission *time* variable.

2. ACTIVITY

Short-term mission *activity* consists of the oral-proclamation and deed-proclamation project (the goer-guests' intended ministry task) planned for a given outreach. An accurate understanding of this activity variable likewise plays a significant part in any attempt to define 'short-term mission.' But please make this important note: the activity variable we refer to is intentionally limited to just the goer-guests' Giving/Sowing portion of the two-way on-field action. This activity variable includes neither the goer-guests' nor the host receivers' portions of the Getting/Reaping side of this two-way on-field serendipity (cf. Chapter 7—The Reciprocity of Give 'n Take).

The Giving/Sowing portion of the activity variable covered in this section is meant to identify whatever work and ministry projects the *goer-guests* are intending to do while on-field (i.e, what this book interchangeably calls the target tasks, intended projects, intended ministry activity, or the intended on-field oral-proclamation and deed-proclamation efforts).

For example, one periodical listed a small sampling of various types of short-terms, semantically identified by such an activity label: "learning ... try us out ... construction ... academic ... performance ... medical and dental ... professional service ... teaching ... discipleship ... justice ... event ... unreached peoples ... Caribbean cruise."[6]

In her *Successful Mission Teams—A Guide for Volunteers,* Martha VanCise lists short-term mission activities she refers to as "opportunities to serve:"[7]

TABLE #3.3

2. ACTIVITY [†]
THE GOER-GUESTS' INTENDED MINISTRY ACTIVITY
SUB-CATEGORIES OF SHORT-TERM MISSION

EVANGELISM	WITNESSING	DISCIPLESHIP	HELPS
1) Proclamation	5) Social Ministry	10) Disciple Making	13) Constr'n & Physcl Labor
2) Church Planting	6) The Arts	11) Education-Giving (Teaching)	14) Other Blue Collar Program Spprt Services
3) Spiritual Warfare	7) Sports Outreach	12) Education-Receiving (Information Acquisition)	15) White Collar Program Support Services
4) Bible Translation	8) Manifestational Gifts		
	9) Multiple Activities with Given Receptor Group		16) Hospitality

[†] includes only the Goer-Guests' **Giving/Sowing** portion of the Two-way On-field Serendipity (cf. Chapter 7)

- Construction
- Vacation Bible School
- Evangelism
- Music Evangelism
- Medical
- Agricultural Assistance
- Craft Instruction

- Religious Surveys
- Literature Distribution
- Youth Camps—Nationals
- Youth Camps—Missionaries' Kids
- Pastoral Training Seminars for Nationals
- Family Seminars for Missionaries

In reality such lists are incomplete, yet still a good attempt at helping us understand short-term mission is often *activity*-driven in terms of the goer-guests' focus and perceived purpose. The activity variable helps navigate the oft-posed question, "what'll ya'll do when ya'll get there?"—and when sufficiently answered helps establish some level of understanding and sense of credibility. The activity variable also helps produce a sense of impending vision for all participants (senders, goer-guests, and host receivers—cf. Chapter 6).

The activity variable helps potential participants decide whether to be a part of a given short-term mission. For example, a family of vocally active believers may desire to go on a short-term mission with *evangelism* activity rather than *arts* (e.g., drama and mime) activity. Or a physician may choose to become a sending supporter by financially contributing toward a short-term mission outreach with *medical* activity rather than *sports* activity. Or a host receiving group may choose not to receive a mission team planning only on *construction* activity because the host receivers learned such construction teams won't build by their time-tested local prevailing standards. Attempting to get a grip on the significantly varied differences implied by the activity variable can help elicit a better understanding, albeit incomplete, of a given short-term mission.

Much like the time variable presented above, the activity variable will dictate a different approach to each aspect of the pre-field, on-field, and post-field process trilogy. But the activity variable by itself—without due consideration of the other seven defining variables—immediately creates potential for problems. For example, if goer-guest participants focus solely on *their* intended activity (without being in a true two-way reciprocity of Giving/Sowing and Getting/Reaping—cf. Chapter 7), they run an unacceptable risk of entering the intended receptor participants' ETHNOS (a political nation, but more specifically, a local ethnic people group) with the same colonialistic, paternalistic, non-serving, know-it-all attitude often prevalent in 19th- and 20th-century Western attempts at mission—clearly a rueful aberration of Biblical mission.

Although we recognize the dynamic creativity of God's people to continually discover new and inventive activities within the realm of short-term mission, we'd still like to conclude the activity variable with a more inclusive list than what we presented above. Our list identifies 16 major sub-categories of potential short-term mission on-field activity, which we've organized under four dominant missiological headings (TABLE #3.3). We realize there will always be cross-over between our four headings, and that differing doctrinal positions may choose to regroup or re-label our list in a fashion deemed more suitable. We briefly explain these goer-guests' intended activities as follows:

Evangelism

EVANGELIZO—to proclaim glad tidings, and *EVANGELION*—good news, the Gospel.

1. *Proclamation* among unchurched people including: preaching, teaching, crusades, media (including especially the *Jesus Film*), creative verbal proclamation of the Good News, Bible and Gospel recordings, broadcasting (radio, television, short-wave, internet), or Gospel literature distribution.

2. *Church Planting* including assistance in various stages of establishing a local indigenous church in an otherwise unchurched region.

3. *Spiritual Warfare* meaning specifically targeted prayer by way of on-site prayerwalking, intercessory prayer, and/or spiritual warfare praying (also included here is Old Testament "destruction"[8] activity specifically ordered by God).

4. *Bible Translation* would include any of the short-term mission program/line activities employed by Bible translation groups such as Wycliffe Bible Translators or Lutheran Bible Translators.

Witnessing

MATUREO—to bear witness to; used as either pre-evangelism or post-evangelism ministry.

5. *Social Ministry* including: mercy ministry (e.g., hospital, orphanage, or prison visitation), medical and dental (and other scientific healing arts), relief (e.g., food or clothing distribution), development (e.g., in agriculture or fresh water), justice, ecology.

6. *The Arts* including: music (vocal or instrumental, solo or group), drama, mime, pantomime, acting, skits, puppetry, drawing/painting/sculpting.

7. *Sports Outreach* including traditional North American athletic activities (i.e., basketball, softball, volleyball, etc.), and athletic activities

originating in other nations (i.e., cricket, football [soccer], etc.).

8. *Manifestational Gifts* including: words of wisdom and knowledge, healing, miracles, discernment between evil spirits and Godly spirits, tongues, and interpretation of tongues (usually such 'manifestational gifts' [cf. endnote #15 of Chapter 2], or signs and wonders, are accepted and readily practiced within Pentecostal/charismatic short-term mission endeavors, while some of the 'manifestational gifts,' such as tongues, are often viewed as controversial and divisive within non-Pentecostal/non-charismatic short-term mission endeavors).

9. *Multiple Activities with a Given Receptor Group* includes any combination of the other 15 listed activities, but all such intended activities are specifically geared toward an intended receptor group or sub-group, such as: children; people with AIDS; physically or mentally disabled persons; a specific socio-economic class (i.e., rural Appalachian poor, or displaced Iraqi refugees now living in Turkey); a specific socio-political class (i.e., Sandinistas in Nicaragua); a specific ethnic people group (i.e., Navaho Indian people living on their tribal lands within Arizona or New Mexico). A hypothetical example of a short-term mission having *multiple activity with a given receptor group* might be: VBS (Vacation Bible School) for a given community's children in the morning, roof reconstruction on the community center during the afternoon, clothing distribution and soccer games in the community's squatter area during the evenings, and medical/dental work during weekends.

Discipleship

MATHETES—a disciple, an imitator, a learner, a pupil.

10. *Disciple Making* including helping followers of Jesus mature in their faith via: teaching/assisting/conducting a children's VBS, adult Bible training school, a church Sunday school; teaching or preaching in an already established church; relational visits to encourage believers to help strengthen their faith by simply "being" with someone else.

11. *Education-Giving (Teaching)* including the teaching of: basic first aid, health, or hygiene; English as a second language (TESL); secular academic subjects to either national children or expatriate missionary children; exchange programs for professors and other academic instructors; teaching professional skills (white collar business skills and blue collar trade skills); and pastoral care to missionary families.

12. *Education-Receiving (Information Acquisition)* including: first-hand observation of on-field mission situations (usually as a 'means' for future decision-making and/or mobilization of potential resources); and information gathering (e.g., Joshua and Caleb in the Promised Land) including research and unreached people group data gathering. In this activity category, host receivers are directly or indirectly discipling goer-guests as their Giving/Sowing portion of the two-way on-field serendipity (cf. Chapter 7—The Reciprocity of Give 'n Take).

Helps

EPIKOURIA—aid rendered by an ally.

13. *Construction Work and Physical Labor* including: engineering, maintenance, repair, excavation, painting, electrical, plumbing, carpentry, masonry, and all trades related to construction and building work; and any other type of physical labor activities.

14. *Other Blue Collar Support Services* including: regional/international courier services, mechanics and facilities/equipment maintenance such as small engine, gas and diesel engine, auto body, janitorial, grounds upkeep, all trades related to plant and facilities maintenance, heating/air conditioning/refrigeration, telecommunications installation, and installation/upkeep/ repair of specialized technology.

15. *White Collar Program Support Services* including: office-related work such as computer programming or data entry, operation of other technology services, accounting, secretarial, management, or administration.

16. *Hospitality* including: dorm parents, child care, guest home facilitation, food services, laundry services.

3. SIZE

The third defining variable is *size*—i.e., the number of goer-guest participants within a given short-term mission. Short-term goer-guests are 'cultural outsiders' who temporarily enter and work within a given on-field *ETHNOS* as individuals, in pairs, as a family, or as a small team or large team. Here, too, all dynamics of pre-field, on-field, and post-field processes will vary in direct correlation to the size variable. Brief examples for each of the five size variables are given below:

1. Individual

Traditional long-term career agencies often need a specialist to perform a specific task (often a short-term *Helps* activity) such as computer programming, printing press installation and training, telecommunications repair, etc. Often this task is completed within a *mini* short-term, *standard* short-term, or *seasonal* short-term period of time. An *individual* teaching English as a second language (TESL) in Japan for the summer (a *Discipleship seasonal* short-term), or in China for a year (a *Discipleship extended* short-term), fits this category as well.

2. Pairs

A good example of short-term mission done in *pairs* are the *Evangelism/Witnessing mini* short-terms of Mark 6:7 (Jesus sends out the 12 two by two) and Luke 10:1 (Jesus sends out the 70/72 two by two). Another example encountered in the early 1980s by one of the authors was two Jamaican itinerant evangelists preaching together in Haiti during the summer (an *Evangelism seasonal* short-term). A third example could be two single European Christian educators assisting the Soviet school system in Kyrgyzstan for 18 months to develop a values-based curriculum (a *Helps extended* short-term).

3. Family

Some Christian physicians plan their annual family vacations to a medically-needy area of the world, accompanied by their medically-trained spouse. Together the husband/wife team performs certain medical activities under the auspices of a given sending entity, usually done in one-, two-, or three-week stints (a *Witnessing standard* short-term). Another example could be a family of five (parents and three children) who spend an entire year (a *Helps extended* short-term) providing child care, maintenance, and secretarial support to a Bible translating organization working in central Africa.

Size of *family* teams depends on the number of participating family members, but usually runs from about two to six. At-home family systems normally dictate the dynamics of a family team while on-field, unless the family heavily integrates with other expatriates or nationals while on-field (in which case its group dynamics would more closely represent the *small* or *large teams* below).

4. Small Team (3–12)

Groups of up to roughly one dozen persons constitute what we identify as a *small team*. Although not a hard fast rule, normal team dynamics in a group

TABLE #3.4

3. SIZE
SIZE SUB-CATEGORIES OF SHORT-TERM MISSION CORRELATED TO RELATED OBSERVATIONS

	(1) INDIVIDUAL	(2) PAIRS	(3) FAMILY	(4) SMALL TEAM	(5) LARGE TEAM
Size	1 person	2 persons	≈ 2–6	≈ 3–12	≈ 13–100+
Sending Entity (SE)	Church / Agency / Self	Church / Agency / Self	Church / Agency / Self	Church / Agency	Church / Agency
Agency Type	Established Traditional	Established Traditional	Established Traditional	Newer Non-Traditional	Newer Non-Traditional
On-field Authority and Operational Structure	Self-determined (within SE's formal structure)	Self-determined (within SE's formal structure)	At-home family systems (within SE's formal structure)	Informal and Loose	Formal and Structured
Goer-Guests' Personal On-field Input	More Input ⟵————————————————————⟶ Less Input				
Length of Time Spent On-field	More Time ⟵————————————————————⟶ Less Time				
Social / Emotional Interchange Among Goer-Guests	More Interchange ⟵————————————————⟶ Less Interchange				
Goer-Guests' Doctrinal / Church Background	Identical Background ⟵————————————⟶ Differing Backgrounds				
Goer-Guests' Originating Geographical Location	Identical Location ⟵————————————————⟶ Differing Locations				
Goer-Guests' Familiarity With Other Goers	Very Familiar ⟵——————————————————⟶ Less Familiar				
Goer-Guests' Personal Ages	Older ⟵————————————————————————⟶ Younger				
Number of On-field Activities [†]	Potential for Fewer # of Activities ⟵——⟶ Potential for Greater # of Activities				
Time of Year Actually On-field	Any Time ⟵————————————————————————⟶ Summer				

© Roger Peterson and R. Wayne Sneed, 1995. Revised 2001. Used by permission.

[†] includes only the Goer-Guests' **Giving/Sowing** portion of the Two-way On-field Action (cf. Chapter 7)—does not include their **Receiving/Reaping** Action; nor does it include any of the Host Receivers' **Giving/Sowing** or **Receiving/Reaping** Action.

of 12 or less allow full emotional and social interchange among each member. Small teams—especially those serving a *mini* short-term—may or may not establish formal leadership within their group while on-field, and may or may not establish formal on-field operational/organizational structures (although more formalized on-field structure would be necessary in *seasonal* and *extended small team* short-terms). In terms of activity, small teams normally focus on one or two primary activities. Small teams sometimes attract more adults than youth, and therefore can be sent on-field any time of the year (as opposed to just during summer break for younger people).

Small teams serving a *mini* or *standard* short-term are becoming increasingly commonplace within many North American churches, especially churches just beginning to involve themselves in mission. One example might be a young growing church now consisting of 150 regular attendees, which organizes a group of six men to spend 10 days (a *Helps standard* short-term) assisting nationals re-thatch a Filipino church which lost its roof during a recent typhoon. Another example might be an organized fellowship of 12 athletes who sense God's call to spend a three day weekend (a *Witnessing mini* short-term) in inner-city Philadelphia playing basketball and baseball as pre-evangelism activities among at-risk teenage youth.

5. *Large Team (13 or more)*
This category consists of more than a dozen individuals (even 100 or more). Normally *large teams* have an established on-field leadership structure, in addition to on-field operational/organizational structures. Emotional and social interchange occurs within the team, but due to its larger number of goer-guests, not to the same extent as a small team. Large teams may focus on just one or two primary activities, but also have greater capacity to focus on several activities at any given time during their on-field outreach. Large teams seldom serve longer than a *mini* or *standard* short-term, and are usually composed of more youth than adults. Summer months, therefore, tend to be the prime time for large teams.

Similar to small teams, large teams are common occurrences within many church and parachurch sending agencies. Large teams are often composed of combinations of individuals and/or families who may not have known each other prior to the short-term mission outreach (i.e., goer-guest participants originate from differing churches and/or from differing geographical locations). Large teams often gather on-field in camp-type environments, similar to summer church camp in operational structure, and similar to outdoor camping in living structure.

The *size* variable dictates unique combinations of characteristics normally common to each one of its five classifications. Although a given characteristic will often times be represented within another classification, TABLE #3.4 provides an overview of the short-term mission characteristics which normally correlate to each of the five respective size variables.

4. LOCATION

The *location* variable relates directly to the on-field site identity of the short-term outreach, and is best understood as analyzed within these five sub-categories: the geo-political nation (or other commonly-used name for the geo-political city or regional area); rural or urban; and domestic or international. The on-field site *location* variable, as defined by the collective understanding these five sub-categories, plays an obviously significant role in the training curriculum used during the pre-field and on-field processes of a given short-term mission (cf. TABLE #3.5).

1.   Geo-political Nation

This is the most visibly obvious and most commonly used location sub-category, such as "I did a short-term to *Sri Lanka*," or "We're going to be prayer-walking in *Cairo*," or "That medical organization sends doctors for a month to *Africa*." It readily, although incompletely, answers the specific "Where?" question inherent to any short-term mission endeavor. We use the term geo-political nation to mean the popular, widely-accepted name which identifies the *geographical* on-site location of the host receiver participants. It can be a nation, state, province, region, territory, locale, city, suburb, village—or combination of any of these locally-accepted identities.

2. Rural or 3. Urban

Former Northern Baptist Theological Seminary Professor and urbanist Ray Bakke points out the unquestionable need for a different ministry methodology between *rural* and *urban* areas by citing primary social identity differences. First, the *rural* areas:

> "In rural areas, people gain identities through [biological and geographical] networks [of primary relationships]: their parents and where they live identify them. In a small town we know everybody. We have a pri-

mary relationship even to the town drunk. We know all the political leaders, the elders, and the children. They all know us—where we live, our parents, sisters, and brothers."[9]

Secondly, the *urban* areas:

"[Because of the] noise, the constant bombardment of sales messages and thousands of casual daily relationships[, people] survive in the city by ... filtering what they accept, and by opting out of relationships and situations. [When we live in] the city we are identified by our jobs, and nearly all our relationships are 'secondary' or casual. Amidst this kaleidoscopic and bewildering environment, we get lost—'when the tide goes out, each shrimp has its own puddle.' ... It is for this reason that unemployment [in the city] is not just an economic crisis, but one of identity. Urban people are insecure, and if they lose their jobs, they suffer more severely than those in rural areas."[10]

Then consider the vast differences in these rural areas: the economically depressed regions of Appalachia, or some Native American Indian reservations, with oftentimes less-than-ideal housing, education, and employment. It becomes apparent that the dynamics of effective urban ministry differ quite substantially from effective rural ministry, and therefore the *rural* or *urban* sub-categories of the on-field site location variable become quite important in any attempt to define and explain short-term mission.

4. *Domestic* or 5. *International*

These final two on-field site location sub-categories are every bit as important as the first three. Within the United States Bakke points out "Los Angeles is now the second-largest 'Mexican' city, while Houston is the fastest-growing one."[11] Such *domestic* mission opportunities abound within every nation—every people group has its own 'Judea and Samaria' (cf. Acts 1:8) containing culturally distant people living in a geographical close locale. Likewise, every people group also has its 'ends of the earth'—classic *international* mission to people living in geographical distant locale. Pursuant to our earlier definition of 'mission,' both *domestic* and *international* mission qualify as opportunities—specialized as they respectively are—for short-term mission.

5. PARTICIPANT DEMOGRAPHICS

Participant demographics can easily become an almost infinite list of identity concepts. Yet for the purpose of understanding short-term mission, we pinpoint five primary sub-categories each for the *goer-guest,* receiving host *field facilitator,* and receiving host *intended receptor* participants:

- age
- gender
- religious identity
- cultural identity
- related experience

One example would be a mixed gender *small team* of inner-city African-American Pentecostal youth, half of whom have no related short-term mission experience doing a *standard Evangelism/Witnessing* short-term outreach to unchurched Eskimo children in a Canadian fishing village, a village which does have the related experience of previously hosting several short-term teams in the past five years.

Another example would be an *individual* middle-class Anglican New Zealander doing an *extended Helps* short-term through a mission agency working among a group of chemically-dependent, marginally-churched Polynesian fisherman in the Marshal Islands.

Accurate analysis and understanding of the goer-guest and receiving host participant demographics of a given short-term mission can contribute greatly to the effectiveness of the *leadership* style and *training* methods used (defining variable #8). Although the intended results of two separately-originating short-term outreaches may be similar, the makeup of each participant trilogy (cf. Chapter 6) may be vastly different. Therefore the leadership and training methods employed for goer-guests—during pre-field preparation, while living and working on-field, and while following up post-field—will likewise need to be contextualized and fit to each given outreach.[12]

When compared with the four preceding short-term mission variables (time, activity, size, and location), two significantly different aspects of the participant demographics variable emerge.

First, participant demographics are simultaneously *externally visible* and *internally hidden* (cf. TABLE #3.1), depending on the perspective of the passive observer. From the passive observer's viewpoint sitting on the *sending-*side of the equation, the goer-guest demographics appear largely visible—while to the same passive observer's viewpoint, the receiving host participant demographics will be largely unknown. Conversely, a passive observer on the *receiving*-side will see the receiving host participant demographics as visible, but incoming goer-guest participant demographics will be largely unknown.

Secondly, unlike the four preceding variables, the participant demographics can seldom be repeated verbatim (especially within small team and large team *size* settings). In TABLE #3.1 we implied 125 major sub-categories ($5^3 = 125$) within just the *participant demographics* variable alone, and the probability of all 125 repeating themselves verbatim on a future short-term mission is very low. Further, each one of these 125 sub-categories contains

---

TABLE #3.5

4. LOCATION and 5. PARTICIPANT DEMOGRAPHICS
ANALYSIS WORKSHEET

---

4. Host Site Location

1) Name of Geo-political Nation (country/region/area/city):_____

(Identity of Intended Receptor Group: _____)

2,3) ❑ Rural ❑ Urban

4,5) ❑ Domestic ❑ International

---

5. Participant Demographics	Goer-Guest Participants	Field Facilitator Participants	Intended Receptor Participants
1) Median Age (or other identifying age characteristic):	_____	_____	_____
2) Male to Female Ratio (or similar gender description):	_____	_____	_____
3) Religious Identity (theological or doctrinal persuasion):	_____	_____	_____
4) Cultural Identity:	_____	_____	_____
5) Related Experience:	_____	_____	_____

---

sub-sub-categories (e.g., both the religious and cultural sub-categories contain an almost infinite number of very unique and specific sub-sub categories). Further yet, all *participant demographics* sub-categories (except gender) are ever-changing, non-static dynamics. This presents an exact replication probability of zero.

The first two of the five primary sub-categories contained within the participant demographics are somewhat self-explanatory—age and gender. But a word now about the remaining three—*religious identity, cultural identity,* and *related experience.*

Religious Identity

Each goer-guest participant has some level of church *(ECCLESIARUM)* affiliation or at least some theological 'position' which that person holds or hopes to be true. But for certain individual goer-guests or their churches (or the goer-guest's sending entity if different from their home church), this identity can be very strong, and enhance or restrict working relationships with Christians of other church affiliations or doctrinal persuasions.

The same may be true for receiving host *field facilitator* participants. Field facilitators in some instances may not be Christian. Even so, the field facilitator still has some level—perhaps even a deep, strong, committed level—of theological identity or spiritual belief which may either enhance or restrict the reciprocity of give and take (cf. Chapter 7) required for effective outreach.

And of course the receiving host *intended receptor* participants have some level of spiritual or religious identity which will directly impact the strategy of the given short-term mission outreach. Often intended receptor participants are not Christian—which is why the oral- and deed-proclamation of God's love (i.e., the intended activity) is somehow being given/sown in their community.

Cultural Identity

When Christian anthropologist Charles Kraft analyzes a culture, he notes two basal levels: (1) the *surface* behavior level, which is directly affected by that given culture's (2) *deep worldview* level. Although it differs vastly from culture to culture (even from the goer-guests' culture to the host receivers' culture as we apply his observations to our short-term mission typology), he sees this second aspect, the deep worldview level, at the very core of a given culture and therefore at the very heart of that culture's entire human life.[13]

Harvie Conn, former Westminster Theological Seminary Professor of Missions, explains we use the term 'culture' to

"refer to the common ideas, feelings, and values that guide community and personal behavior, that organize and regulate what the group thinks, feels, and does about God, the world, and humanity. ...Cultures are patterns shared by, and acquired in, a social group. ...[Even so, there] is a dynamic to human cultures [which contains] gaps and inconsistencies. ...cultural forms (e.g., language, gestures, relationships, money, clothing) are invested with symbolic meanings conventionally accepted by the community. They interpret the forms and stamp them with meaning and value. Each cultural form, ambivalent by itself, thus becomes a hermeneutical carrier of values, attitudes, and connotations. Clothing can indicate social status, occupation, level of education, ritual preparation."[14]

People Groups

The specific *people group*—especially when used in conjunction with the geopolitical nation, such as the *Sunni Islamic White Moors* of Mauritania (west Africa), or the *Tibetan Buddhists* of Nepal, or the *unemployed single Hispanic mothers* of Los Angeles County—provides a potentially helpful semantic handle when *sending entities* or *goer-guests* want to identify a specific *intended receptor* group of people. (But a word of caution: some missiologists view the people group concept as promoting racist church bodies[15]).

What is a *people group*? In 1982 the Lausanne Committee for World Evangelization (LCWE) sponsored a meeting where 40 mission leaders agreed that

"A 'people group' is a significantly large grouping of individuals who perceive themselves to have a common affinity for one another, because of their shared language, religion, ethnicity, residence, occupation, class, caste, situation, or combinations of these. For evangelistic purposes it is the largest group within which the Gospel can spread as a church-planting movement without encountering barriers of understanding or acceptance."[16]

Although a given people group often exists in more than one geo-political area (e.g., there are *Tibetan Buddhists* in Tibet, Ladakh, Mongolia, the CIS [Commonwealth of Independent States]—as well as Nepal[17]), the cultural identity as expressed in the name of a given people group can help provide tremendous pre-field preparation focus, as well as more effective on-field work. Currently missiologists identify approximately 24,000[18] such ethnic people groups around the world, with approximately 10,000 of those deemed as yet unreached with the Gospel (cross-cultural E-2 and E-3 evangelism required). The other 14,000 people groups are deemed reached in the sense they each have an indigenous church of sufficient size and capacity to theoretically reach their own unevangelized people (using same-cultural E-0 and E-1 evangelism). Sending entities and goer-guests are routinely from one or more of these 14,000 reached people groups.

Goer-guests and the sending entity must develop a realistic, honest understanding of their own culture—including the ever-present negative aspects—before trying to understand and work effectively within the parameters of the host receiver's culture. Receiving field facilitators must likewise understand their own culture (baggage, garbage, and warts included) before trying to understand and work effectively—not just with the intended receptor's culture only—but the incoming goer-guests' culture as well.

This is, of course, the great challenge of all cross-cultural mission work: how to work concurrently within two (or three or more) sets of deeply imbedded cultural worldview assumptions, values, and allegiances which govern every surface level behavior—while somehow ushering in some deeper level of God's redeeming love, without destroying the richness of each culture's identity, and yet not compromising on the non-negotiables of the Gospel.

Related Experience

A given goer-guest participant may—or may not—have previous cross-cultural experience, international travel experience, hands-on evangelism experience, or a variety of any other *related experiences* to be encountered during the on-field phase of the short-term mission process trilogy. Goer-guests who have no related experience may tend to be more teachable and trainable (and perhaps more fearful), while goer-guests with just one or two previous short-term experiences may develop a know-it-all attitude and try to skip out on pre-field training. A goer-guest with multiple similar experiences, who joins another church's first short-term outreach, may in fact know much more than the trainers and leaders of that team she is joining.

Likewise an expatriate field facilitator may have received two poorly-trained large youth teams in the past, but has no experience whatsoever with a well-trained small adult team. So what appears on the surface as related experience, is in fact not closely-related at all.

Even the host intended receptors may have—or they may not have—some level of experience with short-term outreach endeavors in their past. Whether such previous experiences have been good or bad, the intended receptor participants will already be transferring their assumptions, attitudes, and expectations to any new incoming short-term endeavors.

TABLE #3.5 combines both short-term mission defining variables #4 and #5 (*location* and *participant demographics*) into an analysis worksheet format, which can be readily used to help better understand two of the eight defining variables of a given short-term mission.

6. SENDING ENTITY

Short-term mission defining variable #6, *sending entity,* is one-half of the 'sender participants' (cf. The Participant Trilogy—Chapter 6). The *sending entity* refers to the organized (whether formal or informal) institutional structure (whether incorporated or not) having primary administrative, managerial, and/or information-sharing responsibility to many of the sending supporters (prayer, financial, and re-entry), all of the goer-guests, and the field facilitators as those aspects apply to the 'sending-side' of a short-term mission.

Although there can—and most often should[19]—be some level of partnership in the 'sending-side' process, we identify 12 functional subsets of short-term mission sending entities (cf. TABLE #3.6) which we group under one of these four major categorical headings:

SE–1 Churches
SE–2 Parachurch Mission Agencies
SE–3 Institutional Non-mission Organizations
SE–4 One's Self

1. Churches (SE-1)

Already there are thousands of churches *directly* sending their own short-term missionaries—*without* the use of their denominational board (SE-2.b—cf. below), or other association/network (SE-2.c), or other parachurch agency (SE-2.a or SE-3.a). Evidence shows that increasing numbers of churches are doing this every year. Even though some missiologists like Ralph Winter believe all world-wide mission efforts "in any part of the world will be most effective only if both [church and parachurch mission agency] structures are fully and properly involved and supportive of each other,"[20] more and more

North American churches increasingly view themselves theologically as having primary, personal responsibility for the Great Commission.

After recently listening to scores of mission executives, church missions coordinators, theological professors, and lay leaders in 10 cities across America, McKaughan, O'Brien, and O'Brien summarized this obvious and increasingly significant trend:

TABLE #3.6

6.1 SENDING ENTITY
THE FOUR SUB-CATEGORIES OF SHORT-TERM MISSION SENDING ENTITIES
(listing their 12 resulting functional subsets, with reference number)

SE–1 Churches	Subset Ref. #
SE–1.a Churches with a Comprehensive Mission Program	1
SE–1.b Churches Doing Short-Term Mission as their Only Mission Program	2

SE–2 Parachurch Mission Agencies

SE–2.a Nondenominational Mission Agencies	
• SE–2.a(1) Traditional Agencies (primary long-term focus)	3
• SE–2.a(2) Non-traditional Agencies (primary short-term focus)	4
SE–2.b Denominational Mission Boards	5
SE–2.c Associations or Networks of Churches	6
SE–2.d Local Society Created Within a Given Church	7

SE–3 Institutional Non-mission Organizations

SE–3.a Christian Parachurch Non-mission Agency Organizations	
• SE–3.a(1) Inter-collegiate Christian Organizations	8
• SE–3.a(2) Individual Christian Colleges & Schools	9
• SE–3.a(3) Other	10
SE–3.b Secular Non-parachurch Organizations	11

SE–4 One's Self 12

"A new day in missions and local church relationships has dawned, and the sun is high in the sky ... local churches express their desire to be the dominant partners in any relationship between church and agency. The local body feels that financial and human resources are theirs, and [that they have] a stewardship responsibility to make sure they are getting the most effective returns on all of it ... there is no misunderstanding that *the center of gravity in missions has moved from the agency to the local church ...*"[21] (italics ours).

Many churches often do have the human and financial resources necessary to structure their own direct short-term mission sending efforts with little or no outside SE-2 or SE-3 agency assistance. Many of these churches also have the capacity to re-program their activities based on the expressed needs of their people. One megachurch pastor noted, "the people in the pew are redefining what missions means, and these people will go elsewhere if we don't change to meet their desires."[22]

We note two important subsets of SE-1 churches. First, the churches which lean toward more of a traditional, comprehensive mission program— as opposed to the second, which are churches which do short-term mission as their only mission program. To many people from the second subset of churches, one- and two-week short-term mission teams are the only understanding of what the word 'mission' means.

Even though hard empirical data is difficult, if not impossible, to substantiate, the direct sending of short-term missionaries by a given church (without denominational or other SE-2 or SE-3 agency assistance) appears to be on an exponential rise. Therefore we conclude that such individual churches are already, and will increase their influence in being, major sending entity players both now and into the foreseeable future.

2. Parachurch Mission Agencies (SE-2)

Ralph Winter defines the parachurch mission agency structure as a "*sodality* [which] is a structured fellowship in which membership involves an adult second decision beyond modality [church] membership, and is limited by [certain qualifying factors]"[23] (italics ours). In other words, parachurch mission agencies are composed of people who have: (1) made a deeper level, 'second decision' regarding Christian missions, and who have: (2) met more requirements (than compared to a church's membership-only requirements) to become members or to participate in the agency's programs.

TABLE #3.7

6.2 'SE–2' PARACHURCH MISSION AGENCIES[†]
EXAMPLES OF 'SE-2' SENDING ENTITIES
PROVIDING SHORT-TERM MISSION

AGENCY CLASSIFICATION	TRADITIONAL AGENCIES[††]	NON-TRADITIONAL AGENCIES[††]
SE-2.a *Nondenominational Mission Agencies*	• Wycliffe Bible Translators • Pioneers • Latin American Missions • Africa Inland Missions • The Evangelical Alliance Mission (TEAM) • Navigators • New Tribes Mission • OMS International	• Adventures In Missions • English Language Institute China (ELIC) • Operation Mobilization (OM) • STEM Int'l • Teen Missions International • Teen Mania • World Servants • Youth With A Mission (YWAM)
SE-2.b *Denominational Mission Boards*	• Assemblies of God, General Council, Division of Foreign Missions • Lutheran Church Missouri Synod, Board for Mission Services • Southern Baptist Convention International Mission Board	• Mission to the World, Presbyterian Church in America
SE-2.c *Associations or Networks of Churches*		• Del Camino Network, Latin America • Union Baptist Association, Houston TX
SE-2.d *Local Society In a Given Church*		• Global Outreach (Perimeter Church), Atlanta GA • Missions & Outreach Ministry (Southeast Christian Church), Louisville KY

[†] Table created from information contained in the "2001–2003 Mission Handbook—18th Edition" (Wheaton IL: EMIS, 2000), and from direct personal research by the authors.

[††] Although most traditional agencies and most non-traditional agencies send both long-term and short-term missionaries, traditional agencies tend to specialize as long-term sending entities, while non-traditional agencies tend to specialize as short-term sending entities.

But as applied to the present short-term mission sending entities we currently observe, Winter's astute historical observation is not comprehensive enough. Therefore we create additional specific subsets to the *parachurch mission agencies* (most of which Winter calls sodalities) which function in the role of a short-term mission sending entity:

- **SE-2.a**—*Nondenominational Mission Agencies* are the nondenominational (or inter- or trans-denominational) parachurch sodalities organized to send cross-cultural missionaries. As an important observation within this category, we further identify nondenominational mission sending agencies in one of two subsets: *traditional* agencies (which historically began their sending efforts only with long-term career missionaries), and the newer *non-traditional* agencies providing short-term mission as their primary sending strategies[24] (cf. TABLE #3.7). Control of mission rests in the hands of its governing Board and its chief executives as established by the charter of the given nondenominational mission agency.

- **SE-2.b**—*Denominational Mission Boards* would be the mission department at the headquarters level of a group of same-name, same-doctrine churches. (Examples would include: United Methodist Church, Global Ministries; Free Will Baptists, Board of Foreign Mission; Assemblies of God, Division of Foreign Missions; Evangelical Free Church Mission; Lutheran World Relief). Each denominational mission board respectively represents hundreds of thousands (even millions) of its church members. Control of mission rests in the hands of its governing Board and its chief executives as determined by the authority and powers granted by its given denomination.

- **SE-2.c**—*Associations or Networks of Churches* are groups of churches (not necessarily from the same denomination or exact doctrinal viewpoints) which form some level of their own organized structure for the expressed purpose of improving their combined joint efforts of cross-cultural mission (e.g., the Del Camino Network in four Latin American nations—cf. www.lareddelcamino.net). Control of mission rests in the hands of more than one church as determined by their specific partnership or association agreements.

- **SE-2.d**—*Local Society Created Within a Given Church* is a separate-ly-named and identifiable society formed inside a given church for the expressed purpose of specializing in cross-cultural mission for that church. The society remains under full control of the given church (e.g., 'Global Outreach' of Perimeter Church in Atlanta).

Often (but not always) it's the SE-2.a and SE-2.b parachurch mission agencies—through their historical experience and specialized on-field work and relationships—which can provide the highest potential for effective on-field ministry for a given mission endeavor whether short-term or long-term (cf. Chapter 6, TABLE #6.1 for our contrasting assessment of each sending entity's particular strengths).

3. Institutional Non-mission Organizations (SE-3)

Although organized and chartered for a primary function and purpose other than Christian mission, such organizations oftentimes have the human and financial resources to structure their own direct short-term mission sending efforts, and may do so with little or no outside SE-2 mission agency assistance (although SE-2.a or -2.b mission agency cooperation may be needed while on-field). Within the SE-3 category we observe two broad subsets of *institutional non-mission organizations* currently functioning at times in the temporary role of sending entities:

- **SE-3.a**—*Christian Parachurch Non-mission Agency Organizations* which we further divide into three functional subsets:

  (1) *Inter-collegiate Christian organizations* whose chartered purpose is to evangelize and disciple college students across as many secular college campuses as possible. Such organizations' respective size, strength, and relationships to other nations of the world now easily affords them the ability to send their own short-term mission outreaches, even though sending missionaries was not the expressed sole purpose of their founding charters (i.e., InterVarsity Christian Fellowship, Campus Crusade for Christ, Fellowship of Christian Athletes, etc.).

  (2) *Individual Christian schools, colleges, and seminaries* which officially organize, sponsor, and send their own students on short-

term mission outreaches, often giving academic credit to those who go. Although such schools were founded for the purpose of classroom-based Christian education, such schools now see the immense educational value to be attained on the field, and often engage themselves as active short-term mission sending entities. Christian colleges send thousands of short-termers annually, and must be considered very serious, significant short-term mission sending entities. Examples of just a few of these SE-3.a(2) colleges include:

- Wheaton College
- Bethany College of Missions
- Messiah College
- John Brown University
- Bethel College
- Trinity International Univ.
- Taylor University
- Gordon College
- Master's College
- Azusa Pacific University
- Vanguard University
- Northwestern College (IA)
- Northwestern College (MN)
- Biola University
- Point Loma College
- Oral Roberts University[25]

(3) *Other institutional non-mission organizations* which include Christian radio stations; church-affiliated hospitals; any locally-chartered campus fellowship organized around athletics, Bible study, unmarried singles, or other common interests; and all other Christian-based affinity groups whether incorporated or not.

- **SE-3.b**—*Secular Non-parachurch Organizations* which include all for-profit organizations, secular humanitarian aid organizations, and other organizations—none of which were founded and chartered to intentionally advance Christianity (e.g., community medical hospitals; secular schools; and other non-church, non-parachurch secular institutions of which some employees or members happen to be Christian and who persuade their organization to officially sponsor short-term endeavors, often because of a humanitarian focus).

4. *One's Self (SE-4)*

Normally when goer-guest participants (as individual, pairs, family, small team, or large team) head out to do a short-term mission, they have been sent either by their respective church acting in its SE-1 capacity, or by an SE-2 mission agency (or ideally, by a collaboration of both church and agency). Historically there have been exceptions such as Gladys Aylward's solo launch into ministry, or Bruce Olson's solo into South America,[26] and others. Never barring the inexplicable work of the Holy Spirit, the self-sent solo mission efforts seem usually to be the exception. Yet it is fully possible—though normally neither Biblically nor logistically advisable—to send one's self without the official sending covering of church and agency.

A Concluding Observation Regarding Sending Entities
Similar to variable #5 (participant demographics) in terms of passive observation, the sending entity is simultaneously externally visible and internally hidden. While on-field, passive locals don't normally observe the sending entity *per se* (i.e., internally hidden)—unless the entity is a parachurch agency with an obvious on-going, on-field presence. Conversely on the sending-side, a local passive observer may well be aware "First Church downtown sent a bunch o' folks somewhere last summer" (i.e., externally visible)—but at the same time was unaware that First Church actually used an SE-2.a mission agency based out-of-state (i.e., internally hidden) to plan and organize the pre-field and on-field process.

7. MISSION PHILOSOPHY

We explain the seventh defining variable, *mission philosophy,* within three primary sub-categories:
- Personal Mission Definition
- Ministry Values
- Ministry Expectations

A participant's[27] personal definition may not actually be written out *per se*; yet it most certainly exists. A personal mission definition (whether written or not, whether conscious or not) flows out of a given participant's values, then manifests itself through that participant's expectations by way of the ministry roles and intended activity the participant believes should take place. (As this pertains to goer-guests, such resulting on-field ministry action is what this book calls the goer-guests' Giving/Sowing intended activity).

When thought through and identified as such, a stated *mission philosophy* helps answer the 'why-are-we-in-this-thing?' question, and pries open doors to evaluative self-critique which can help strengthen and greatly improve the effectiveness of a given short-term endeavor's entire process trilogy, including its final outcomes. ILLUSTRATION #3.2 visually diagrams the mission philosophy formation process.

Within the short-term mission process, there are essentially four dominant sets of participants which consciously (or subconsciously) ask, and consciously (or subconsciously) answer, this 'why' question—i.e., these four already have a mission philosophy whether they realize it or not. They include: (1) the sending entity; (2) the goer-guest participants; (3) the receiving host field facilitator participants; and (4) the receiving host intended receptor participants. Each of these four brings into the short-term mission effectiveness equation its own *mission philosophy*—one or more definitions based on respective values and expectations.

When the definition, values, and expectations are not necessarily uniform between the goer-guests and sending entity, or between the sending entity and the receiving host field facilitators—or when they're not adequately understood by the sending entity and the receiving host field facilitators regarding the receiving host intended receptor participants—the stage gets set for problems. Therefore we strongly encourage at least the first three of the four sets of participants indicated above (and in churched and partially evangelized mission field settings the intended receptor participants as well) to take the time necessary to learn the following about themselves and the other participants:

1. Personal Mission Definition

In the previous chapter we spent a fair amount of time attempting to systematically build a "line upon line, precept upon precept" understanding of our definition of mission (we also included definitions of several others as well). But a personalized written *mission definition* only serves its users when it accurately represents the values and expectations we discuss below. We strongly recommend that all three (or all four, when applicable) sets of participants we refer to in this section take the time to study Scripture, pray, and ask the Lord to reveal the deep *ministry values* that explain the *ministry expectations* you have as you play your *ministry role*. This is especially necessary for on-field goer-guests who perform the intended Giving/Sowing activities of whatever it is they define as 'mission.' Useful tools to help you in this process are the questions posed in context of the MISTM-Grid contained in Chapter 9. If put into writing, your written definition helps summarize these answers, and has potential to become another very helpful starting tool when trying to best match yourselves for maximum Kingdom impact. When the mission definition of goer-guests, field facilitators, intended receptors, and the sending entity are all in relative alignment, the given outreach has high potential for maximum impact.

Once again we'll provide our critical definitions here to help re-ignite your thinking process as you begin to understand and develop your own definition:

Mission (active verb—full definition)
  Sending messengers (missionaries) away from their 'normal' home culture as soon as possible, and into another culture and people (intended receptors), for the express purpose of proclaiming with word and deed (the intended activity) the Good News that sets any person free from anything that binds them.

Mission (active verb—simplified definition)
  Sending active Gospel messengers into another culture.

ILLUSTRATION #3.2

7. MISSION PHILOSOPHY
FORMATION OF A PERSONAL MISSION DEFINITION

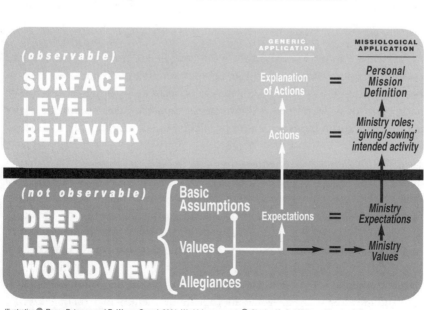

Illustration © Roger Peterson and R. Wayne Sneed, 2001. Worldview concepts © Charles Kraft, 1984; used by permission.

Missionary

A person sent into another culture to be an active Gospel messenger in both word and deed.

2. Ministry Values

Broadly speaking, *values* are one of the deeply-imbedded aspects of any culture's worldview;[28] such values almost always differ significantly between the goer-guests' culture and the host receivers' culture(s). Christian anthropologist Charles Kraft highlights some deeply-imbedded contrasting values which exist within all spheres of differing cultures' lives, such as:

- *the personal sphere* (individual rights and freedoms vs. family loyalty)
- *the economic sphere* (capitalism vs. "dickering" which places a high premium on developing personal relationships between buyers and sellers)
- *the political sphere* (democratic government based on 51% majority vs. consensus requiring 100% agreement by certain leaders)
- *the family sphere* (marriage based on individual romantic attraction vs. marriage arranged on the basis of the overall best interests of two families)
- *the religious sphere* (individual conversion vs. group consensus conversion)[29]

However, in terms of short-term mission, we are narrowing the focus to specific *ministry* values that the sending entity, goer-guests, and host receivers consciously (or more often subconsciously) bring to the whole short-term mission process trilogy. These ministry values permeate every action taken throughout the entire pre-field, on-field, and post-field process.

MINISTRY VALUES: Sending Entity

Some driving and shaping *ministry values* that a sending entity might hold could be operational integrity, organizational accountability, disciple making, people empowerment, serving, loving, giving, working for justice, mercy, etc.— or—that the intended receptor participants are basically ignorant, that Western technology can solve every problem, that we have all the answers, or controlling, or using people as machines, etc. One sending entity may highly value pre-field training—and spend substantial efforts producing top-notch curriculum and effective trainers—while another sending entity may marginalize the value of such training and expend very little resource preparing its goer-guest participants. The ministry values of the sending entity will play an especially profound effect on how, and for what purpose, its goer-guests are trained.

MINISTRY VALUES: Goer-Guests

A goer-guest's ministry values may emanate from a well-grounded, lifetime study of God's Word—or—be syncretized and intermingled with his own culture's worldview so thoroughly that the goer-guest's Christianity resembles very little of Biblical Christianity. Goers-guests' ministry values could range from Kingdom priority, God glorification in word and deed, turning the other cheek, the necessity of praise and worship for spiritual warfare, persistent prayer, outreach and evangelism, reconciliation, justice, stewardship of the world's natural resources, development of close personal relationships, personal empowerment of the Holy Spirit, etc., to job security, financial wealth, technology over relationships, occasional prayer (as long as someone else is doing it), personal rights, personal comfort, individualism, superiority, racism, etc. To further complicate the issue, short-term mission is often done with multiple people (i.e., in pairs, small teams, or large teams), with each goer-guest participant holding their own varying ministry values. Whatever ministry value a given goer-guest holds to, will profoundly effect his expectations of not only himself, but his expectations of the other goer-guests (i.e., his teammates) and all other participants as well.

MINISTRY VALUES: Host Receivers

Host receiver field facilitators' ministry values will likewise cover a wide spectrum. Certain ministry values may manifest themselves toward the goer-guest participants, while other ministry values may manifest themselves toward the host receiver intended receptor participants. Such ministry values could demonstrate themselves in relationship priority, trust, truth, assistance, guidance, training, partnership, patience, equality—or—inferiority/superiority, impatience, frustration, judgement, etc. Host receiver intended receptor participants' values may manifest themselves toward either the goer-guests or the host receiver field facilitators within the ministry context as welcomed assistance, thankfulness, warmth—or—mistrust, greed, hate, etc.

3.   *Ministry Expectations*

Except, perhaps, for a self-sent individual short-term endeavor, short-term mission rarely occurs outside of some degree of structure, some degree of organization. Within this context, organizational behaviorists Paul Hersey and

Kenneth Blanchard define organizational *expectations* as

> "... the perceptions of appropriate behavior for one's own role or position or one's own perception of the roles of others within the organization ... the expectations of individuals define for them what they should do under various circumstances [during the short-term mission] and how they think others [e.g., the sending entity, goer-guests, or host receivers] should behave in relation to their positions."[30]

They point out when "a person has *shared expectations* with another person[, it] means that each of the individuals involved perceives accurately and accepts a personal role and the role of the other"[31] (italics ours). In other words, when goer-guest participants share the same expectations as the sending entity and the field facilitator participants, there is a high likelihood all three participant subsets will successfully perform their given short-term mission roles with maximum effectiveness. The same behaviorists also emphasize "if expectations are to be compatible, it is important to share common goals and objectives."[32]

But what happens if there are conflicting expectations? Anthropologist Kraft says conflicting expectations lead to role conflict.[33] It's obvious that unidentified or unresolved conflict leads to unmatched ministry expectations, resulting in less than effective ministry.

For example, during the last moments of the pre-field process, goer-guests, receiving hosts, and the sending entity are all consciously (or subconsciously) envisioning upcoming on-field roles in context of what will happen, how it will happen, to whom it will happen, when it will happen, where it will happen, and why it will happen. When all participant subsets have arrived at an accepted consensus with respect to the given short-term mission's goals and objectives, a healthy state of mutual *ministry expectations* is in the making. But when these parties fail to discuss their goals, hopes, and dreams, there is an increased likelihood that competing agendas—what Kraft calls role conflict—may squelch an otherwise effective short-term mission outreach.

MINISTRY EXPECTATIONS: Sending Entity

The sending entity may effectively convey one or more of its clearly-defined ministry expectations while it trains and prepares its goer-guests pre-field. Or it may emanate a plethora of mixed, confusing expectations depending on which person from the sending entity you talk to. If the sending entity is an

SE-2.a or SE-2.b parachurch agency which has on-field employees or official representatives (whose function may then become that of the host receiving field facilitator), these employees or representatives may expect to be in charge of the entire short-term outreach during its on-field process. Why? Because in their previous related experience (cf. defining variable #5), they were in that leadership role. As a result, they 'play the role of team leader' without ever consulting the goer-guests leaders (who likewise are trying to 'play the role of team leader' while on-field—just like they successfully did back home during pre-field training).

MINISTRY EXPECTATIONS: Goer-Guests
Goer-guests may expect to see hundreds of intended receptor participants 'playing their role as unsaved heathen' who will flock to hear stories about Jesus, or the goer-guests may expect to 'play their role as superior construction experts' and erect an entire church building in five easy days. Some goer-guests may expect to get a tax-deductible trip for divvying out tracts on a tropical beach. Other goers may expect to conduct VBS with children or bring soap and towels to an orphanage—and expect the intended receptors to 'play their role as needy, thankful children.' One goer may expect to befriend a teenage communist and love that person to Christ, while another expects to teach English for a year and personally befriend an influential member of the host receiver school's administrative staff. Another short-term team may have some of their goer-guests expecting to sleep in private rooms with private baths, while other goer-guests on the same team expect to 'live like the local people,' by roughing their entire on-field process living in the crowded, thatched-roof homes of national intended receptor participants.

MINISTRY EXPECTATIONS: Host Receivers
Host receiver intended receptor participants may expect to 'play the role of paid worker' and be employed by the goer-guests on certain construction projects, or to 'play the role of generous host' by sharing their meager food and limited floor space with the goers—expecting the goers to 'play the role of grateful guest.' Other intended receptor participants expect goer-guests to know nothing of the local language or customs, and to have to tolerate these obnoxious guests for fear of offending someone perceived to be important. Or the host receiver field facilitators may expect goers to 'play the role of baby sitter for the missionary kids'—even though the goers expected to 'play the roles of evangelist and teacher.' Some intended receptor participants can't

wait to make friends with people from a far-off land. Others may envision hanging around the medical clinic project, in hopes to spend hours and hours each day just talking and getting to know their visiting guests as they play their role in a people-are-more-important-than-projects scenario.

A Concluding Observation Regarding Mission Philosophy

The values, expectations, and mission definition that make up the *ministry philosophy* of the sending entity, goer-guests, and host receivers are almost always internally hidden from the passive observer on both the sending-side and receiving-side of the equation. Even more unfortunate is that these elements of ministry philosophy are hidden all too often from the participant members themselves, resulting in mediocre ministry at best. Once again, you may want to work through questions posed in context of Chapter 9's MISTM-Grid to help all parties flush out their hopes, dreams, objectives, and goals. Once the results of these items are on the discussion table, they still need to be prayed through, deliberated, and prioritized—and then synthesized into an agreement (or some other useful format) beneficial to all involved. (This process can actually help produce your very own written mission definition.)

8. LEADERSHIP EFFECTIVENESS AND TRAINING EFFECTIVENESS

The eighth and final defining variable used to understand short-term mission is *leadership effectiveness and training effectiveness*. Closer examination of this variable (cf. TABLE #3.1) reveals that—for our short-term mission definition purposes—we've reduced this very complex and multi-layered variable to just three primary sub-categories:

1. **Leadership effectiveness** upon the *goer-guests* (during the entire pre-field, on-field, and post-field process trilogy);
2. **Training effectiveness** upon the *goer-guests* (during the entire pre-field, on-field, and post-field process trilogy); and
3. **Training effectiveness** upon the *host receivers* (both the field facilitator and the intended receptor participants when applicable).

Note that these three sub-categories making up variable #8 are highly subjective and much more difficult to quantify as a 'defining variable' *per se*. All three vary greatly from one example to the next—depending upon the given situation. It is actually the composite of the first seven variables that provides the correct recipe for each of these three sub-categories.

1. Leadership Effectiveness Upon the Goer-Guests

Although leadership clearly involves people, we're using the term to mean not just people but process as well. In other words, we mean everything that influences the goer-guests throughout all pre-field, on-field, and post-field phases of the short-term mission. Professor of Leadership and missiologist Bobby Clinton defines leadership as "a dynamic process in which a man or woman with God-given capacity influences a specific group of God's people toward His purposes for the group."[34] We agree, and therefore intend the leadership aspect of our defining variable #8 to mean the comprehensive, overall impact of the total composite of all leadership and their leadership acts[35]—wherever, however, and through whomever it occurs during the entire process trilogy of a given short-term mission. Because leadership is such a specialized, dynamic discipline evolving throughout a given leader's lifetime, space won't permit us to do in-depth justice to leadership theory. Therefore we'll note that this sub-category, *leadership effectiveness upon the goer-guests*, is better understood within the meaning of these four descriptors:

    (A) Quantity of Leadership Personnel
    (B) Quality of Leadership Personnel
    (C) Leadership Style Adaptability
    (D) Related Leadership Experience

(A) Quantity of Leadership Personnel

The number of leaders required for a given short-term mission depends:

- primarily upon the *size* (defining variable #3)
- secondarily upon the *intended activities* (defining variable #2)
- thirdly upon the *participant demographics* (defining variable #5), especially with respect to the age and gender sub-categories of the goer-guests
- fourthly upon circumstances unique to a given short-term mission

(B) Quality of Leadership Personnel

Higher *quality* of leadership correlates directly to increased potential for maximum impact short-term outreach. In multiple leadership situations (i.e., when the *quantity* of leadership is not merely one person, but several as obviously required in large team situations), the collective *quality* of all leadership emanates in part from mutually agreed upon:

101

- job descriptions
- chain of authority and command
- accountability systems among all leaders

(C) Leadership Style Adaptability

Are there one or two always-correct styles of leadership for short-term mission endeavors? With more than 777 million variations, the obvious answer should be "No!" During the last several decades empirical research

> "has clearly supported the contention that there is no one best leadership style. Successful and effective leaders are able to adapt their style to fit the requirements of the situation."[36]

What we're calling *leadership style adaptability* is what Hersey and Blanchard call 'situational leadership.' They note that "all situational approaches require the leader to behave in a flexible manner, to be able to diagnose the leadership style appropriate to the situation, and to be able to apply the appropriate style."[37]

(D) Related Leadership Experience

We also recognize that the more closely-related leadership experiences a leader has with respect to a given short-term mission endeavor, that the greater the likelihood her leadership acts will be in tune with situations needing those acts. Because of the vast number of short-term mission variations, it is impossible for any leader's experiences to be perfectly matched to a given short-term mission. Even so, we find the following five arenas of related leadership experience help maximize a given leader's potential for effective influence, effective decision-making, effective leadership acts, and effective implementation of appropriate leadership styles:

- Small-group leadership experience
- Overseas or similar cross-cultural experience
- Team-driven leadership experience
- Intended activity (cf. defining variable #2) experience
- Participant demographic (cf. defining variable #5) experience

2. Training Effectiveness Upon the Goer-Guests

Professional educators realize that what we call *training effectiveness* is really learning. Learning is the effective transfer of knowledge, skill, or attitude from someone who knows or has (trainer, teacher, or leader), to someone who does not yet know or does not yet have (trainee or student or follower). A good educator also realizes the best and most effective learning takes place when the trainee is 'hungry'—that is, when a student has a perceived personal need for specific information or a specific skill. When a trainee sees little, if any, personal gain to be made from the subject matter being taught, that person has little motivation to learn.

Training goer-guests requires the trainer to create a learning environment that facilitates as much 'hunger' in trainees as the trainer can realistically create. However, there's much more to effective learning than simply creating and capitalizing on the hunger. We identify six crucial arenas that help make effective training possible for goer-guests:

(A) Understanding How Trainees Learn
(B) Quality of Trainers Doing the Training
(C) Timing of Training Delivery
(D) Correctly-planned Training Curriculum to be Used
(E) Quality of Training Curriculum Used
(F) Variety of Appropriate Training Methodologies Used to Deliver the Training

(A) Understanding How Trainees Learn
Leaders who train short-term mission goer-guests will be much more effective if they grasp the following three insights into adult learning:[38]

i.   *Trainee Learning Assumptions* (that learning is not one-way, but a collaborative effort between the trainer and trainee, that trainees' previous experience counts, that trainees learn best when they have a perceived need to know and can make real-world applications, and that self-esteem or other personal internal motivational factors will take place as a result of learning).

ii. *Trainee Learning Styles* (feelers, observers, thinkers, and doers).

iii. *Trainee Learning Modality Preferences* (visual, print, aural, interactive, tactile, and kinesthetic).

(B) Quality of Trainers Used Doing the Training
In his book *Preparing to Serve—Training for Cross-cultural Mission*,

Anglican missionary trainer David Harley helps flush out a summary of trainer qualities by first reminding us that just *one* stand-alone quality—however significant—is not enough:

- *Academically-qualified Missiologist:* "Those who are most qualified in the academic discipline of missiology are not necessarily the most suitable people to train missionaries."
- *Theologically-degreed Pastor:* "It cannot be assumed that all those who have a theological degree or have trained to be pastors know how to teach."
- *Experienced Long-term Missionary:* "Missionaries may have 10 or 20 years of experience, but if they cannot interpret their experiences of success and failure in order to teach others, they will not make good trainers."
- *Former Missionary:* "If former missionaries are inept and boring communicators, they will fail to stimulate the [trainees'] interest."[39]

From this same chapter, "Who Does The Training?", we've organized eight of Harley's key observations of *trainer qualities* as follows:

- Good cross-cultural, first-hand field experience
- Cross-cultural sensitivity
- Good communication skills (able to make the curriculum material relevant and intelligible; able to use a variety of appropriate training delivery methodologies)
- A sensitive, mature Christian with a gift for training [the spiritual gift of teaching]
- Good grasp of the specific subject being taught [at the readiness level of the follower-trainees]
- An ability to work well with others
- An ability to spend time with the trainees (approachability and availability for discussion, questions and answers, sharing of ideas)
- A current, continued direct involvement in the subject matter they are teaching (practitioners, not just theorists or has-been practitioners)[40]

(C) Timing of Training Delivery

Is there a more effective time than another during the process trilogy to deliver given training items (i.e., given knowledge or skills)? We contend there is. So does Lawson. She explains Malcolm Knowles' andragogical learning assumption #4: "learning activities must be clearly relevant to the *immediate* needs of the [trainee]. To be effective, deliver *just-in-time* training..."[41] (emphasis ours).

The goer-guests' 'hunger' level for certain information and skills needed will peak naturally by itself at certain times during the process trilogy. Sagacious trainers recognize this, and where possible attempt to provide those respective pieces of knowledge transfer at those ideal times. As a matter of fact, sometimes the ideal time for training goer-guests is *not* pre-field, but rather on-field!—while the goer-guests are in the middle of their front-line intended activities.

As we pointed out in Chapter 1, our dominant western academic training model is the train-first—then-go-do-the-job model. Because we highly value mistake-free delivery of our missiology (and that's a good thing), this train-first model appeals to our conventional wisdom. And when such wisdom is challenged, we appeal to parallel wisdom, saying things like, "You don't want brain surgery from a first-year medical student, do you? Then why should we send 'first-year' missionaries who don't yet have *all* their training?"

But the contemporary short-term mission movement has helped us realize that the Bible does indeed challenge us to consider a different missiological training model—the train-as-you-go model. In Chapter 10 we'll explore this a little deeper, but for now simply note that in Luke 9 and Luke 10, the 12 and 70/72 disciples' 'hunger' level for new knowledge and skills increased directly as a result of Jesus' use of the train-as-you-go model.

(D) Correctly-planned Training Curriculum

There are five key subsets of curriculum that trainers need to develop for short-term mission goer-guests. They are:

- Cross-Cultural Training
- Personal Preparation
- Logistics Training
- Intended Activities Preparation
- Financial Preparation

TABLE #3.8 below provides a somewhat expanded list of these primary, generic curriculum items. Most short-term mission endeavors should consider this list as foundational for development of their correctly-planned training curriculum.

TABLE #3.8

8.1 TRAINING THE GOER-GUESTS
SUGGESTED 'CORRECTLY-PLANNED CURRICULUM' ITEMS
CORRELATED TO 'TIMING OF TRAINING DELIVERY'

SUGGESTED CURRICULUM ITEMS	PRE-FIELD	ON-FIELD	POST-FIELD
1. Cross-Cultural Training			
General: theory, simulation games, simulated settings	①		
Specific: host nation/people specifics	1	②	
Specific: language training & rehearsal	1	②	
Specific: re-entry training	1	②	3
2. Personal Preparation			
Biblical Basis for Mission	①		
Purpose of Outreach	①		
MISTM Theory: goers' responsibility to all participants	1	2	③
Personal Spiritual Preparation	①	2	
Team Covenant Development†	①		
Team Building/Team Spiritual Preparation†	①	2	
Prayer & Spiritual Warfare Training	1	②	3
Debriefing		①	②
Follow-Up Training & Integration	1	2	③
3. Logistics Training			
Airline or Other Round Trip Travel Arrangements	①		
Travel Documents	①		
Prescriptions, Immunizations, Health, & Hygiene	①		
On-Field Housing, Transportation, Food	①		
On-Field Dress & Clothing	①	2	
On-Field Site Orientation	1	②	
Packing	①		
Risk & Liability Issues	①	2	
Customs & Immigration	①	2	
Policies: cancellation, dating, smoking/drinking, photos & video, personal CD players, begging, etc.	①	2	
4. Intended Activities Preparation *			
Mutually-Determined Activities: training & rehearsal	①	2	
Other Intended Activities: training & rehearsal	1	②	
5. Financial Preparation			
Budget Development	①		
Fund-Raising: plans, implementation, management	①		
Money Due Deadlines	①		

KEY: Sequential numbers indicate the process flow of training; circled numbers indicate when primary focus of training should occur.

† Assumes small team or large team short-term outreaches as defined in this book. * cf. Defining Variable #2, 'Activity.'

(E) Quality of Training Curriculum Used
Reading a third-generation photocopy is about as enlightening as the neighbors' summer vacation slide show fired up just before midnight. Books that fall apart, notebook binders that don't hold their content, handouts that aren't well-organized, incorrectly-sized type fonts, web-page text and video footage and photographs that haven't been edited—these quality-controllable items can help make or break the 'hunger' needed for effective knowledge transfer.

Every short-term outreach has a limited budget. Yet failure to include funding for well-developed, inviting-to-read, easy-to-grasp training curriculum will only impede the probability of achieving maximum impact in the given short-term outreach. Spend the time and money needed to develop good, applicable material and related media that real people can really use, and from which they can actually learn.

(F) Variety of Appropriate Methodologies Used to Deliver the Training
The stand-up-in-front-of-the-class, lecture-only model of training delivery remains as functional as a square wheel. Unfortunately this model gets pommeled into us through constant exposure to school classroom environments, pulpit preaching, political proselytizing, and other sit-and-be-quiet-and-listen-to-me settings. Lecture/listen can work effectively—but only when used judiciously as merely one of the arsenal of appropriate training delivery methodologies.

We organize appropriate training methodologies into four subsets of related items. Note that one or more items from each of these four subsets occur simultaneously when effective learning is actually taking place. But it's up to the trainer—having accurately diagnosed the 'readiness level' of the learners—to identify specific methodologies from each of these four subsets and pull those items together to work in harmony:

i.   *Learning Location Settings* (classroom settings, retreat-type settings, simulated on-field settings, private study settings, and on-site settings).

ii.   *Trainer Tools* (white boards, flip charts, audio/visual media, trainer's physical presence/appearance, chairs/benches/tables/desks, and sensory objects).

iii. *Assembly and Seating Techniques* (large group, small groups, one-on-one, individual desks, group tables, seating and standing variations).

iv. *Knowledge Transfer Techniques* (lecture/listen, multiple trainers, case studies, creative drama, interactive discussion, jigsaw self-training, Q&A, up-front presentations/reports/drama, assessment and feedback gathering for trainers, training and learning games, skill practices/rehearsals, and observation).

3. *Training Effectiveness Upon the Host Receivers*[88]

The 'six crucial arenas' ('A' through 'F' above) concerning training effectiveness upon the *goer-guests* are essentially the same for the *host receivers*.

Note that our content and explanation as previously given assume a western-based sending entity's and goer-guests' perspective. For example, much of the electronic technology, trainer tools, and learning location settings may not be as readily available, nor as appropriate in the host receivers' culture.

A second caveat concerns the potentially vast differences between each of the two subsets of host receivers, the *field facilitators* and the *intended receptors*. Where both subsets are on the economic and educational scale will play a major part in the trainer's contextualization of their training material. Here, too, the trainer has to accurately assess the overall 'readiness level' of the given host receiver subset he is training.

As we consider the *training effectiveness upon the host receivers* we present below, we'll simply assume the general content of the previous section, noting only specific curriculum items unique to training host receivers. Note also that trainers for the field must possess a 'multi-cultural savvy.' They need (repeat, *need*) a sensitive and reasonably accurate understanding with respect to at least three cultures:

- The incoming *goer-guests'* culture—and especially their unique demographical profile
- The host receiver *field facilitators'* culture
- . The host receiver *intended receptors'* culture

(A) *Curriculum for Training Field Facilitators*

If field facilitators are expatriate long-term career missionaries, their pre-arrival training should have included a required course on 'receiving and effectively leveraging your ministry using short-termers who interrupt your longer-term career work.' (Missionary training schools which fail to include such a course are setting their candidates up for failure. Whether you're ready or not, short-term missionaries *are* coming to your field.)

If field facilitators are local national people, either the sending entity or on-field mission board needs to provide essentially the same course: 'receiving and effectively leveraging your work using short-termers who interrupt your plans.'

If you are a field facilitator for short-term missionaries, and you have not yet received such training, then help your sending board (sending entity) organize and plan a training seminar for you and other colleagues, to help maximize the marvelous leverage available through correct use of short-termers. Such training should cover nine primary areas, contextualized to the uniqueness of given field location and culture:

i. Logistical Support for Short-Termers
ii. Program Delivery Support for Short-Termers
iii. Identifying Your Strategic Field Activities Leveragable through Short-Termers
iv. Blending Your Field-supplied Leadership with Their Sending Entity-supplied Leadership
v. Risk Management and Security Issues for Short-Termers
vi. Cross-cultural Training: Grasping the Short-Termers' Worldview
vii. Recruiting from Short-Termers for Field Needs
viii. Outcomes Follow-up
ix. Relational Issues

(B) Curriculum for Training Intended Receptors
We know of no material yet available for training and helping the intended receptors prepare for, receive, and effectively work with short-term missionaries. The little material that is available tends to focus on field facilitators.

Therefore we'll suggest the following guidelines, including some ideas for stimulant resources which—although written primarily for field facilitators—can help short-term mission practitioners begin structuring training elements for intended receptors:

i. PARTNERSHIP ASSUMPTION
We first assume there exists some level of partnership between the sending entity and the field facilitators.

ii. FIELD RELATIONSHIPS ASSUMPTION
We further assume that field facilitators are already in some working, mutually-beneficial relational level with intended receptors.

iii. TEACHING RESPONSIBILITY BELONGS PRIMARILY TO FIELD FACILITATORS LEADERS

AND INTENDED RECEPTORS LEADERS

Whatever needs to be taught to intended receptors is best taught by the people with whom they are already in relationship. Ordinarily that will be their own leaders, and leadership from the field facilitators (sometimes these two are one and the same).

iv. POSSIBLE CURRICULUM ITEMS
- Understanding the Incoming Culture of the Short-Termers
- Policies and Guidelines Related to Working with the Short-Termers (begging, asking, money, swapping addresses, reporting problems, on- and off-limit locations, etc.)
- Purpose and Expected Benefits to All Participants

v. RESOURCE 'STIMULANT' SUGGESTIONS
- The 25-item 'VWAP Destination Set-Up Sheet' compiled by Chris Eaton and Kim Hurst[42]
- Chapter 5 'Hosts' of the Ditch Townsend book *Stop Check Go*[43]
- Stan Nussbaum's *The ABCs of American Culture* and Sarah Lanier's *Foreign to Familiar*[44] (both books are great resources to help non-Americans better understand the American culture)

Definition Summation

REGARDING 'short-term' (as it is used to modify the word 'mission'), we identified eight defining variables which contain 69 major sub-categories. When multiplied together, this gives us 777 million variables—too many!—to arrive at any one definitive definition of 'short-term mission.' Even so, we'll now propose a practitioner's definition of 'short-term mission' that we'll continue to develop throughout the remainder of this book:

"the God-commanded, repetitive deployment of swift, temporary non-professional missionaries."

Endnotes
Chapter 3

1. *(p. 65)* We use the phrase 'mission community' to mean all parts of the entire *ECCLESIARUM* intentionally involved in *MISSIO DEI*. This includes individuals as well as groups (both formal and informal) such as churches, denominations, mission sending agencies, missionaries, mission support services, mission trainers and educators, mission schools, mission intercessors, mission funders and supporters, etc. We further intend the phrase 'mission community' to include all of the above irrespective of educational or experiential levels, including experienced traditional missiologists and nonconformist newcomers to missiology.

2. *(p. 66)* **Samuel Wilson and Ed Dayton, eds.**, *13th Edition Mission Handbook* (Monrovia CA: MARC, 1986), p. 578.

3. *(p. 67)* **Andrew Atkins**, "Work Teams? No, 'Taste and See' Teams" (*Evangelical Missions Quarterly*, 27(4), October 1991), p. 385.

4. *(p. 67)* In all fairness to Youth With A Mission, the initial four month Discipleship Training School is often conducted in an on-field context. Yet a primary focus of that initial four month DTS is *discipling* its goer-guest participants prior to their initial two month on-field ministry outreach (hence our 2:1 ratio).

5. *(p. 67)* Roger Peterson has been actively involved in short-term mission since 1980, Wayne Sneed since 1981, Gordon Aeschliman since 1977, and our editor Kim Hurst since 1985. For all three authors and our editor, this includes involvement as goer-guest followers, goer-guest leaders, and sending entity leaders (organizing and training).

6. *(p. 71)* **Gordon Aeschliman, ed.**, "Lots of Short-Term Trips" (*The Short-Term Mission Handbook*, Evanston IL: Berry Publishing, 1992), p. 14.

7. *(p. 71)* **Martha VanCise**, *Successful Mission Teams—A Guide for Volunteers* (Birmingham AL: New Hope, 1996), p. 26.

8. *(p. 73)* In the Old Testament (only), we apply the Spiritual Warfare "activity" label to also include those very specific "human warfare" instances where God clearly instructed His people to "utterly destroy" or to "devote to the Lord" (as translated in the RSV and NIV) certain cities, objects, or even peoples (cf. Joshua 6:17,18,21; 8:26; 10:1; 11:11,12,20,21; 22:20; Judges 1:17). The original Hebrew term used in these passages refers to the irrevocable giving over of pagan things or pagan persons to the Lord by totally destroying them, so that those pagan things/peoples would not cause God's chosen people to sin by committing spiritual prostitution (idolatry).

9. *(p. 80)* **Ray Bakke**, *The Urban Christian* (Downers Grove IL: InterVarsity Press, 1987), p. 42.

10. *(p. 80)* *Ibid.*, pp. 42–43.

11. *(p. 80)* *Ibid.*, p. 33.

12. *(p. 81)* Leadership style is most effective not when leadership consistently utilizes his/her own personal default style preference, but rather when his/her leadership style is intentionally altered and adapted to one that best matches its followers' maturity/developmental level in any given context [cf. **Paul Hersey and Kenneth H.**

Blanchard, *Management of Organizational Behavior* (Englewood Cliffs NJ: Prentice Hall, 1988), pp. 270–303]. Similarly, anthropologist Chuck Kraft stresses communication is most effective when it is 'receptor-oriented' because of continual interpretive assessments taking place by listeners. Kraft explains:

"When a speaker tries to get across a message, in addition to interpreting what he/she says, the receptors interpret clothing, tone of voice, posture, the setting in which the interaction takes places, the time of day and whatever is going on inside of them. The meanings assigned to all of these elements, then, become a part of the message communicated" [**Charles H. Kraft**, *Anthropology for Christian Witness* (Maryknoll NY: Orbis Books, 1996), p. 146].

13. *(p. 83)* Cf. **Kraft**, p. 11. Kraft further subdivides this second aspect (worldview) into three sub-categories: basic assumptions, values, and allegiances.

14. *(p. 84)* HARVIE M. CONN, "Culture" entry contained in: **A. Scott Moreau, ed.**, *Evangelical Dictionary of World Missions* (Grand Rapids MI: Baker Books, 2000), pp. 252–254.

15. *(p. 84)* Cf. the A. SCOTT MOREAU "Culture" entry contained in: **Moreau**, p. 746.

16. *(p. 84)* In 1982 the Lausanne Committee for World Evangelization (LCWE) sponsored a meeting in Chicago where 40 mission leaders agreed that

"A 'people group' is a significantly large grouping of individuals who perceive themselves to have a common affinity for one another, because of their shared language, religion, ethnicity, residence, occupation, class, caste, situation, or combinations of these. For evangelistic purposes it is the largest group within which the Gospel can spread as a church-planting movement without encountering barriers of understanding or acceptance" [**Frank Kaleb Jansen**, *Target Earth* (Kailua-Kona HI: University of the Nations; and Pasadena CA: Global Mapping International, 1989), p. 108].

17. *(p. 84)* Taken from *Adopt-A-People Clearinghouse Prayer Card* (Colorado Springs CO: Adopt-A-People Clearinghouse, 1995).

18. *(p. 85)* Presently one of the primary 'think tanks' with respect to *people groups* is the U.S. Center for World Mission founded in 1976 by missiologist Ralph D. Winter in Pasadena, California. According to a fax message sent from the USCWM's Executive Director Greg H. Parsons to Roger Peterson on December 15, 1995, 14:32 PST, the

"Total count of peoples in the world is estimated at 24,000 (these are peoples that need a viable church planting movement—not the language groups or merely ethnic groups)."

19. *(p. 86)* We recognize the church (the *ECCLESIARUM*) to be God's appointed agent on earth for mission (*MISSIO ECCLESIATO*), and in that sense the church always has primary responsibility for sending out its members (cf. Matthew 16:18, John 21:15–17, and Acts 13:1–3) in accordance with the Great Commission. Yet we recognize historically that mission has largely been done by sub-sets within the church, i.e., by groups of highly-committed Christians who have organized for the express purpose of mission, and normally have done so as a task-focused arm of either a given church or given denomination, or a group of related churches. The parachurch (*para*—like, or similar to), as a task-focused arm of the church, is therefore also a bona fide agent for mission. [For a more in-depth discussion of the missiological necessity of the parachurch and the legitimacy of both the church and parachurch structures (although the following author strongly prefers the 'modality/sodality' concept as opposed to 'church/parachurch' when discussing sending aspects of

Christian mission), consult the RALPH D. WINTER article, "The Two Structures of God's Redemptive Mission," found in: **Ralph D. Winter and Steven C. Hawthorne, eds.**, *Perspectives on the World Christian Movement* (Pasadena CA: William Carey Library, 1999), pp. 220–230.]

20.   *(p. 86)*   *Ibid.*, p. 220. Local church leaders mobilizing their respective churches for mission with*out* the use of a parachurch mission agency may want to ponder the contents of Winter's entire article (cf. *Ibid.*, pp. 220–230)—a brief historical and Biblical assessment of the mission sending relationship between church and parachurch.

21.   *(p. 88)*   **Paul E. McKaughan, Dellanna W. O'Brien, and William R. O'Brien**, *Choosing A Future For U.S. Missions* (Monrovia CA: MARC, 1998), p. 27.

22.   *(p. 88)*   *Ibid.*, p. 30.

23.   *(p. 88)*   **Winter and Hawthorne.**, p. 224.

24.   *(p. 90)*   Some *non-traditional* mission agencies utilize short-term mission as their exclusive strategy in their particular role of fulfilling the Great Commission, while other *non-traditional* mission agencies send not only short-termers, but long-term career missionaries as well. An example would be Youth With A Mission (YWAM) which, internationally, sends tens of thousands of short-termers annually—but which also currently has more than 10,000 long-term career missionaries in approximately 800 locations in approximately 134 nations of the world (these year 2000 statistics verified by December 04, 2002 e-mail from the YWAM International Communications Office in Colorado). The interesting observation is this: YWAM, which sends more short-termers on an annual basis than any other sending entity, is also one of the world's largest long-term career missionary sending entities.

25.   *(p. 92)*   This list of schools which function temporarily in the role of *SE-3.a(2) sending entity* is far from complete. The majority of the schools listed were derived from the list of attending participants in one of the annual *Fellowship of Short-Term Mission Leaders* conferences held every October (cf. http://www.fstml.org for information on the annual conference). Other schools listed were based on the authors' first-hand knowledge.

26.   *(p. 93)*   Cf. Chapter #1: p. 22 on Gladys Aylward; and pp. 26–27 on Bruce Olson.

27.   *(p. 93)*   Cf. Chapter #6—The Participant Trilogy, and Chapter #9—The MISTM-Grid. Remember, the short-term mission 'participants' are not merely the *goer-guest participants* alone, but include the *sender participants* and *host receiver participants* as well.

28.   *(p. 96)*   **Kraft**, p. 11.

29.   *(p. 96)*   *Ibid.*

30.   *(p. 98)*   **Paul Hersey and Kenneth H. Blanchard**, *Management of Organizational Behavior* (Englewood Cliffs NJ: Prentice Hall, 1988), p. 147.

31.   *(p. 98)*   *Ibid.*

32.   *(p. 98)*   *Ibid.*

33.   *(p. 98)*   **Kraft**, p. 316.

34. *(p. 101)* **J. Robert Clinton**, *The Making of a Leader* (Colorado Springs CO: Navpress, 1988), p. 14. Clinton footnotes his own definition and further explains *leadership* as a:

> "... dynamic process over an extended period of time in various situations in which a leader utilizing leadership resources and by specific leadership behaviors, influences the thoughts and activities of followers toward accomplishment of aims usually mutually beneficial for leaders, followers, and the macro context of which they are a part" (p. 213).

Clinton also defines what he means by the term *leader*:
> "A Biblical *leader* is defined as a person with God-given capacity and God-given responsibility to influence a specific group of God's people towards His purposes for the group" (*Ibid.*, p. 213).

35. *(p. 101)* Clinton defines *leadership act*:
> "... the specific instance at a given point in time of the leadership influence process between a given influencer (person said to be influencing) and follower(s) (person or persons being influenced) in which followers are influenced toward some goal [**J. Robert Clinton**, *Foundations of Leadership* (Pasadena CA: Fuller Theological Seminary School of World Mission, In-Service Program ML Syllabus, Notes #2), p. 12].

36. *(p. 102)* **Hersey and Blanchard**, pp. 101–102.

37. *(p. 102)* *Ibid.,* p. 106.

38. *(p. 103)* The three insights presented in this section are selectively extracted from adult learner concepts found in: **Lawson, Karen**, *The Trainer's Handbook* (San Francisco CA: Jossey-Bass/Pfeiffer, 1998), pp. 22–30.

39. *(p. 104)* **C. David Harley**, *Preparing to Serve—Training for Cross-Cultural Mission* (Pasadena CA: William Carey Library, 1995), pp. 47, 51.

40. *(p. 104)* *Ibid.,* pp. 47–57.

41. *(p. 105)* **Lawson**, p. 25.

42. *(p. 110)* Cf. **Chris Eaton and Kim Hurst**, *(Leader's Manual) Vacations With a Purpose* (Colorado Springs CO: Cook Ministry Resources, 1991), pp. 52–59.

43. *(p. 110)* Cf. **Ditch Townsend**, *Stop Check Go* (OM Publishing, 1996), pp. 130–134.

44. *(p. 110)* Cf. **Stan Nussbaum**, *The ABCs of American Culture* (Colorado Springs CO: Global Mapping International, 1998). 55 pp., paperback (available at www.gri.org), and cf. **Sarah A. Lanier**, *Foreign to Familiar* (Hagerstown MD: McDougal Publishing, 2000), 128 pp., paperback, ISBN 1-581580-022-3.

CHAPTER **4**

APPLYING
OUR DEFINITION

1 God-commanded   2 Repetitive Deployment
3 Swift   4 Temporary
5 Non-professional Missionaries

O LAY THE BASIS FOR PROVIDING WHAT WE HOPE CAN
be a helpful, usable definition for short-term mission practitioners, we devoted Chapter 3 to a somewhat in-depth examination of
the eight primary defining variables and their 69 major sub-categories. These
defining variables and their sub-categories are all contained within 777 million
variations of what people commonly refer to as 'short-term mission.' As the
chapter's concluding result, we then proposed our working definition of
short-term mission:

> "the God-commanded, repetitive deployment of swift, temporary
> non-professional missionaries."

117

Our definition summarizes the three previous chapters. More important-ly, it provides us with a strategic user's definition, helping practitioners better apply its potential benefits (as opposed to its lurking-nearby pitfalls).

This brief chapter will now look separately at each of the five key con-cepts contained within our definition: (1) God-commanded, (2) repetitive deployment, (3) swift, (4) temporary, and (5) non-professional missionaries.

(1) GOD-COMMANDED

Mission is a God-commanded responsibility of every church worldwide. Nowhere is that responsibility made any easier to understand than in God's Great Commission. The New Testament provides us with seven versions of that command,[1] all squarely built on a sturdy Old Testament foundation of God's mission to redeem the lost world (cf. Chapter 2).

The church is composed of people, the highest degree of God's creation. In Chapter 1 (God's Fools) we argued strongly that God calls the people of His church—His real people, His real fools, His entire Body—to take part in His mission to redeem the world. No Christian is exempt from that call. God will not issue waivers due to old age or young. He won't excuse on account of gender, race, culture, education, social status, economic status, or experi-ence. *Every* follower of Christ is a commissioned member of God's royal priesthood. *Every* member of His priesthood has been called to declare God's wonderful deeds.

Short-term mission is currently the one mission structure available to the entire church worldwide which, if properly put into practice, could actually release all of God's real people into the world He so loves. Can you imagine the world's 800 million Great Commission Christians[2] set loose across the globe over the course of the next five years? It breaks down to roughly 13 mil-lion people a month at a time. If logistically that's too many, then consider just a tenth—1.3 million short-termers every month. Could it be done? It'd be messy, it'd be confusing, and there'd be millions of problems (literally). But could it be done? The massive problems it would create still pale in compari-son to problems four to five billion people have who aren't yet walking in the full reality of God's love and His redemptive plan for all of creation.

Many Biblical texts strongly suggest that short-term mission is an often-used missiological means to God's ends of increased God-glorification and worship. Moses, the spies, Nehemiah, Jonah, Jesus, the women, Paul, Barnabas, and Peter are perhaps the most obvious examples. Chapter 10 (A

Biblical and Theological Basis) will develop our theological case much further.

But an important note: just because something is called 'short-term *mission*' does not justify everything using that name (cf. Chapter 8). We contend that if the *primary* purpose of a short-term 'experience' is to disciple the goer-guests, or to provide a cross-cultural experience (important as both these agenda are), then the outreach should *not* be called a 'short-term *mission*' (cf. Chapter 2—Defining 'Mission'), but rather a 'cross-cultural *trip*.' This book is about short-term *mission*.

(2) REPETITIVE DEPLOYMENT

As we alluded to in footnote #9 of Chapter 2, and will explain in much greater detail in Chapter 10 (A Biblical and Theological Basis), the Apostle Paul's methodology of mission was one of repetitive deployment. Over the course of seven separate short-term endeavors, Paul performed his preaching, evangelistic, and visitation missionary activity. He won converts to the faith, successfully planted multiple churches, and returned on subsequent short-terms just to see how everyone was doing.

Repetitive deployment contains two elements. The first element is doing more than just one short-term mission. The second element refers to the field location. Some repeat short-termers go back to the same location; others return—but to new fields they've yet to visit. The Apostle Paul did both.

Repetitive Deployment (same field)

Bob and Dee were medical professionals called to live and work in a northern midwestern city. Permanent overseas career work was not an option. But going overseas once a year to Haiti was an option they could manage. Not just once, but several times the family (including three daughters) made their mission journey overseas to help improve the lives of Haitian people. And every time they went they became more effective inside the local culture. On-going, repetitive deployment to the same field was practical, doable, and a wise expenditure of time and financial resource for their family. Missiologically, God's Kingdom in Haiti expanded because of their repetitive efforts.

Repetitive Deployment (new fields)

Dick and Juanita Brown[3] have a growing passion for prayer, for unreached peoples, and for mobilizing others into mission. So they have made arrangements with their home church and with a mission agency to send trained teams of short-termers into a variety of 10/40 Window nations. While on-field, the Browns and their team members spend a great deal of time in on-site prayer and in other strategic activities. Then they return home, where the Browns begin recruiting the next group for another nation somewhere in the 10/40 Window. The Browns intend to saturate this part of the world with thousands of man-hours of on-site prayer, by taking different short-term teams to different nations as many times as they can.

As another example, Rich is responsible for his college's mission outreach program. Every summer Rich organizes 10 to 12 groups of students, and makes arrangements in the same number of field locations to send his students to work. Multiple groups every summer. New students every summer—but predictable, repetitive deployment of short-term missionaries which the college's field partners can rely on.

(3) SWIFT

Perhaps the greatest asset short-term mission brings to the table is its ability to swiftly, rapidly place missionaries on-field. Traditional career missionaries often spend years in pre-field training. Short-termers can be deployed within just a few weeks or months.

Certain types of work may require extended training for maximum effectiveness, such as Bible translation or frontier church planting within an unengaged unreached people group. But many types of strategic, Kingdom-advancing mission work in certain fields do not require years and years of training; many fields are "ripe unto harvest" right now, and simply need laborers—now! Not theologians, not missiologists, not strategists, not deep thinkers—but laborers, people willing to sweat, work hard, and do whatever strategically needs to be done. (Remember, Jesus' only *requirement* for missionary service is empowerment of the Holy Spirit ... everything else—no matter how much sense it makes or how good it sounds—is man's requirement.)

Kathy did her first short-term as a young woman. She and fellow church members helped build an orphanage for needy children in a Caribbean nation. A couple years later Kathy did a second short-term to another part of the world where she and her teenage colleagues helped build a much-needed road in Papau New Guinea. In both instances Kathy and her teammates were effective in their mission; in both instances Kathy was quickly deployed into these effective outreaches after just a couple months of preparation.

Reggie[4] was a young, budding rock star (or so he thought). Seeing Kingdom-potential inside this young man, one November his pastor's wife invited him to go on their church's first overseas short-term mission (scheduled to depart the next month after Christmas). Reggie said, "No, because my band is all booked up." Two weeks later his band began breaking up. With less than a month to go, Reggie got trained, prepared, and raised his entire support and headed overseas with that church team. His team made good progress on its assigned building project (which was completed in less than two years with local labor and other short-term teams). Reggie was swiftly deployed as an effective team member into an effective short-term mission in less than a month's time.

When a field is crying for laborers, it takes years to form and send *career* missionary teams. Some career teams will fall apart during their pre-field training, bonding, and deputation process. Worse yet, they fall apart the first year on the field, producing virtually no Kingdom return on the hundreds of thousands of dollars supporters invested in their intended efforts. But in just a few months short-termers can be recruited, trained, and sent. And there are times—many times!—when the rapid, swift short-term strategy is the better financial and missiological strategy to employ.

(4) TEMPORARY

Rather than using a fixed element of time such as 'less than two years,' or 'up to four years,' or 'one to three weeks,' we contrast the short-term missionary's on-field time commitment against the traditional long-term career missionary's on-field time commitment, by suggesting the use of the word *temporary*.

Although every church is responsible for the Great Commission, and every believer in the church is commanded to "Go!", it stands to reason that not every person is called into *lifetime* overseas missionary work. It also stands to reason that not every person is qualified for lifetime overseas missionary work. How do we reconcile this juxtaposition of God's ideal vs. human reality?

Short-term mission offers 'unqualified' people (God's fools) legitimate opportunities to respond to the Great Commission. Opportunities for *temporary* engagement in front-line activities are essential for church members not called nor qualified for *lifetime* cross-cultural missionary work—if we want to help the church obey everything that Christ has commanded.

A short-termer's on-field work is temporary by design and by intentionality. Although long-term career work can be cut short for various reasons, long-term career missionaries tend to view their on-field contribution in primarily one location over the course of their lifetime. Short-termers view their on-field contribution as temporary, fully expecting to return back home and re-engage in whatever primary activity they left behind.

Career missionaries often buy one-way tickets, because they're not sure when or if or how they'll return back home. Short-term missionaries almost always buy round trip tickets, because they know exactly when they're coming back home.

Temporary is not meant to suggest either good or bad. It is meant merely to help provide understanding of what short-term mission is and isn't, and of how it can best be used as a bona fide missiological strategy when long-term career strategies are not the right option.

(5) NON-PROFESSIONAL MISSIONARIES

The primary definition of the word 'professional' revolves around the concept of payment received for services rendered, or as one dictionary's first explanation states, "engaged in an activity as a means for livelihood or for gain."[5]

Long-term career missionaries receive a monthly salary. While some denominations or agencies pay a fixed guarantee, many career missionaries raise their monthly support themselves. Either way, they are paid wages for the service they provide. From the U.S. Internal Revenue Service's perspective, they are either employees or subcontractors, and are taxed accordingly; they're professionals by definition.

Most short-term missionaries are not paid a salary or wage. They are volunteers who donate their time. By definition, that makes short-term goer-guests *non-professional* missionaries. (Short-termers who work for several months or a few years may, however, receive a salary).

The term 'professional' also connotes a certain competence and expertise in the person's place of business or work. Because of more extensive training, long-term career missionaries are assumed to have a competence and expertise—and are therefore assumed to be professionals. On the other hand, some short-termers do not have the same extensive training, and do not therefore have a professional level of competence and expertise with respect to *missiology*. Therefore it is correct to call short-term missionaries *non-professional* missionaries. But make no mistake—if they're doing *mission* (as opposed to a cross-cultural trip)—they're missionaries just the same.

Non-professional does not make a person no good or useless. On the contrary—these are the *primary* types of people God calls to participate in MISSIO DEI (cf. Chapter 1—God's Fools). Bill Hamon summarizes this very well: "God does not call the qualified, but qualifies the called."[6]

The world of God's mission has a place—and has a need!—for both the professional and non-professional missionary. And the non-professional is still God's number one choice, because the fools who succeed only do so because it's obvious to everyone else that it's God Himself working through them.

Summary

WE'VE developed a five-item definition which essentially covers all 777 million variations of short-term mission. First, mission itself is *God-commanded*. Whether it's 'long-term' or 'short-term' has no bearing whatsoever on the fact that mission is God-commanded. Second, short-term mission is marked by easy and available opportunities of *repetitive deployment* (to same locations and to different locations). Third, short-term missionaries can be deployed *swiftly* and without delay. Fourth, short-term mission is an intentional *temporary* engagement within another culture. And fifth, short-term missionaries are normally non-paid volunteers who donate their time; they are *non-professional missionaries.*

Endnotes
Chapter 4

1.   *(p. 118)*   Cf. Endnote #1 of Chapter 1.

2.   *(p. 118)*   800 million Great Commission Christians is a "safe" estimate, according to an October 24, 2002 e-mail response received by Roger Peterson from the U.S. Center for World Mission, Pasadena. Great Commission Christians are 'mature-enough Christians' who, theoretically, are actually capable of evangelizing unsaved persons.

3.   *(p. 119)*   Fictitious names used; story is true.

4.   *(p. 121)*   Fictitious name used; story is true.

5.   *(p. 122)*   **Jess Stein, ed. in chief**, *The Random House College Dictionary* (New York NY: Random House, Inc., 1975), p. 1057.

6.   *(p. 123)*   **Dan Davidson and Dave Davidson; and George Verwer**, *God's Great Ambition* (Waynesboro GA: Gabriel Publishing, no date), pages not numbered, paperback, ISBN 1-884543-69-3.

THE PROCESS TRILOGY

1 Pre-field   2 On-Field   3 Post-field

I N FEBRUARY 1995, I (ROGER PETERSON) PRESENTED A 'HOW-TO-do-it' workshop on short-term mission at the Heartland MissionsFest in Tulsa, Oklahoma. I'll never forget one of the attendees, a local mission pastor. I challenged everyone to avoid myopically limiting short-term mission merely to just what happens 'over there.' I stressed that short-term mission will fail unless you include all the things that should happen *before* you get there, and all the things that should happen *after* you get back home. I used my hands to illustrate the point. I created three imaginary left-to-right boxes in thin air, assigning the words pre-field, on-field, and post-field to each respective box. That pastor's "I get it!" light clicked 'On!' so obviously, that I sensed the Lord was using him to confirm a concept God was beginning to extract from my

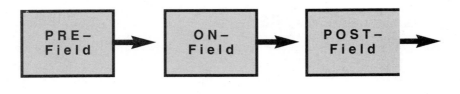

ILLUSTRATION #5.1

THE PROCESS OF SHORT-TERM MISSION
A WESTERN, LINEAR VIEW OF THE THREE
PRIMARY PROCESSES OF SHORT-TERM MISSION

heart. His confirmation helped me realize these 'boxes' and labels had great potential to help others as well. ILLUSTRATION #5.1 provides the ink-on-paper representation of what my hands tried to demonstrate that day in Tulsa.

A Western Sending Entity Orientation
Although the 'process trilogy' represented by the graphic can be used by any participant involved in any of the 777 million variations of short-term mission, it represents the perspective of the senders and goer-guests. (Host receivers are already 'on-field'—before, during, and after the short-term outreach. From a host receiver's perspective, process trilogy terms for a short-term could, on some occasions, be pre-invasion, invasion, and post-invasion!)

The drawing itself is also limiting. The very nature of a framed box implies concepts containing items of rigid structure and order. The boxes and their attached arrows suggest neatly controllable segments of time. Furthermore, the boxes suggest three equally-sized segments—when in reality, the concepts, responsibilities, and events implied by each box often flow over and intermingle with the other boxes.

Even so, ILLUSTRATION #5.1 is valid and extremely helpful to the short-term mission practitioner. It strongly implies that a short-term mission is not a single event—but rather a *process* of interrelated events and responsibilities over the course of time. The middle box (on-field) may well be the primary focus of a given short-term outreach, but its placement in the middle means something has to occur before you get there. The unframed right-hand portion of the last box (post-field) rightly suggests that the impact of the short-term mission—whether good or bad—never ceases, but continues indefinitely.

Certain events, certain commitments, certain decisions, certain responsibilities, certain actions need to occur at certain times. The time slots represented by these boxes help short-term mission practitioners better organize these certain items. The arrows attached to each box help the practitioner realize that the effect of whatever they've done, or failed to have done, is carried forward into the relationships and events represented by the next box.

PRE-FIELD

Pre-field represents the entire period of time before the actual on-field portion of the short-term outreach begins. Pre-field exists from the moment of conception (regardless of who conceived the outreach). But pre-field has different implications for different members of the participant trilogy (cf. Chapter 6—The Participant Trilogy).

Sending Supporters

All six subcategories of sending supporters (cf. Chapter 6) have critically important roles pre-field, in order to effectively send the goer-guests on-field:

1. *Prayer Supporters*
   During the pre-field portion of the process trilogy, prayer supporters should first and foremost be "led by the Spirit" as they pray. Second, prayer supporters should pray regularly (ideally every pre-field day). Prayer items should generally revolve around these four areas:
   - For Holy Spirit filling and empowering in the short-term goer-guests, as effective witnesses for Christ (cf. Acts 1:8).
   - For goer-guests' health, personal issues, financial support, logistical concerns, training effectiveness, and any other goer-guest or sending entity request.
   - For field facilitators, the intended receptors, and all on-field site items as requested by the sending entity and field facilitators.
   - For effective on-field debriefing and post-field follow-up for both the goer-guests and the host receivers.

2. *Financial Supporters*
   Financial supporters need to make every effort to submit their contributions on time, and in the manner the sending entity recommends.

3. *Logistical Supporters*

Logistical supporters make arrangements with goer-guests during the pre-field process, to provide certain 'back home' logistics help for goer-guests during their on-field outreach. This can include making advance commitments to: provide airport drop-offs and pick-ups, care for pets, cut the grass, milk the cows, pick up the mail, pay the bills—or whatever needs to be done 'back home' for the goer-guests while they're on-field.

4. *Emotional Supporters*

"I believe God wants you to go!", or "I think you should join our church's short-term outreach!", or "keep working on that Russian language!", or "God really can provide the money you need!" are examples of the crucial role emotional supporters play during the pre-field process for goer-guests. When key family members or other influential persons provide such emotional support, a goer-guest can be greatly encouraged during difficult pre-field moments of preparation. An encouraging word spoken at the right time can help free goer-guests from ungodly self-doubt and worry.

5. *Communication Supporters*

Short-term missionaries need someone 'back home' who will call or write or produce communication newsletters to the other 'back home' sending supporters and all others with whom the short-termers need to stay in touch. This is especially crucial for short-term outreaches lasting longer than two months. So during the pre-field process, communication supporters make all those necessary arrangements with the goer-guests prior to their departure.

6. *Re-entry Supporters*

Re-entry supporters are those persons specifically chosen to meet with the returning short-termers after they come back home. Re-entry supporters ask 'intelligent questions'[1] about the on-field portion of their short-term outreach, and listen closely and carefully to every word. During the pre-field process, goer-guests must 'sign up' these people. (The sending entity is responsible for providing the re-entry supporters with that list of 'intelligent questions.')

Sending Entity

Seth Barnes, founder and president of Adventures In Missions, has sent more than 40,000 short-termers in the last 12 years.[2] With all that experience, Barnes still reduces the sending entity's multitude of pre-field responsibilities into just three overarching themes:[3]

1. *Design (mutual design)*

   The outreach must be designed in a collaborative partnership between the sending entity and host receivers (field facilitators). It is a cooperative design consisting of specific mission opportunities and mission projects (i.e., intended activities) which both parties believe to be beneficial to the intended receptors, and which both parties believe can be accomplished by the goer-guests. Both parties acknowledge and plan for certain desired benefits to themselves (such as discipleship of the goer-guests, or financial or other asset provision to the field facilitators)—provided these desired personal benefits don't diminish in any way the planned benefits for the intended receptors.

2. *Recruiting / Screening / Selecting*

   Goer-guests must be recruited and selected according to the mutually-designed, pre-determined criteria of step one.

3. *Preparation and Training*

   The sending entity sees to it that goer-guests it selects are trained in conjunction with the mutually-designed plans of step one. Training curriculum (cross-cultural training, personal preparation, logistics training, intended activities preparation, and financial preparation—cf. TABLE #3.8) are tailored to work this plan.

Goer-Guests

Goer-guests' primary pre-field responsibilities are three-fold:

1. *Prayer*

   "Pray without ceasing" (I Thessalonians 5:17) is step number one!

2. *Securing Sending Supporters*

   Goer-guests need to recruit and secure the commitment of (up to six subcategories of) sending supporters (cf. Chapter 6—The

Participant Trilogy) whom they will need, in order to effectively accomplish their mission outreach.

3. *Preparation*

   Pre-field preparation for short-term goer-guests consists of receiving, understanding, and accurately applying all training supplied by their sending entity. As a reminder, training consists of five key subsets of preparation: cross-cultural training, personal preparation, logistics training, intended activities preparation, and financial preparation (cf. TABLE #3.8).

Field Facilitators

Here again Seth Barnes helps us reduce the multitude of pre-field responsibilities for field facilitators to just three themes:

1. *Design (mutual design)*

   As indicated above, the short-term outreach must be mutually designed as a collaborative effort between the sending entity and field facilitators. Both parties focus primarily on the intended receptors and appropriate missiological provision to the intended receptors. Collaborating together, they determine intended activities both parties believe can be accomplished by the goer-guests.

2. *Setup*

   What the field facilitators and sending entity designed in step one, is what the field facilitators need to implement for goer-guests when they come on-site. This requires advance setup efforts *prior* to the goer-guests' arrival, tailored to the mutually-designed plan. Such setup will normally revolve around three of the nine items we listed in 'Training Effectiveness Upon the Host Receivers' (cf. section #3 of Chapter 3, variable #8). Those three include providing pre-arrival setup support concerning:
   - Logistical Support for Short-Termers
   - Program Delivery Support for Short-Termers
   - Risk Management and Security Issues for Short-Termers

3. *Preparation and Training*

   Field facilitators also need training in order to facilitate true mission through the goer-guests to the intended receptors. As alluded to in step two above, those nine training items are listed and explained in the previous chapter. But to briefly note, the remaining six of field facilitators' 'pre-field' training items are:

- Identifying Your Strategic Field Activities Leveragable through Short-Termers
- Blending Your Field-supplied Leadership with Their Sending Entity-supplied Leadership
- Cross-cultural Training: Grasping the Short-Termers' Worldview
- Recruiting from Short-Termers for Field Needs
- Outcomes Follow-up
- Relational Issues

ON-FIELD

On-field represents the period of time that short-term goer-guests are on-site with respect to their intended mission. It exists from their moment of arrival, to their moment of departure. On-field can also be viewed as the period of time when goer-guests are actually on location with their host receivers.

Sending Supporters

Sending supporters now shift from their pre-field responsibilities to their on-field responsibilities:

1. *Prayer Supporters*

   While goer-guests are on-field, prayer supporters must still be "led by the Spirit" and pray regularly. Prayer supporters' four 'default' prayer items should include:
   - Spiritual warfare and Kingdom effectiveness in mission; pray that God will produce Kingdom growth within intended receptors through the efforts of this mission outreach.
   - Goer-guests' personal health, safety, boldness in the Spirit, humility in serving, and submission to all on-field leadership.
   - Unity within, and humility among, the on-field leadership trio (cf. section #6 below).
   - Effective on-field debriefing and appropriate post-field follow-up for especially the goer-guests and the host receivers.

133

2. *Financial Supporters*
   Financial supporters are technically done, and—if not already—could now consider becoming prayer supporters during the on-field portion.

3. *Logistical Supporters*
   Logistical supporters now carry out all 'back home' arrangements made for goer-guests while goer-guests are on-field.

4. *Emotional Supporters*
   Although emotional supporters are technically done (and could also become prayer supporters during the on-field portion), opportunities to continue speaking words of encouragement to goer-guests may present themselves through phone calls or e-mail exchanges with the field. "Stick in there!—I know God will use you!", or "We just prayed for you this morning!"

5. *Communication Supporters*
   Communication supporters now carry out all 'back home' communication responsibilities agreed upon for their goer-guests while goer-guests are on-field.

6. *Re-entry Supporters*
   Re-entry supporters should begin looking and praying through the (sending entity-supplied) list of 'intelligent questions' they'll be asking goer-guests upon their return back home.

Sending Entity and Goer-Guests
From the perspective of the sending entity and its goer-guests, 'on-field' usually consists of an intermingling of these six specific items:
1. Programmed Delivery of Goer-Guests' Intended Activities
2. Programmed On-field Team Meetings
3. Programmed Cultural Interaction
4. Non-programmed Cultural Interaction
5. Non-programmed Receiving
6. Leadership Influence

1. Programmed Delivery of Goer-Guests' Intended Activities
The on-site program delivery of goer-guests' intended activities (cf. Chapter

3, variable #2) for intended receptors is often the primary *intended* outcome of pre-field training. Again, for these program activities to achieve success, their design had to have been mutually planned by the sending entity and field facilitators. Success also assumes that all goer-guests achieved adequate, proper training (cf. Chapter 3, variable #8), and that they retain the effects of such training and know how to properly apply what they've learned. Success further assumes goer-guests' mission philosophy (cf. Chapter 3, variable #7) is essentially in line with their sending entity's and field facilitators' mission philosophy.

2.   *Programmed On-field Team Meetings*
Team meetings are a significant piece of most goer-guests' on-field process. On-field team meetings apply to all size variables of short-term mission, except the individual. The coming together for worship (which is always a form of spiritual warfare), the 'therapy' of an affinity-group discussion, the getting-our-heads-together, the programmed structure of active listening and intentional learning from host receivers and other leaders contribute greatly to the goer-guests' on-field effectiveness.

   Although they vary depending upon the experience of the sending entity (and field facilitator), on-field team meetings routinely occur once or twice a day—often first thing in the morning, and/or last thing in the evening. Such meetings may run from a few minutes to an hour or longer. Items which are appropriate for on-field team meetings are generally the routine daily items, which are practical or necessary to the outreach's continued success. These items often include:

- devotions
- praise and worship (singing)
- prayer
- Bible study or teachings
- problem-solving
- mutual encouragement and support

- announcements
- additional training
- mission teachings
- discussion
- making or amending plans
- active listening/observing by all leaders to everything said and done

   A few on-field team meetings run much longer, and become the primary activity of an entire morning or day. These meetings often focus on bigger training items which are necessary to successful on-field outreach, and for which the 'Timing of Training Delivery' (cf. Chapter 3, variable #8) is more effective on-field (as opposed to pre-field). Those items include:

- on-site orientation
- re-entry preparation
- debriefing session(s)

- amending intended activities
- extended teaching or instruction related to the local culture

3. Programmed Cultural Interaction

Planned, programmed interaction with the people and places represented by the local culture should be a major objective of the sending entity (and host receivers). Local people, local shopping, local sites of interest, local points of historical significance, local community events, local rites of passage, local food and beverages, local plants and vegetation, local animals, local poverty, local wealth, local government services, local music, local language, local media (radio, television, newspapers, magazines), local art, local transportation, local roads, local restaurants, local parties and celebrations—these are merely a few of the cultural items that contribute significantly to the goer-guests' on-field effectiveness.

As leaders (sending entity leaders and host receiver leaders) help goer-guests enter into, process, and begin understanding the local culture, goer-guests begin to apply their pre-field and on-field training in real life situations. This expands worldviews, challenges paradigms, exposes racism, increases knowledge. And God gets bigger. The result? Goer-guests become more effective.

4. Non-programmed Cultural Interaction

While making announcements at the National Short-Term Mission Conference[4] one year, Kim Hurst told conference participants, "what happens *in between* this conference's programmed events may well be the most important thing you encounter this weekend." Kim understood how God uses serendipitous 'chance' encounters between certain people whenever a group gathers because of a 'programmed' event (cf. Chapter 7).

The same holds true for short-term mission. Non-programmed occurrences—during free time, during space in between programmed events, and even the unscheduled 'chance' encounters or events occurring during programmed time—easily find their way into goer-guests' paths dozens of times each day. These are often cultural opportunities which God can use to sharpen skills, build deeper friendships, open doors, and create opportunities for Kingdom growth in any of the participants (especially goer-guests and intended receptors). Wise leaders will build allowance into the programmed schedule to accommodate these unscheduled, non-programmed cultural interac-

tion opportunities. These usually are *not* interruptions to the on-field program—but rather a hugely important serendipitous piece of the program God
Himself has designed.

5. Non-programmed Receiving

Goer-guests often return home exclaiming, "I received more than I gave!", or
"I learned so much more from the local people than I ever taught them!" Host
receivers often experience similar unintended personal growth and insight:
"The Americans (Canadians, Europeans, Asians, etc.) really *don't* dress and
talk like what we see on T.V.!", or "I learned that many [Americans] cry, they
hurt, and have problems, too!", or "They explained who Jesus is!"

Here again, the seasoned leader recognizes that a significant piece of the
on-field outreach winds up as a reflective process within short-termers' and
host receivers' hearts. Good leaders realize their goer-guests and intended
receptors often experienced significant—even life-changing—growth during
the on-field outreach. This non-programmed receiving will be the focus of
Chapter 7 (The Reciprocity of Give 'n Take).

6. Leadership Influence

On-field leadership is the linchpin of every short-term mission team's outreach. A poorly designed program can still have effective delivery (and effective
results) with good leadership. But even the best designed program is prone to
failure with poor on-field leadership (cf. Chapter 3, variable #8).

The on-field, team-driven leadership will vary with each short-term situa-
tion, but is generally a trio of leadership representation. The leadership trio
consists of:
  •   Sending Entity Leadership (Goer-Guest Leaders)
  •   Field Facilitator Leadership
  •   Intended Receptor Leadership

  a.   *Sending Entity Leadership.* The sending entity (cf. Chapter 3, vari-
       able #6) may be a church working independently (an SE-1), or may
       be that same church working in partnership with an SE-2 parachurch
       mission agency. Given the second scenario, the church may be sup-
       plying two or three of its own leaders, while the parachurch mission
       agency is supplying one or two of its leaders. Summary: the sending
       entity *partnership* could be supplying anywhere from one, to a com-
       posite of five or more leaders—each of whom assumes certain on-

field authority. (If the sending entity is a partnership like we're describing, there are in effect four 'groups' or four potential agendas of on-field leadership assumptions—as opposed to the trio of three indicated above).

b. *Field Facilitator Leadership.* The field facilitators may—or may not—be a direct part of the SE-2 sending entity. Either way, it is likely there are one or more persons assuming a leadership role during the on-field outreach. Often, this person is the on-site staff person, missionary, national pastor, or other national leader.

c. *Intended Receptor Leadership.* If the intended receptors are people or a given people group actively participating in the on-field outreach, they will also have one or more of their leaders (e.g., mayor, chief, elder, other national pastors) who may be 'represented' by the field facilitators, but who may desire active leadership presence during the given short-term mission. In unreached groups or regions of high security concerns, the leadership from the intended receptors will probably not be an active part of the on-field leadership trio.

It is essential that this trio (or four 'groups' as in (a) above) of on-field leadership have daily meetings. These four agenda items are mandatory in each daily leadership meeting:

- *Issues and Problems:* What issues, concerns, and problems have arisen since we last met? What is our plan of action concerning problem resolution?
- *Today's Game Plan:* Is today's plan still in motion? What tweaks do we need to make to today's plan? Which leaders are responsible for what part of today's plan?
- *Tomorrow's Game Plan:* Are we on track concerning tomorrow's plans? What adjustments might we need to make today, with respect to meeting tomorrow's game plan?
- *Prayer:* This is the first thing, last thing, and most crucial thing you do in each daily leadership meeting.

Although it will vary in each situation, generally the on-field leadership responsibilities will flow best as follows:

Field Facilitator Leaders &
Intended Receptor Leaders

- logistical arrangements made with local people (housing, (food, ground transportation)
- on-field site orientation
- cultural guidelines and local rules reinforcement
- employment of local people (cooks, drivers, interpreters, guides, workers, foremen, etc.)
- mentoring the goer-guests
- recruiting for field needs
- handling local political or governmental requirements
- on-field security instruction
- financial disbursements on behalf of goer-guests expenses

Sending Entity
(Goer-Guest) Leaders

- team dynamics of the goer-guests
- discipline and conflict resolution within the goer-guests
- daily goer-guests' team meetings (worship, prayer, activity assignments)
- general 'baby-sitting' of all goer-guests 24/7
- liaison for issues between goer-guests and field facilitators, and between goer-guests and intended receptors
- communication liaison with SE leadership remaining back home
- management of goer-guests' luggage, personal items

POST-FIELD

Although the line between on-field and post-field is often blurred for some members of the participant trilogy, post-field means everything that occurs during the period of time the on-field portion of the outreach ceases to exist.

Post-field continues indefinitely for every member of the participant trilogy, but perhaps the greatest continuation finds its impact in goer-guests and intended receptors.

Sending Supporters

Some of the sending supporters' roles were completed pre-field and on-field. Yet the following post-field responsibilities for sending supporters still remain:

1. *Prayer Supporters*
   During the first one to two weeks post-field, prayer supporters should attempt to touch bases with (1) the goer-guest(s) they prayed for, (2) the sending entity, and (3) the goer's re-entry supporters to see what specific intercessory prayer items may now be needed during re-entry and post-field follow-up (e.g., needs, problems, future plans).

2. *Financial Supporters*
   Financial supporters' role is complete.

3. *Logistical Supporters*
   Meeting and picking up goer-guests as they arrive home at the airport (or bus station or church parking lot) is perhaps the first postfield logistical task. During the next couple days, other logistical supporters should contact their respective goer-guest(s), to report and debrief the assigned logistical task(s) they completed while goer-guests were on-field.

4. *Emotional Supporters*
   Emotional supporters' role is essentially complete.

5. *Communication Supporters*
   Communication supporters' role is essentially complete (the returned goer-guests should now assume personal direct responsibility for all needed communication).

6. *Re-entry Supporters*
   Re-entry supporters now swing into action. Ideally, re-entry supporters are prepared with a list of 'intelligent questions'[5] to ask their respective goer-guest(s). Re-entry supporters make a date (with sufficient time—at least two or three hours) in an emotionally safe and interruption-free environment. They sit down to listen, really listen to goer-guest's answers. If re-entry supporters suspect any concerns or other issues needing follow-up, the supporters help steer goer-guests to the appropriate people (e.g., the mission pastor, the counselling pastor, etc.). Re-entry supporters need to remain on standby for one or two other meetings, prepared to pick up their active role of supportive listening to goer-guests. (If more than three meetings are necessary, a professional referral may be in order.)

Sending Entity

The sending entity has five major areas of post-field follow-up responsibility. Some are direct, non-delegable responsibilities, while others can only be accomplished by empowering other people outside of the sending entity's direct control. Those five post-field responsibilities are:

- Empowering All Participant Trilogy Members for Their Respective Follow-up Responsibilities
- Debriefing Sending Entity Leaders (Goer-Guest Leaders)
- Following Up on All Goer-Guests (Leaders and Followers) and Helping Them Integrate Back Home
- Assuring Proper and Timely Reporting Back to All Sending Supporters
- Evaluation with Field Facilitators

(All five of these areas of responsibility are imbedded within the next section, including paragraphs #1 through #6 below.)

The sending entity is responsible to see to it that post-field follow-up occurs with all members of the participant trilogy. If the sending entity cannot do follow-up directly itself, it is still responsible to see to it that the appropriate participant trilogy members do so, and to provide direction or training to assist in that process. For example, if the sending entity is a church (SE-1), the church can—and must!—do *direct* personal follow-up with each goer-guest. But if the sending entity is a mission agency (SE-2), the agency loses direct contact with goer-guests once they return home. Even so, the agency can—and must!—do *indirect* follow-up, by supplying appropriate church leadership with the training and tools they need to do local post-field follow-up with their own goer-guests.

NOTE: In the portion of the section that follows, the *italicized* paragraph titles are the participant trilogy members needing post-field follow-up. Within each corresponding paragraph, **bold** type indicates the participant trilogy member responsible for that follow-up:

1. *Sending Supporters*
   - Pre-field trainers and goer-guests leaders should have instructed **goer-guests** how to follow-up with their sending supporters. Personal thank you notes or phone calls to each supporter goes a long way.
   - If the sending entity has names and addresses of sending supporters, the **sending entity** should send an 'official' thank you, photo, and brief written report of what God accomplished through the goer-guests on the mission outreach.
   - If the **sending entity** has a regular gathering of its people (e.g., a Sunday church service, or weekly campus chapel) where many sending supporters are likely to be present, a follow-up presentation of

what God accomplished through the goer-guests on the mission outreach is an appropriate supplement to the above.

2. *Sending Entity*
   Based on the intended receptors' evaluations of the on-field outreach, **field facilitators** must evaluate the sending entity, with respect to how well goer-guests achieved the mutually-designed outreach. **Goer-guests** must likewise evaluate their on-field experience with the sending entity, in a manner that allows honest surfacing of any leadership issues or other unresolved concerns. If the sending entity was a partnership formed, for example, between a community hospital (SE-3) and a mission agency (SE-2), leadership from **each sending entity partner** needs to debrief each other once back home, to make sure no gaps, issues, or details remain unattended.

3. *Goer-Guest Leaders (Sending Entity Leaders)*
   Sending entity executive leadership must take special time to debrief each goer-guest leader it sent on-field. It's imperative to learn what on-field commitments may have been made to host receivers by goer-guests, so that goer-guests can be held accountable to such commitments. It's also important for the executive leadership to hear every concern or critique goer-guest leaders may need to report.

4. *Goer-Guests (Followers and Leaders)*
   (a) DIRECT
       Regardless of which type of sending entity was used, it's the **home church** that has the relationship with, and responsibility for, their returning goer-guests to do post-field follow-up and re-entry integration. As we argued in the first two chapters, mission is the call and responsibility of every church. Therefore, in the post-field process of short-term mission, every church must continue its call and responsibility to its members.
   (b) INDIRECT
       Although SE-2 agencies, SE-3.a(2) schools and other sending entity groups can provide some post-field follow-up, only the home church can stick with it and see it through on a personal one-on-one basis. So **agencies, schools,** and **other groups** must do whatever they can do directly themselves (via postal

mail, e-mail, scheduled reunion meetings, etc.), but more importantly must provide post-field follow-up to goer-guests *indirectly* by empowering each of their short-termers' home churches.

It's unfortunate that many churches don't provide adequate follow-up and integration opportunities for returning short-termers. Previous research indicates incredible potential benefits begin to accrue immediately—to the local home church, community, and world (and therefore to the Kingdom of God)—all correlated to the short-term mission outreach.

In 1991, Peterson and Peterson found statistically significant and "substantial changes in prayer, financial giving, commitment to world mission, mission-related activities and education, and in feelings about returning to the mission field ... as a result of [goer-guests'] short-term mission."[6] Their study specifically found that post-field, short-term goer-guests':

Prayer
- prayer for a specific missionary by name increased ....+ 83%
- prayer for a specific geographical location increased ....+ 149%
- prayer for a specific people group increased ....+ 141%
- mission focused prayer overall increased ....+ 237%

Giving
- monthly missions giving increased $22.80 ....+ 93%
- perception of their "sacrificial" giving increased ....+ 400%

Local Involvement
- local outreach to internationals increased ....+69%
- mission-related support activities increased ....+64%
- mission-related education increased ....+32%

Return to the Field
- feelings ("likely" or greater) about returning to the field 77%
- actual return to the field (short- and long-term) 32%
  - —returned within a 1 year time frame 50%
  - —returned within a 1–2 year time frame 35%
  - —returned within a 2–3 year time frame 10%
  - —returned within a 3–4 year time frame 3%
  - —returned within a >4 year time frame 2%

It's the trend observed in the last five lines of data where we want to draw your attention. Fully one-half of those who returned to the mission field, did so within one year of coming home from their short-term mission. The percentage of those returning diminished markedly with each ensuing year. These data strongly suggest that each church must implement a follow-up program right away, after goer-guests come home from their short-term mission outreach. (Note that the goal of the church's follow-up program should not exist only to field returning missionaries. The "return to the field" data merely suggests the sooner any follow-up is implemented, the greater the likelihood of facilitating favorable Kingdom responses—whatever course that may take.)

What components should a church have in its follow-up program for its returning goer-guests? Here are the must-haves which should be readily available to the short-term goer-guest from the moment he first reports back to his home church:

- Private debriefing and reporting (via re-entry supporters)
- Public debriefing and reporting (via Sunday services, Sunday school, church small groups)
- Reunion party (include short-termers from outside the church)
- Issues counselling (for personal and spiritual issues which may have surfaced on-field)
- Career-path counselling (for short-termers who sense God calling them in a new or different career)
- Educational counselling (for short-termers who sense God calling them to new or different training and education)
- Practical, stretching service opportunities with local ethnic peoples outside of the home church's walls (e.g., service opportunities that parallel on-field experiences—soup kitchens, hospital visitation, teaching English to immigrants, community clean-up projects, etc.)
- Practical, stretching service opportunities within the home church's own walls (service opportunities that build on the on-field experience, e.g., Sunday school teaching, small group leadership, mission committee participation, drama ministry, music ministry, etc.)
- Practical, stretching opportunities for intercessory prayer and strategic financial giving (opportunities that build on lessons learned during the on-field portion of the outreach)
- Mentoring and personal discipleship
- Opportunities to launch new parallel ministries back home

- Resourcing opportunities to return back to the field (longer on-field time, more responsibilities)
- Resourcing opportunities for further mission training (e.g., Perspectives on the World Christian Movement, Bethany College of Missions, Fuller School of World Mission, etc.)
- Opportunities to host visiting missionaries or international guests
- Opportunities to mobilize others to do their first short-term mission
- Making sure goer-guests honor all on-field commitments made to host receivers

5. *Field Facilitators*

   After the sending entity debriefs its goer-guest leaders and reviews its goer-guests' evaluations, the **sending entity** must follow-up with their field facilitator partners, with respect to how well the mutually-designed outreach was achieved.

6. *Intended Receptors*

   Field facilitators must listen to comments (evaluations) from the intended receptors, concerning the on-field experience they had with the on-field leadership, the goer-guests, and their intended activities. Since field facilitators are the people who remain on-site after goer-guests return home, **field facilitators** are the ones who must follow-up on every outcome of the short-term mission on-field outreach, whether good or bad. On the positive side, new converts need discipling and need a good local church. On the negative side, field facilitators need to support the intended receptors as they correct whatever problems were caused by the goer-guests.[7]

Goer-Guests

Goer-guests have three post-field follow-up responsibilities:
- Integrating Themselves Back Home
- Following Up with Sending Supporters
- Following Up with Commitments Made On-Field

Integrating Themselves Back Home

Working from knowledge gained during their on-field re-entry preparation, on-field debriefing, and home church post-field follow-up, goer-guests are now responsible to 'unpack' many things God taught them throughout their short-term mission. Integrating these lessons into the routine of normal life (or—changing from a normal state of life to a permanently abnormal state) becomes the challenge for each goer-guest. This can be a difficult, messy, even life-long process for some returning goer-guests (which is why their home church must come alongside them).

Goer-guests should first and foremost seek to work out their re-entry issues and follow-up plans through the post-field programs offered by their home church. And since most churches don't have good post-field programs, returning short-termers may become the people to launch such programs within their own church. (Use the previous page as a guide in developing such a program.)

Integrating themselves back home is often the most difficult piece to accomplish, because a missionary—even a short-termer—no longer fully 'fits' any culture, including her home culture of origin. Family, friends, and work colleagues may have a hard time understanding certain behavioral and attitudinal changes that often accompany a short-termer's attempt at getting back into the 'normal' swing of things. That's why the home church must come alongside each returning goer-guest, helping them integrate their own personal changes into whatever the reality of life is for them at the given place and time.

Following Up with Sending Supporters

Another follow-up imperative for goer-guests involves contacting each of their respective sending supporters. Prayer supporters need to hear how their prayers were answered. Financial supporters need not only a personal thank you note, they need to know how their financial investment furthered the Kingdom of God. Logistical supporters need to be thanked specifically for doing whatever it was they did. Emotional supporters need thanks for their words of encouragement. Communication supporters need to be thanked for handling correspondence and missionary prayer letters. And re-entry supporters need to be thanked for listening to the stories.

For some, a quick personal e-mail will be sufficient. For others, a nice personalized thank you card or letter is better (hand delivered or postal mailed). Some will appreciate a phone call. A photograph or two (or directions to a web site with photos), a small souvenir, a formal written report (no longer than two full pages is best), or invitation to the public sharing event (e.g., church service presentation) will also be appropriate for supporters that invested more of their time, finances, or energies in goer-guests.

Following Up with Commitments Made On-Field
Within a week after arriving back home, goer-guests must sit down, go through their on-field journal, and organize a 'to-do' list for all the commitments they made to field facilitators and intended receptors back on the field. Wherever possible, goer-guests should submit a copy of this list to their sending entity—especially the appropriate home church leadership—to allow full disclosure and accountability among all participants.

Generally such commitments may include:
- promise to send photographs
- promise to write
- promise to provide financial or other asset assistance
- promise to return back to the field

In certain 'unreasonable' situations, the sending entity leadership may need to suspend certain commitments its goer-guests may have made, and provide the correct avenues for goer-guests and other appropriate leaders to apologize and make amends with appropriate host receivers. To promise anything, however good the original intention of the heart may have been—and then to fail to follow through—happens far too often, and is nothing short of deception and lies. Goer-guests must be encouraged to flush out every commitment they made, into an arena of accountability for the sake of the Kingdom of God.

Field Facilitators
Field facilitators have two primary post-field follow-up responsibilities:
- Debriefing and Evaluating the Sending Entity
- Debriefing and Following Up with Intended Receptors

Debriefing and Evaluating the Sending Entity
After debriefing the intended receptors, field facilitators need to assess to what degree the mutually-designed outreach was achieved. Field facilitators then need to pass along that evaluation to the sending entity. Then together, the field facilitators and sending entity debrief each other with respect to successes, unresolved issues, missed expectations, and make future plans for their next mutually-designed short-term mission.

Debriefing and Following Up with Intended Receptors
Field facilitators are the key on-site people to follow up with intended recep-

tors. To what degree did the mutually-designed mission get accomplished? And at what expense to the field—especially to intended receptors? What needs to be done differently next time around? What promises—realistic or unrealistic—did goer-guests make to the intended receptors?

Because of the very nature of short-term mission (swift, temporary deployment of non-professional missionaries), chances are good that goer-guests made more than one mistake on-field. What were those mistakes? Field facilitators need to apologize and make good on those errors in behalf of goer-guests. Field facilitators also need to pass along this information to the sending entity, who in turn must follow-up with its goer-guests.

Intended Receptors

Intended receptors need to debrief the field facilitators on their perception of the mission outreach.

If the intended receptors were overtly involved in the on-field outreach, they need to know that field facilitators will be willing to 'hear their side of the story, and do something about it' if the goer-guests created any problems or uncomfortable situations.

If the intended receptors were not overtly involved (as is often the case in nations of high security concern or restricted access), formal debriefing and follow-up probably cannot take place. Field facilitators (and sending entity leaders) need to prayerfully discern their degree of success with intended receptors.

If the intended receptors were objects of God's creation (water which has become polluted, forests that have been rapidly harvested but not replaced, etc.) or objects of man's creation (corrupt civic structures, or oppressive systems, etc.), formal debriefing needs to take place with appropriate representatives from those respective spheres.

Summary

SHORT-TERM mission is not an isolated event *in* time. It is a process *over* time that includes all participants. From a western sending perspective, short-term mission begins pre-field (which is primarily mutual design, recruiting, planning, preparation). It continues on-field (primarily the program delivery and reciprocity of give and take between all cultures present on-field). And short-term mission continues post-field (with debriefing, re-entry, and follow-up needed for all participants).

Endnotes
Chapter 5

1. *(p. 130)* Cf. **Lisa Espineli-Chinn**, *Reentry Guide for Short-Term Mission Leaders* (Orlando FL: Deeper Roots Publications, 1998), specifically "Post-return Debriefing" (pp. 35–37); "Helping Spouses and Children in Reentry (pp. 42–48); and "Settling-In Exercise (pp. 62–63). Cf. also the "Appendix" of **Duane Elmer**, *Cross-Cultural Connections* (Downers Grove IL: InterVarsity Press, 2002), pp. 205–207.

2. *(p. 131)* (http://www.adventures.org).

3. *(p. 131)* Extracted from in-person conversations between Seth Barnes and Roger Peterson (and from small group discussion notes in which Barnes participated) at the FSTML (Fellowship of Short-Term Mission Leaders) Annual Conference held October 2–6, 2002, at the Simpsonwood Conference and Retreat Center in Atlanta, Georgia. Peterson has expanded on Barnes' concepts; (for more FSTML information go to: http://www.FSTML.org).

4. *(p. 136)* An annual January weekend training conference for short-term mission sending entities (primarily SE-1 churches) and their goer-guest leaders; (for NSTMC information go to: http://www.NSTMC.org).

5. *(p. 140)* Cf. Endnote #1 above.

6. *(p. 143)* **Roger P. Peterson and Timothy D. Peterson**, *Is Short-Term Mission Really Worth the Time and Money?* (Minneapolis MN: STEM Ministries, 1991), pp. i–28.

7. *(p. 145)* Wayne Sneed has field facilitator colleagues in Brazil, to whom this appalling short-term event actually took place:
    "In 1985 a team from Florida came to build a wall. The team never asked what the orphanage home really needed, they just wanted to build a block wall because that's what they knew how to do. The orphanage home felt obligated to let them do what they wanted. So they said, 'OK, build a wall over here.' The team did, and took hundreds of pictures of their project to put in their report to the home church back in Florida. After the team left [the Brazilians] tore the wall down. None of the team noticed the wall was built in the middle of [the orphanage's] soccer field" (extracted from a personal e-mail sent by Wayne Sneed to Roger Peterson, by request, dated December 30, 2002).

THE PARTICIPANT TRILOGY

1 Senders   2 Goer-Guests   3 Host Receivers

MUCH HAS ALREADY BEEN DISCUSSED CONCERNING the participant trilogy in previous chapters. Yet it is imperative that short-term mission practitioners understand who it is, exactly, that makes up this trilogy, and why it is they all are considered to be full-fledged 'participants.'

Participants are not merely those who go on the short-term mission outreach. Are students the only educational participants in a classroom?...(what about the teacher)? Are people who sit in the pews on Sunday the only participants in a worship service?...(what about the ushers, or preacher, or organist, or music minister?...what about the sound and video crews—aren't they participants, too)?

As a matter of fact, using the word 'participant' to imply only those who go on a short-term mission outreach is actually a misappropriation of Scripture.

III John 6b–8 (RSV)

"You will do well to send them on their journey as befits God's service. For they have set out for His sake and have accepted nothing from the heathen. So we ought to *support* such men, *that we may be fellow workers* in the truth" (emphasis ours).

It doesn't take a seminary degree to figure out this one. *Any person who supports* another person—for the purpose of sending that person out for the sake of the Gospel—is a *fellow worker* with that sent person (we call that sent person a 'goer-guest'). So if the sent person (goer-guest) is considered a short-term mission participant, then according to III John 6–8, so are all that person's sending supporters.

Matthew 10:41 (NIV)

"*Anyone who receives* a prophet because he is a prophet will receive a prophet's reward, and *anyone who receives* a righteous man because he is a righteous man will receive a righteous man's reward" (emphasis ours).

Matthew 10:40–41 (THE MESSAGE)

"We are intimately linked in this harvest work...Accepting a messenger of God is as good as being God's messenger. Accepting someone's help is as good as giving someone help."

Those who receive a prophet (God's messenger) get to enjoy the same reward as the messenger gets. *Receiving* someone's help is as good as giving it. It seems fairly clear to us that *receivers* of short-term missionaries (especially *willing* receivers) are viewed by God as equal participants in His harvest plan, because both are entitled to the same reward.

SENDER
Participants

MOST mission literature blurs two distinct mission sending concepts into one confusing term: 'senders' ('sending'). In actuality there are *two* sub-categories of senders, and *two* different sets of responsibilities. The *sending supporters* and *sending entity* are described and differentiated below:

SENDING SUPPORTERS

Sending supporters are normally individual people (or couples or families; and sometimes a business organization or other group) who voluntarily respond *on an individual basis* to one or more of six means of supporting a short-term missionary. These six means of support were originally identified by Neal Pirolo[1] for long-term career missionaries, but work perfectly in the short-term mission arena as well. Those six are:

1. Prayer Supporters
2. Financial Supporters
3. Logistical Supporters
4. Emotional Supporters
5. Communication Supporters
6. Re-Entry Supporters

1. Prayer Supporters

Prayer supporters intercede for given goer-guests and all aspects of the short-term outreach (cf. Chapter 5 for specific pre-field, on-field, and post field intercessory prayer items).

2. Financial Supporters

These are the individual folks (and organizations) who write a contribution check or who take part in fundraising events by purchasing a product or service where the proceeds are given to offset the mission outreach expenses.

ILLUSTRATION #6.1

Participant Trilogy Members

THE THREE MAJOR CLASSIFICATIONS OF SHORT-TERM MISSION PARTICIPANTS, SHOWING THEIR SIX RESPECTIVE SUBSETS OF PARTICIPANTS

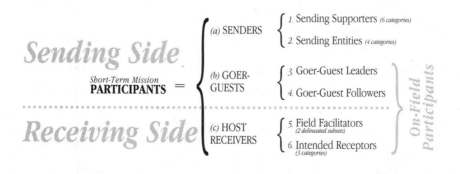

3. Logistical Supporters

Logistical supporters make arrangements with goer-guests during the pre-field process, to provide certain 'back home' logistics help for goer-guests during their on-field outreach. Examples include airport drop-offs and pick-ups, pet care, check their vacated home (especially important during the cold winter months in northern climates), and whatever needs to be done 'back home' for the goer-guests while they're on-field.

4. Emotional Supporters

As we mentioned in the previous chapter, encouraging statements such as "I believe God wants you to go!", or "I think you should join our church's short-term outreach!", or "keep working on that Russian language!", or "God really can provide the money you need!" are examples of the crucial role emotional supporters play during the pre-field process for goer-guests. When key family members or other influential persons provide such emotional support, a goer-guest is greatly encouraged during difficult pre-field moments of preparation, and freed from ungodly self-doubt and worry.

5. Communication Supporters

Short-term missionaries need someone 'back home' to call, write, or produce communication newsletters to the other 'back home' sending supporters and all others with whom the short-termers need to stay in touch. This is crucial for seasonal and extended short-term outreaches (months or years), but seldom necessary for mini and standard outreaches (days or weeks).

6. Re-Entry Supporters

Re-entry supporters are those persons specifically chosen to meet with the returning short-termers after they come back home. Re-entry supporters are prepared with a list of 'intelligent questions'[2] to ask their respective goer-guest(s). As discussed in the previous chapter, re-entry supporters make a date (with sufficient time—at least two or three hours) in an emotionally safe and interruption-free environment. They sit down and listen, really listen to the goer-guest's answers. If re-entry supporters suspect any concerns or other issues needing follow-up, these supporters help steer goer-guests to the appropriate people (e.g., the mission pastor, the counselling pastor, etc.). Re-entry supporters need to remain on standby for one or two other meetings, prepared to pick up their active role of supportive, understanding listening to goer-guests.

SENDING ENTITY

The *sending **entity*** is an **organization** or similar structure having its own identifiable name (e.g., First Church, or ABC Mission Agency, or The Lay Ministry Training School, etc.). The sending entity is often viewed as the sponsor. Usually it's an organized (whether formal or informal) institutional structure (whether incorporated or not) having primary administrative, managerial, and/or information-sharing responsibility to many of the sending supporters (especially the prayer, financial, and re-entry sending supporters), all of the goer-guests, and the field facilitators. The sending entity manages the bulk of pre-field and post-field aspects for participants on the 'sending-side' of the short-term mission equation, acting as key 'sending-side' liaison with its field facilitator partners on the 'receiving-side.'

In Chapter 3, defining variable #6, we spent seven pages describing what the four major short-term mission sending entities are, specifically including their 12 functional subsets (cf. TABLE #3.6). We won't take time to re-describe them in this chapter, other than to contrast their respective strengths and weaknesses as compared with each other as shown in TABLE #6.1.

G O E R - G U E S T
Participants

A T FIRST pass, the term 'goer-guest' seems a bit awkward. Wouldn't the selection of just one of those words be easier for the short-term mission practitioner to use? Perhaps. Yet the choice of this two-word term is very intentional, and fabulously pregnant with meaning.

Goer

Perhaps the single word which best summarizes Christian mission (cf. Chapter 2) is the verb "Go!" And because that "Go!" command is given to all believers, the believers who respond then become the semantic counterpart to that verb—the noun 'goers.' Use of the word 'goer' also helps differentiate between other members of the participant trilogy. Using the word 'goer' helps us clearly realize we're *not* talking about the senders or the host receivers. Referring to the short-term mission participant who physically goes to work in the on-field site as a 'goer' is a theologically correct, accurate use of that term.

Guest

To finalize the design and terminology of the MISTM-Grid (cf. Chapter 9), one

TABLE #6.1

Sending Entity Contrasts
Comparing Strengths and Weaknesses
of the Four Primary Types of Sending Entities

OVERALL

SE-1 Churches

S = Cradle to grave resp'bility to goer-guests

1. SE-1.a Churches *(comprehensive mission program)*

S = Recruiting/mobilizing of *all* ages

2. SE-1.b Churches *(STM-only program)*

W = Multiple programs & foci; potential for self focus over intended receptor focus

SE-2 Parachurch Mission Agencies

S = Operates for one primary focus (intended receptors), with greater capacity (than SE-1 Churches) for lifetime on-field follow-up

SE-2.a Nondenominational Mission Agencies

3. •SE-2.a(1) Traditional Agencies *(long-term focus)*

W = Less able (than SE-1 Churches) to provide lifetime follow-up to goer-guests

4. •SE-2.a(2) Non-traditional Agencies *(short-term focus)*

5. SE-2.b Denominational Mission Boards

6. SE-2.c Associations or Networks of Churches

7. SE-2.d Local Society Created Within a Given Church

SE-3 Institutional Non-mission Organizations

S = Mission becomes integrated with other programs & foci

SE-3.a Christian Parachurch Non-mission Agency Organizations

S = SE-3.a(2) schools have natural capacity for pre-field & post-field training; recruiting/mobilizing the historical *ideal* age (late teens, early 20s)

8. •SE-3.a(1) Inter-collegiate Christian Organizations

9. •SE-3.a(2) Individual Christian Colleges & Schools

10. •SE-3.a(3) Other *(e.g. Christian radio stations, Christian hospitals)*

W = Less able (than SE-1 Churches) to provide lifetime follow-up to goer-guests

11. SE-3.b Secular Non-parachurch For-Profit Organizations

12. SE-4 One's Self

S = Can immediately follow the Spirit

W = One person can't realistically do it all

KEY:

S = Strength

W = Weakness

(NOTE: A given strength or weakness should not be used to make a case either for or against any type of Sending Entity. Rather, attempt to leverage all strengths where possible, and acknowledge—and shore up!—the weaknesses.)

PRE-FIELD   ON-FIELD   POST-FIELD

PRE-FIELD	ON-FIELD	POST-FIELD
S = Spiritual preparation, care, and bonding of goer-guests (goer-guest-oriented training of the goer-guests) *W* = Goer-guest preparation focus can overshadow what should be the primary focus on intended receptors	*S* = Care/nurture/discipleship of goer-guests *W* = Goer-guest focus can be at expense of intended receptors' best interests	*S* = Greatest potential for best possible lifetime follow-up with goer-guests *W* = Harder to maintain good on-field follow-up program for intended receptors
S = Greater potential for mutu-ally-designed outreach beneficial to all participants (receiver-orient-ed training of the goer-guests) *S* = Greater ability for good administration, setup, logistics planning *W* = Often can't apply intimate knowledge of goer-guests (like their Church can) to planning	*S* = Intended receptor focus beneficial to all participants *S* = Greater ability for good administration of field programs & field logistics support *W* = Since goer-guests aren't an agency's primary focus, goer-guests can feel slighted	*S* = Greater capacity for life-time on-field follow-up with intended receptors *W* = Less able to provide lifetime follow-up to goer-guests
S = Bonding of goer-guests often exists due to involvement in the given affinity group's other activities (goer-guest-oriented training of the goer-guests) *S* = SE-3.a(2) schools have greater potential for in-depth training in mission *W* = SE-3.a(3) and SE-3.b groups present a less-experi-enced knowledge of mission *W* = Goer-guest preparation focus can overshadow intended receptors	*S* = Care/nurture/discipleship of goer-guests *S* = SE-3.a(2) schools educa-tion of their goer-guests *W* = Goer-guest focus can be at expense of intended receptors' best interests	*S* = The nature of the given affinity group naturally allows some reasonable follow-up of goer-guests *W* = Harder to maintain good on-field follow-up program for intended receptors because charter calls for focus in some other arena
S = Can speed up pre-field preparation time *W* = Likely to miss important, beneficial preparation items	*S* = Can do whatever he/she wants to do, whenever, wherever *W* = Total independence eventu-ally works against self	*S* = Can theoretically custom design own follow-up program *W* = Not likely to do it; and no one to share experience with

of the several things Wayne Sneed and I (Roger Peterson) did was to submit its terminology to other people in order to obtain their insight and critique. One person was our short-term mission colleague and cross-cultural specialist Lisa Espineli Chinn, the current Director of International Student Ministries of InterVarsity Christian Fellowship–USA (IVCF), Madison, Wisconsin. Lisa was born and raised in Quezon City, Philippines (near Manila). After completing graduate studies at Wheaton College in Wheaton, Illinois, Lisa returned home and served as campus staff worker for IVCF–Philippines for seven years. As what this book calls a field facilitator, Lisa garnered extensive experience with Westerners working as career and short-term missionaries through IVCF–Philippines. Lisa then returned to the United States as a campus staff worker with IVCF–USA, specializing and was involved in training American students going on short-term missions. Lisa married an American (who is ethnically Chinese), and has become a gorgeous tapestry of Filipino, (some Chinese), and American—one of those wonderfully unusual bi-cultural people who seem to extract only the best God has to offer from Asian and Western cultures.

While working in her Asian culture which values humility and servant-hood (those are *deep* Biblical values, are they not?), Lisa received and hosted short-termers who had been trained to come alongside her local people, and who exemplified unusual servant attitudes. Their demeanor ran against the stereotype of the Western pride and 'take over' attitudes so common in most other types of short-term endeavors.

Perhaps that's why Lisa struggled with one of the earlier draft versions of the MISTM-Grid we asked her to critique. It used only the single word 'goer' and only the single word 'receiver' to title two of the participant groups. To Lisa, the single word 'receiver' showed a one-sided experience instead of a mutuality that should characterize any short-term mission. She consulted with some of her international colleagues (people who typically would be on the host receiving end of short-term missions). They, too, felt the simplistic use of 'goer' and 'receiver' created an 'us/them' mentality, and that such simplistic terms may serve only to reinforce an American assumption of American dominance, and an American assumption of field subordination.

Even though Wayne and I believed our single words 'goer' and 'receiver' had a solid Biblical footing, we both recognized God's wisdom coming to us through Lisa. If a short-termer from any culture sees herself as the power-house, who's going to help those poor needy people, that short-termer may crush much of what God wants to do during that outreach. But if the short-termer sees herself as a guest, she is more likely to be thankful, humble, servant hearted, non-assuming—pleasant and effective to work with.

A guest is sojourner (one who sojourns). Webster gives us just two brief definitions for sojourn: "a temporary stay," and "to stay as a temporary resident."[3] And just like the word 'goer,' the word 'guest' also has a well-established Biblical basis in its synonymic usage as 'sojourner.'

The Old Testament contains more than 20 passages[4] concerning the "stranger who sojourns…". Scripture's use of the words 'stranger' and 'sojourn' in each of these 20+ passages clearly implies a *guest*. So referring to the short-term mission participant who physically goes to work in the on-field site as a 'guest' is a theologically correct and accurate use of that term.

Finally, in small and large teams, goer-guests are usually referred to as 'team members' (which is perfectly fine). Yet for the purpose of this book, we'll stick with the term goer-guest simply because individually-sent short-termers don't fit into a typical 'team member' category.

Here are the two sub-categories of goer-guests in most short-term missions:
- Goer-Guest Leaders
- Goer-Guest Followers

GOER-GUEST LEADERS

Most size variables (cf. Chapter 3, variable #3) of short-term mission send one of more leaders with their goer-guests. Pairs may split leadership; a parent may lead in family short-terms. One or more leaders are often sent with small and large teams—especially church-based teams. If any of these size variables use an SE-2 agency, that agency may also send its leader(s). (Goer-guest leaders do *not* include the field facilitator leaders.)

Goer-guest leaders are any and all leaders supplied by any of the sending entities involved. They go on-field just like other goer-guests, but have certain leadership responsibilities with respect to the short-term mission. Goer-guest leaders are especially common in small and large team outreaches.

GOER-GUEST FOLLOWERS

The term 'goer-guest followers' is seldom used in this book, except when distinguishing between the goer-guest leaders and goer-guest followers. Note that many of the goer-guest leaders will many times need to submit to other leadership—either other goer-guest leaders, or host receiver leaders. That makes those 'leaders' followers just like other goer-guest followers.

HOST RECEIVER
Participants

HOST RECEIVERS include everyone who lives on-site in the short-term mission on-field location. It consists of missionaries, other expatriate people, local national leaders, local national people, intended receptors, and any of the organizations they represent (civic structures, local businesses, NGOs [non-governmental organizations], local churches, local schools, unreached people groups, etc.). We organize host receiver participants into two sub-categories. Each sub-category has its own additional subsets of host receivers as follows:

- Field Facilitators
  - Local/National People and Organizations
  - Same-Culture Expatriate People and Organizations
  - Other-Culture Expatriate People and Organizations

  the relationship is either:
  ❑ SE-related
  ❑ SE-contracted

- Intended Receptors
  - Human Beings (people groups, individuals)
  - Non-human Elements of God's Creation (vegetation, waters, etc.)
  - Structures and Systems of Man's Creation (civic structures, corporate structures, systems that create oppression and injustices)

It's imperative we differentiate the broader category of host receivers into its two primary sub-categories—the *field facilitators* and the *intended receptors.* Many short-term endeavors wind up on-field only to serve the field facilitators (i.e., the missionary or the national contact pastor or other leader) and not the intended receptors. Of course our field facilitators need to be served—but the primary reason they are already on-field is, in theory, to serve their intended receptors. Short-term mission practitioners must push to do the same, focusing their resources to leverage Kingdom outcomes first and foremost for the intended receptors.

FIELD FACILITATORS

Field facilitators are individuals and/or their organizations who serve as on-field liaison for all on-field short-term mission arrangements. They may be highly structured and organized, or loosely structured. They are responsible for all receiving-side management, administration, set-up, program support, logistical support, and field follow-up for a short-term outreach. Field facilitators mutually design every short-term outreach in conjunction with the sending entity. They may—or may not—be direct members of the intended receptor group.

Sending Entity Relationship
Field facilitators are either related in some ongoing function to the sending entity, or they are contracted on a per job basis.

SE-related facilitators may actually be sending entity on-field employees or regular on-field subcontractors. Or they may be related through third party relationships or through on-going partnership agreements. SE-related field facilitators and their related sending entity hold some degree of mutual accountability with each other, and often refer to each other as "*our* group back in [the States]," or as "*our* folks on the field."

SE-contracted facilitators do not necessarily have any repeat relationships. SE-contracted field facilitators are often 'hired' for a one-time job, when a sending entity enters a new country or region without any as-yet formalized on-field relationships.

Cultural Identity
Field facilitators have one of three primary cultural identities. Either they belong to, and are members of the local intended receptor's culture (as Chechnyans are in Chechnya, for example)—or they are expatriate people born into another culture and nation, but who have come to live and work in a different culture (as Lebanese businessmen are in Haiti, for example).

But as it impacts short-term mission, expatriate field facilitators are either expatriates from the same culture as the goer-guests (as American missionary field facilitators in Kenya would be to American short-termers in Kenya)—or they are expatriates from an entirely different culture (as German missionary field facilitators in Brazil would be to Korean short-termers in Brazil).

Some short-term outreaches are composed of goer-guests from a multitude of nations and cultures, as is the case in many YWAM (Youth With A Mission) or OM (Operation Mobilization) outreaches. And in the case of both these same sending entities which both have ocean ships used in their respective outreaches, the field facilitators they work with in every port of call are also from a variety of nations, and are obviously new facilitators every time the ships dock.

Whether related or contracted, and regardless of culture, field facilitators are crucial members of the participant trilogy. They're the on-site experts, without whom the sending entity and goer-guests would not be able to do effective mission.

INTENDED RECEPTORS

Most often the intended receptors are a 'targeted'[5] group of people—people with HIV/Aids, orphans, a specific unreached people group, street children, prostitutes, or any other commonality which tends to naturally assimilate its own kind together.

Missionaries (both long-termers and short-termers) and sending entities often have a 'burden' for, or a call to, a certain nation or a certain group of people. These people then become the intended receptors, the 'target' of the missionaries' and sending entity's intended activities.

Intended receptors can also be anything in the world which God has created. Lakes and rivers are polluted (a human violation of Scripture's command). Forests and other natural resources are often extracted and pillaged from developing nations at great expense to its indigenous people's own good. Intended receptors of a short-term mission's efforts can also be the sinful, oppressive, and unjust systems which man creates through corrupt governments and greedy corporate businesses. Wherever and however sin abounds throughout the world provides an opportunity for short-term missionaries to do something Godly about the problem.

Summary

WE BELIEVE the Bible views *senders, goer-guests,* and *host receivers* all in the same camp—that of being fellow workers who are intimately linked together for the harvest, each receiving from God the same reward for their efforts. *Senders, goers,* and *receivers* are all equal 'participants' in short-term mission. Short-term mission can't be done with just one or two of the participant groups. All three are mandatory in God's plan. They make up what we call the short-term mission 'participant trilogy.'

Endnotes
Chapter 6

1.   *(p. 153)* Cf. **Neal Pirolo**, *Serving as Senders* (Emmaus Road, International, 1991), 207 pp., paperback, ISBN 1-880185-00-8. Our fourth category of Sending Supporters (Emotional Supporters) is what Pirolo terms a 'moral' supporter in his book. However, we feel our term 'emotional' is a more accurate label for this particular type of support.

2.   *(p. 154)* Cf. Chapter 5 endnote #1.

3.   *(p. 159)* *Webster's New Ideal Dictionary* (Springfield MA: G. & C. Merriam Co., 1973), p. 504.

4.   *(p. 159)* Cf. in the KJV: Exodus 12:48, 12:49; Leviticus 16:29, 17:8, 17:10, 12:12, 18:26, 19:33, 20:2, 25:6, 25:45; Numbers 9:14, 15:14, 15:15, 15:16, 15:26, 15:29, 19:10; Joshua 20:9; Ezekiel 14:7; *et al.*

5.   *(p. 162)* The use of the word 'target' or 'targeted' is offensive to many host receivers. Such words are often associated with archery and guns, and therefore carry an overtone of sport, or of killing. However our use of these words is borrowed from western marketing concepts, with our intention being that of focus on someone or something specific—for the express purpose of the Gospel.

CHAPTER 7

THE RECIPROCITY OF GIVE 'N TAKE

the Two-way On-field Serendipity between Goer-Guests and Host Receivers of:

1 Giving/Sowing   2 Getting/Reaping

"THE GIFT OF FINDING VALUABLE OR AGREEABLE THINGS not sought for"[1] is how Webster describes the word serendipity. Serendipity occurs in many corridors throughout life—in shopping centers, at county fairs, the neighbor's back yard, and on airplanes. Serendipity occurs in grocery store check-out lines, waiting for the bus, at community pancake breakfasts, sitting outside watching a parade, in jail cells, during fishing tounaments. Serendipity even occurs—*always* occurs—on short-term mission outreaches.

People bump into other people during the normal routines of life. It happens when a person—who has his own agenda (which results in intended activities)—attempts to move forward in that agenda.

Let's take Rick,[2] for example. A handsome bachelor in his early 50s, Rick had long forgone the idea of getting married. When he switched jobs, his new company in Minneapolis arranged to send him to Paris for two weeks of intensive training. Rick hadn't seen Europe since he was a kid, and was thrilled that his tall, lanky, people-person HR Director was more than willing to have the company foot the bill all the way to France and back.

Rick took a taxi the morning of departure. His driver was a newly-arrived Somali immigrant named Hazem. During the ride to the airport, Rick discovered Hazem had briefly driven taxi in Paris before coming to Minnesota last month. On one of his taxi runs he'd actually transported three tourists from Minnesota to see the Eiffel Tower. The tourists were great people, Hazem said. They'd even bought him lunch on the way to the Tower. When Hazem told them they were different from other tourists, the Minnesotans replied that they were followers of Jesus, and that Jesus had given them a special love for Muslim people. Hazem remembered them clearly, because those three had treated him with genuine love and respect—and because the most gracious of the tourists was a tall, very tall man with a bald head and long curly sideburns who tipped him an extra 50 Euros. Hazem felt really drawn to that guy's authentic smile and warm personality. But, another fare was waiting to leave.

Now it was Rick's turn to talk. He took a chance. Did Hazem happen to get any of their names? And was the tall man with long curly sideburns by any chance named Sam ("Sam the Man") Nordquist?

Hazem nearly hit the car in front of him—yes that was his name, Sam the Man! Turns out that Sam the Man is also the tall, lanky Human Resource Director who just hired Rick.

Rick didn't know Sam was Christian. Hazem didn't know Rick knew Sam. Sam didn't know the taxi driver from Paris just moved to Minneapolis. Rick rang up Sam on his cell phone and asked if he remembered a taxi driver during his last France trip. "The Somalian driver? Yes I do. I had really wanted to stay in touch with that guy, but someone else jumped in his cab before I could get his address." Although Hazem didn't know Jesus and had no American friends in Minneapolis, Rick realized Hazem's life was about to change.

Rick's agenda had been getting to the airport—but he discovered another valuable gift: his taxi driver knew Rick's new boss, and together they both held the keys to the Somali man's deepest needs.

Hazem's agenda had been earning a fare—but he discovered another valuable gift: his passenger worked for the lanky tourist he'd been so drawn to in Paris, and his passenger was going to get all three of them together next month.

Sam's agenda had been to hire the best person for the job—but he discovered another valuable gift: his new employee just reconnected him with a Muslim man he'd like to have befriended, and with whom he'd like to have had the opportunity to answer questions about Christ.

Serendipity on Short-Term Mission Outreaches

We noted in Chapter 5 that for the sending entity and goer-guests, 'on-field' usually consists of a commingling of these six specific items:

1. Programmed Delivery of Goer-Guests' Intended Activities
2. Programmed On-field Team Meetings
3. Programmed Cultural Interaction
4. Non-programmed Cultural Interaction
5. Non-programmed Receiving [serendipity]
6. Leadership Influence

Two of these—'programmed cultural interaction' and 'non-programmed cultural interaction'—are occurrences that unfold themselves into the serendipitous 'non-programmed receiving' that is the topic of this chapter.

Goer-guests *always* experience some sort of serendipitous encounter with people, places, and things they 'bump' into on-field. As sending entity leaders prepare them to go, goer-guests and their sending supporters tend to discuss the upcoming outreach as a certain 'project' to a certain nation. "They'll be teaching at a school in Nairobi," or "We'll be pouring footings for a new feeding center in Honduras" are classic examples of how senders and goer-guests talk about the upcoming on-field outreach.

The goer-guests' agenda (their intended 'giving/sowing' activities—e.g., teaching at a school, or pouring the footings) usually winds up being accomplished to some degree or another. But just like Rick, Hazem, and Sam, on-field participants almost always discover the priceless gift of finding incredibly valuable, agreeable things in the other culture—things they never sought for.

In Chapter 5 we discussed the importance of a collaborative partnership in designing the short-term outreach. A common mistake many short-term practitioners sometimes make is to assume this mutual design consists merely of planning just the 'project' (the intended activity). But the mutual design must also take into account much more (cf. the 6-point list above). The mutu-

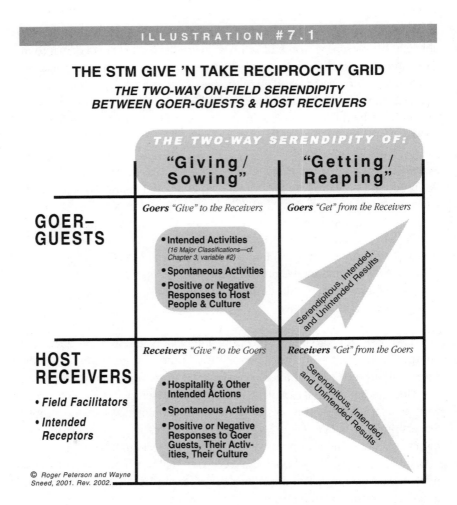

al design should plan for 'unplanned serendipity' (the non-programmed receiving mentioned in that list)—because serendipity is what always occurs whether you plan for it or not.

On-field 'Giving/Sowing' Action

Serendipity occurs on-field when goer-guests and host receivers both attempt to move forward in their own agenda. Each 'gives' and 'sows' into the lives of the other (assuming the outreach has been mutually designed). According to Luke 6:38, a return on that 'giving' investment into someone else's life becomes inevitable. The return comes back as "good measure, pressed down, shaken together, running over" (RSV) into the lap of the original giver. That good measure of return, which has been pressed down and shaken together so it holds even more to the point of running over, is the same valuable gift of finding something not sought for that Webster calls serendipity. ILLUSTRATION #7.1 depicts how serendipity often occurs in short-term mission outreaches.

Goer-Guests' 'Giving/Sowing' Action
Although a bit oversimplified, goer-guests' on-field 'giving/sowing' action can usually be reduced to three primary concepts:

1. *Intended Activities*
    These are routinely one or more of the 16 items we identified within short-term defining variable #2 of Chapter 3. The intended activity(s) for the goer-guests should have been mutually planned by collaboration between the sending entity and the field host. Pre-field training should have helped prepare goer-guests to effectively deliver this programmed activity while on-field. Whatever intended activities (whether right or wrong) are performed by goer-guests, are 'given' and 'sown' into the lives of host receiving people. There will be serendipity—a return on this investment back to goer-guests.

2. *Spontaneous Activities*
    Since it's unrealistic to think anyone can carefully plan every minute of every hour of every day goer-guests are on-field, it stands to reason that goer-guests will wind up doing a lot of unplanned things during the outreach. Some of those will be little things. Other things will be huge and quite significant. Some will be correct. Some of those things will be exceedingly incorrect. Whatever spontaneous activities (whether right or wrong) are done by goer-guests, are 'given' and 'sown' into the lives of host receiving people. Goer-guests will receive a return on this investment.

3. *Positive or Negative Responses to Host People and Culture*
    Even taking into account proper pre-field training, every person, place, and situation that differs from a goer-guest's definition of 'normal' will result in positive or negative reaction. Whatever positive or negative responses to the host culture (whether right or wrong) are

169

given by goer-guests, are 'given' and 'sown' into the lives of the host receiving people. There will be a return on this investment, too.

Host Receivers' 'Giving/Sowing' Action
In the broadest possible context, there are also three primary 'giving/sowing' actions performed by host receivers during a short-term outreach:

1. *Hospitality and Other Intended Actions*
   Because the incoming goers are guests, the service of hospitality is often the number-one function of field facilitators and intended receptors. Hospitality expectations and other intended actions on the part of host receivers should have been mutually designed during pre-field planning. Whatever amount of hospitality (or lack thereof which can happen in some restricted-access or other resistant fields), and whatever other intended actions are performed by host receivers, they are 'given' and 'sown' into the lives of their goer-guests. There will be a return for host receivers on their investment.

2. *Spontaneous Activities*
   Not every minute of the outreach can be planned. Therefore host receivers likewise wind up doing many unrehearsed, impromptu activities because it seems at the time the right thing to do. And some of those things will be right. And some wrong. Whatever spontaneous activities (whether good or bad) are done by host receivers, are 'given' and 'sown' into the lives of the goer-guests. There will be a return to host receivers on this investment.

3. *Positive or Negative Responses to Goer-Guests, Their Activities, Their Culture*
   Field facilitators and intended receptors will embrace many of the goer-guests and their activities and actions in a whole-hearted, welcoming manner. But the attitudes and actions of some goer-guests can smack of indifference, pride, and selfishness resulting in an understandable negative response from host receivers. Whatever positive or negative responses are given by host receivers to the goer-guests and their temporarily imported culture (whether such a response is justified or not), are 'given' and 'sown' into the lives of goer-guests. Yes, there will be a return on this investment as well.

On-field 'Giving/Sowing' Action Summary
Goer-guests and host receivers 'give' and 'sow' into the lives of each other through their planned intended program activities, through their unplanned spontaneous activities, and through their positive or negative responses to these activities and to each other's culture. Goer-guests and host receivers each receive a serendipitous return on their wise, positive 'giving' investments.

The Serendipitous Return on Investment
The Luke 6:38 "good measure" return accrues to goer-guests when they 'give' to host receivers. The same "good measure" return accrues to host receivers when they 'give' to goer-guests. Such is the reciprocity available within a short-term mission outreach that has been mutually designed by the sending entity and host receivers. It is a reciprocity originally composed by God, a reciprocity of give and take, a reciprocity of sowing and reaping. Galatians 6:7/RSV reminds us it is God who produces this return on investment: "...for whatever a man sows, that he will also reap."

Goer-Guests' Serendipitous Return
We've identified four "good measure" pleasant, agreeable (serendipitous) returns which routinely accrue to goer-guests in most short-term outreaches:

1. *Kingdom Growth*
    Kingdom growth in goer-guests almost always takes place within two distinctions:

    *   First, goer-guests often learn much more about the character and nature of God while on-field in a mission outreach setting. Their 'normal' routine approach to life gets upset (in a good way) while on-field. Goers are often stretched by temporarily living together in community. They also encounter more opportunity to pray and ask God for intervention, blessings, miracles—and many goer-guests report phenomenal results. In outreaches where there are already local believers, goer-guests are often humbled by local Christians' faith (especially in poverty situations). Living through the reality of these and other similar on-field encounters results in a greater understanding of Who God is, and exposure to new ways in which He may choose to work.

171

- Second, these same experiences often expand goer-guests' understanding that God really does love the *entire* world, and really does want to redeem *all* of creation everywhere (and not just their home culture). Their previous myopic vision for God's world has widened. Scales have fallen from their eyes. Goer-guests are becoming World Christians.[3]

2. *Worldview Expansion*

It seems that many Americans are prone to pride, self-sustenance, independence, selfishness, personal rights, and a host of other 'founding spirits' that 'made our country great' (supposedly). Most of our high school graduates speak just one language, and can't locate more than a half dozen other nations on a world map (how quickly can you locate Gabon or Tuvala or the capital city Dushanbe[4]—without the use of the world wide web or other index?). The same on-field experiences that created Kingdom growth now become the encounters that expand the general worldview of 'average' American Christians. No longer do goer-guests view other nations' political, economic, and social issues in terms of how they affects *us* in the United States—but in terms of how it affects *their* citizens. No longer do goer-guests boast only about Mt. Rainier or Niagara Falls—but they're quick to point out Mt. Kilimanjaro and Iguazú Falls as well.[5] Goer-guests who return back to their home country begin to see themselves as 'world citizens.' Ironically, this new self-perception benefits their home nation as well.

3. *Deeper Insight on Self (from God's perspective)*

In one of our earlier publications, Peterson (Peterson and McDonough[6]) wrote about the 'gift discovery' occurring within goer-guests as a result of the on-field portion of their short-term mission. God has gifted each of His children in a different way for building up the body of Christ. However, each person's gifts may not be immediately obvious even to the individual. One of the beneficial outcomes of a short-term mission is being exposed to ministry opportunities in a cross-cultural environment. Goer-guests take part in ministry outside of their daily routine. God then uses such situations to bring to the surface specific gifts and abilities of which these goer-guests were previously unaware. God also provides an awareness that there may very well be other as-yet identified ministry opportunities for which goer-guests now realize they may be gifted and in which they may greatly enjoy.

4.   *Broadened Basis of Friends*
The on-field process almost always consists of living, working, ministering, praying, sweating, crying, worshipping, and sharing together with goer-guest teammates, and with host receiving people. A tight bonding between the on-field participants—a 'soul-knitting' much like David and Jonathan experienced[7]—takes place rapidly. The people involved in a given short-term mission often wind up post-field as their own unique affinity group, even months and years after the on-field outreach. Each person has similar shared experiences, and for many they were lifetime mountaintop experiences. It's difficult to fully explain some of those feelings and experiences to 'outsiders,' but the 'insiders' know intuitively the warm and precious depth of meaning certain words, pictures, stories, or other people elicit when these friends get together.

On April 4, 1979, I (Roger Peterson) had a parallel bonding experience similar to what often happens during a short-term mission—one that very few 'outsiders' will ever *really* understand. I was aboard TWA flight #841 that barrel-rolled into an upside-down 45-second nosedive (cf. Addendum "E").[8] Even though we miraculously leveled out just four seconds away from crashing into the ground, we still had to prepare for an emergency landing. Since our airplane had been badly damaged during that accelerated decent, preparing for the 'emergency landing' actually meant preparing for a crash landing.

I have never seen *death* in another living person's face before. But in those final few moments of preparation for our 'emergency landing,' I saw death in the face and eyes of one of the flight attendants who—still on the clock (a paycheck I'm sure she thought she'd never collect)—went through her cabin duties, handing out blankets and pillows to each passenger to 'soften' the blow of the forthcoming impact. She was lifeless, emotionless as she mechanically performed the duties required in TWA's emergency manual she thought she'd never really have to use. We had to get rid of our shoes, pull pens and

173

sharp objects from our pockets (preparation to use the evacuation slides). We even had to get rid of neck ties. Then on final approach the closing instructions came to us something like this: "Clasp your hands behind your head, and put your head down, *now...*", and in the brief seconds it took me to comply, I 'saw' the events of my life, the hopes and dreams I still had, and the family I loved and didn't want to leave—it all swept through me in the blink of an eye. Inside my soul and spirit I bid good-bye to the light of my earthly life and pleaded simply with God not to have to fight my way through flaming jet fuel and its monstrous, hellish effects. In the awesome eternity of that brief moment, I felt the actual spiritual presence of God's arms wrapping themselves around me. His inaudible voice instantly placed a crystal clear understanding in the ears of my heart that simply said, "You will be alright." I knew then for certain (with resolute, absolute certainty) that I would either immediately be with God in heaven—or that I would walk away from the plane unharmed. God didn't reveal which one, but instead allowed me to taste the sweet victory, the savory "peace of God, which passes all understanding" (Philippians 4:7). Such peace cannot be manufactured when facing your own death. It comes *only* from God. It comes *only* from trusting Him totally.

Three years later, CBS Television got ahold of all the cockpit crew, all but one of the cabin crew, and 39 of the of the 82 passengers. They spent untold hours interviewing each one of us. After they scripted the entire event from the passengers' and crew members' first-hand accounts, and from other official accounts, they flew us all to Hollywood, California. A limousine driver met my incoming flight, and took me to the studios where all the airplane cutaway shots and luggage check-in shots were filmed. We each got our scripts and we each portrayed our actual selves as CBS filmed their one-hour documentary special, *The Plane That Fell From the Sky.*[9]

Most of those three days of filming were spent sitting around the studio waiting for our few minutes in front of the lights. That gave us ample time to personally talk with fellow passengers and our heroic flight crew. Although it had been nearly four years since our 35,000-foot drop out of the sky, each of us instantly bonded to one another. None of us *had* to explain how we felt during that nosedive and emergency landing in Detroit. For those of us who did explain, we had attentive ears, fully focused; and we understood each other completely, intuitively. We'd been there together. We had survived together. We were like lost friends finally getting back for a reunion—even though most of us hadn't spent any time whatsoever getting to know each other since that ominous April evening (which God turned into my *second* salvation).

Short-term mission readily facilitates this same type of deeply-connected bonding to other on-field participants. The primary serendipitous return for most goer-guests' investment into the lives of intended receptors, is a new cadre of lifelong, richly- and permanently-conjoined friends who intuitively, non-judgmentally understand what each other experienced.

Host Receivers' Serendipitous Return
Host receivers likewise have four very similar "good measure" returns:

1. *Kingdom Growth*
    In unchurched or unevangelized regions of the world, many intended receptors will come to faith in Jesus Christ as a result of the short-term mission outreach. Intended receptors and field facilitators also receive other forms of Christian growth through discipleship, teaching, and training efforts from some goer-guests. Although intended receptors may not necessarily be expecting Kingdom growth in their lives, that is often one of the eternal benefits they 'get' by way of 'giving' their hospitality and friendship to goer-guests.

2. *Worldview Expansion*
    Cross-cultural interaction between goer-guests and host receivers doesn't produce an expanded worldview for just the goer-guests, but for field facilitators and intended receptors as well. Any time various cultures commingle with each other—especially in the context of a mutually designed short-term mission plan—the contrasts, uniquenesses, and methods used to achieve the plan all work together to expand all participants' worldviews. The on-field outreach often serves to help intended receptors realize that not all

people from the goer-guests' culture smoke, drink, and curse like their counterparts seen on television.

3. *Gifts of Material Blessing*
    Gifts of financial support, food, clothing, building supplies, Bibles, toilet tissue, and a plethora of other items the West often takes for granted, are often the surprise blessing host receivers 'get' from goer-guests they have befriended. Of course an unhealthy dependency can take place here. But through the commitment of ongoing partnership, prayer, and accountability, host receivers can be recipients of these serendipitous blessings.

4. *Broadened Basis of Friends*
    Host receivers can form many genuine friendships with goer-guests they host over the years. The often intense setting of an on-field outreach provides a quick ramp-up to deep, abiding friendships as people work, process, pray, and play together.

Summary

A CLASSIC MISTAKE many short-term endeavors make is to think the goer-guests are the only participants providing a program, that they are the only participants planning to do something for someone else. Whether planned or not, the reality of short-term mission is that host receiver participants likewise have something to give in return to goer-guests. For many goer-guests, this comes as a pleasant, serendipitous surprise. For many host receivers, what they receive from the incoming goer-guest participants also comes as a pleasant surprise. A healthy short-term mission always consists of a reciprocity of give and take—a two-way serendipity on the field between the goer-guests and the host receivers—of giving/sowing, and of getting/reaping.

Endnotes
Chapter 7

1.   *(p. 165)* *Webster's New Ideal Dictionary* (Springfield MA: G. & C. Merriam Co., 1973), p. 481.

2.   *(p. 166)* The story is completely fictitious, created only to anecdotally explain how routinely serendipity takes place.

3.   *(p. 172)* The term 'World Christians' has been often used by the mission community during the past twenty-plus years, thanks in part to **David Bryant**, *In The Gap* (Downers Grove IL: InterVarsity Press, 1979), p. 73. Bryant writes,
> "World Christians are day-to-day disciples for whom Christ's global cause has become the integrating, overriding priority for all that He is for them. Like disciples should, they actively investigate all that their Master's Great Commission means. Then they act on what they learn. World Christians are Christians whose life directions have been solidly transformed by a world vision."

A decade later **Paul Borthwick**, *A Mind For Missions* (Colorado Springs CO: Navpress, 1989), p. 15, penned,
> "A world Christian breaks the mold of a self-centered way of thinking. A world Christian understands that Jesus calls us to deny ourselves (Luke 9:23) so that we might respond to a world of greater need beyond ourselves."

At the annual EFMA (Evangelical Fellowship of Mission Agencies) Executive Retreat in September 1998 in Atlanta, USCWM (U.S. Center for World Mission) founder RALPH WINTER suggested to Co-author Peterson during a breakfast conversation that the term should now be modified to read 'Daily World Christians,' in order to more accurately convey the full meaning of the original term as used within the context of our present-day society; (for EFMA information go to: http://www.EFMAmissions.org and for USCWM information go to: http://www.USCWM.org).

4.   *(p. 172)* Cf. http://www.google.com as one source for obtaining more information.

5.   *(p. 172)* *Ibid.*

6.   *(p. 172)* **Daniel P. McDonough and Roger P. Peterson**, *Can Short-Term Mission Really Create Long-Term Missionaries?* (Minneapolis MN: STEM Ministries, 1999), p. 28.

7.   *(p. 173)* Cf. I Samuel 18:1 in the KJV and the RSV.

8.   *(p. 173)* Facts pertaining to this true story were extracted from a variety of published sources too numerous to list (dozens of newspaper articles; magazine articles; information posted to the world wide web; television reports; National Transportation Safety Board reports). Many of these sources contain conflicting information. However, every effort has been taken to tell this story as accurately as possible from the author's (Peterson's) perspective, including his own personal recollection and his own personal review of these available publications.

9.   *(p. 174)* CBS Television's one-hour documentary *The Plane That Fell From the Sky* was produced by Paul and Holly Fine, and aired on CBS network stations July 14, 1983.

SHORT-TERM *MISSION* VS. CROSS-CULTURAL *TRIPS*

Intended Receptor Focus? or Self Focus?

JUST BECAUSE SOMETHING IS CALLED 'SHORT-TERM *mission*' does not justify every endeavor using that phrase. If the *primary* purpose of a short-term is for goer-guest leaders to disciple their goer-guest followers, or if the *primary* purpose is to provide an educational cross-cultural experience (important as both these agenda are), then the outreach should *not* be called a 'short-term *mission.*' Why? Re-read Chapter 2, (Defining 'Mission').

What you're doing is a cross-cultural *trip*. And nothing is wrong with a cross cultural trip—just don't call it a mission. And if you're a parachurch mission sending entity (an SE-2), don't give out *mission*-based tax receipts to financial supporters—unless you're doing a mission, a genuine, bona fide mission.

SE-1 Churches & Goer-Guest Leaders

When something else becomes priority and takes precedence (like discipling your goer-guests), your goer-guest leaders run a high risk of using the local culture to meet first their own agenda, and using the field facilitators to meet first their own needs, and using what should have been the intended receptors to meet first their own desires.

This is nothing more than pillaging the locals. Only cultural imperialists do that sort of thing.

To jump in and get satisfied the way you want, all at someone else's expense, is called abuse. It's called violating someone else's rights, it's called molesting other people's emotions, it's called betraying the host receivers with your promise of 'mission' when all you wanted to do was use the host nation and use the already-overworked field facilitators to create a mountaintop spiritual high for your short-termers.

No, nothing's wrong with creating a spiritual high—just don't be an imperialist to get it.

If you're certain God has called you to take your youth group overseas for an intense last-chance discipleship outing before they graduate from high school, then have the integrity to tell your field facilitators that you want to set up a 'cross-cultural discipleship trip'—don't pretend it's a mission. Don't even call it a mission.

SE-3.a(2) Schools

If you're a professional educator who's seen the undeniable educational growth that accrues to students who go overseas, you also run a high risk of plundering the local people as a cultural imperialist. There's no question a student's personal knowledge, skills, and worldview attitudes improve as much in a month overseas as it does in a semester in your classroom back home. So if your only priority is your students' education, be honest about that with your field facilitators. Then by all means go ahead and set up a 'cross-cultural education trip'—just don't call it a mission, even if you're the Academic Dean of a Christian college.

Field Facilitators

It's great that you're a field facilitator who loves to work with short-termers. Just make sure you're setting up actual 'mission' with their sending entity. For example, what activities do you plan to have goer-guests work on?—repairing the local church roof?, or painting *your* house? Or what supplies will you have goer-guests transport to the field?—sewing machines to help intended receptors create needed jobs, or M&Ms and Fruit Loops for *your* family?

Of course many goer-guests would be thrilled to use their on-field time to help you with needed repairs, or to provide your family with special treats. Just make sure your personal needs don't continually trump the needs of the intended receptors.

There are times when it will be a priority for you to set up a cross-cultural, come-and-help-me 'trip.' Just don't call it a mission unless you can definitively leverage your goer-guests efforts to the benefit of the intended receptors. This is an ethical issue that tampers with conflict of interest. So be honest with yourself, and do your best to leverage everything you can to the benefit of the intended receptors you came to serve.

Chapter Conclusion

A T THIS point it may well be worth your while to re-read our 'Mission Philosophy' section (cf. Chapter 3, variable #7). If your bottom-line definition of 'mission' is something other than what we implied in Chapter 2, that's O.K.—just make sure all other participant trilogy members are singing from the same piece of 'mission' music you are.

We still contend that anything called 'Christian mission' must involve all its participants in the manner that best serves God's desires for the intended receptors. This means the sending supporters, the sending entity, the goer-guest followers and leaders, and the field facilitators all do their role which focuses principally on benefits to the intended receptors.

When we provide genuine mission first and foremost and do so with humble servant hearts, when we rally all our mutual efforts and energies toward the intended receptors we're professing to serve, then we're really seeking first the Kingdom of God (cf. Matthew 6:33). When we do genuine mission first, then all these other things will be added unto us and will accrue to our blessing. Goer-guests *will* get discipled. Students *will* gain knowledge and expanded worldview. Field facilitators *will* get personal needs met. All on-field participants *will* encounter an incredible cross-cultural, life-changing experience.

It's simply a case of not putting the cart before the ox.

CHAPTER **9**

THE MISTM-GRID

Maximum Impact Short-Term Mission

SOLOMON SAID IT BEST. THERE IS NOTHING NEW UNDER the sun. This is also true of the MISTM-Grid. Although it's a creation of my (Wayne Sneed) own doing, it comes from ideas and concepts which are becoming more and more well known throughout the short-term mission movement. However, taking some of these best ideas and fitting them into one tool, a grid, might be something that's just now becoming familiar to you.

The initial prototype of this tool came to me during a leadership meeting with the Fellowship of Short-Term Mission Leaders (FSTML).[1] As we were discussing the annual FSTML Fall Conference, several people were throwing around short-term mission terms, philosophies, and anachronism like they were simple things even a child knew and understood. I'm no great philosopher, so I started writing them all down, hoping not to look foolish in front

ILLUSTRATION #9.1

The MISTM-Grid
MAXIMUM IMPACT SHORT-TERM MISSION

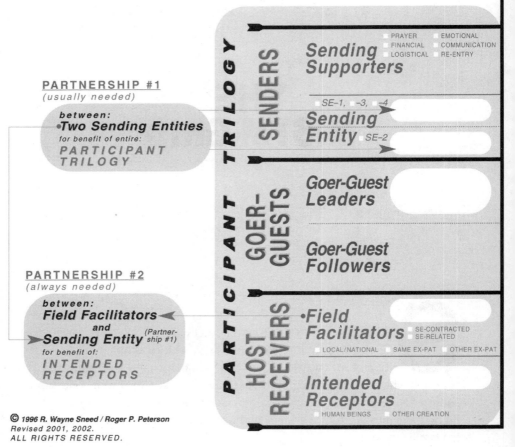

PARTNERSHIP #1
(usually needed)

between:
•Two Sending Entities
for benefit of entire:
PARTICIPANT TRILOGY

PARTNERSHIP #2
(always needed)

between:
Field Facilitators
and
Sending Entity *(Partnership #1)*
for benefit of:
INTENDED RECEPTORS

For limited reproduction permission, please consult Endnote #4 at the end of this Chapter.

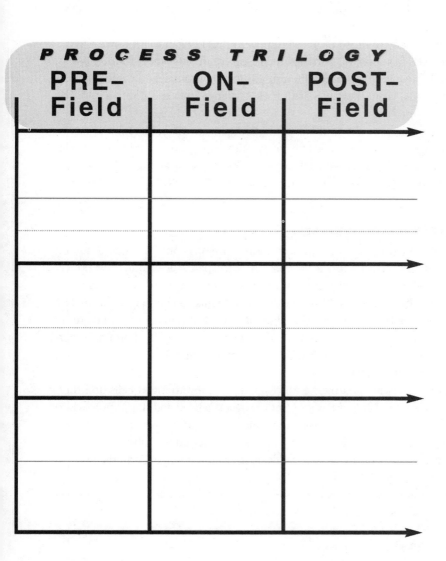

PROCESS TRILOGY

PRE–Field	ON–Field	POST–Field

For limited reproduction permission, please consult Endnote #4 at the end of this Chapter.

of my friends. Later, in the privacy of my own office, I'd research and discover what they all meant.

Since many of those terms were new to me, I began to jot down the different classifications of participants involved in any short-term mission. Before I knew it, I had three different participant groups, and three different time periods. From there, it wasn't rocket science to fit these into a grid that made sense to me.

Since that time the grid has been worked, reworked, tested, and retested nearly a dozen times. The specific wording now contained in the MISTM-Grid has been prayed over, talked over, consulted, argued, and pondered until we have come to what you now see in ILLUSTRATION #9.1.

MISTM-GRID OVERVIEW

The MISTM-Grid (Maximum Impact Short-Term Mission) has been designed as a tool to help all short-term mission participants flesh out their ethical responsibility to other participants involved in a given short-term mission. As potentially helpful as the MISTM-Grid can be to mission participants from any culture, it's important to acknowledge that the Grid is just a tool—a culturally-bound tool, designed from a Western, linear-thinking sending entity perspective. It presents a generalized overview which will not fit every short-term mission situation 100%.

Boundaries implied by the MISTM-Grid's neatly-arranged cells and their plumbed, squared lines are not meant to suggest a fixed and static approach to mission. Mission must be a living, dynamic, Holy Spirit-infused process where all participants—especially the sending entity, goer-guests, and field facilitators—maintain a posture of humble flexibility and tolerance for ambiguity.

The following two sections have been covered in more detail in previous chapters, but are summarized here for quick review.

Process Trilogy (cf. Chapter 5)

A given short-term mission consists of much more than its on-field outreach. It exists as an identifiable 'group' or 'mission' from the moment of its inception, to well beyond its time spent on-field. From a western perspective, the left-to-right linear time process of a short-term mission can be viewed as follows:

Pre-Field ⟶ On-Field ⟶ Post-Field ⟶

Certainly there is some overlap between these three phases. But the three distinctions of short-term mission 'process' help us understand (especially when placed in context of the X-axis of the MISTM-Grid) that all participants have certain ethical responsibilities to all other participants during all three phases of a short-term mission.

Participant Trilogy (cf. Chapter 6)

Based on such Scriptures as III John 5–8 and Matthew 10:40–42, the Y-axis design of the MISTM-Grid helps us realize that participants of a short-term mission are not merely those who go. Strong evidence in the Bible suggests that those who send, as well as those who receive, are equal participants with those who go. Therefore the three primary sets of short-term mission participants are:

- Senders
- Goer-Guests
- Host Receivers

These three mega-sets of short-term mission participants make up the participant trilogy. Yet to fully understand ethical responsibility within a short-term mission, each of these three mega-sets must be delineated into their second level of identification. There are two delineations each for all three mega-sets of participant trilogy members:

- Senders = {
  Sending Supporters *(6 categories)*

  Sending Entity *(4 categories)*
}

- Goer-Guests = {
  Goer-Guest Leaders

  Goer-Guest Followers
}

- Host Receivers = {
  Field Facilitators *(2 delineated subsets)*

  Intended Receptors *(3 categories)*
}

Following are abbreviated definitions for some of the participant trilogy members (cf. Chapter 6 for complete definitions):

Sending Supporters (SS)
Adapted from Neal Pirolo's *Serving as Senders*,[2] sending supporters are individuals (primarily) who help support goer-guests by way of:

1. Prayer Support
2. Financial Support
3. Logistical Support
4. Emotional Support
5. Communication Support
6. Re-entry Support

Sending Entity (SE)
Sending entities are institutional organizations (usually) which provide the pre-field and post-field administrative structure for goer-guests. Sending entities have the management and communication responsibility for everything and everyone on the 'sending-side' of a short-term mission. Sending entities mutually design every short-term outreach in conjunction with the field facilitators. Sending entities are grouped into four major categories:

- SE-1 Churches
- SE-2 Parachurch Mission Agencies
- SE-3 Institutional Non-mission Organizations
- SE-4 One's Self

Field Facilitators (FF)
Field facilitators are field missionaries or national host leaders who serve as on-field liaisons for the on-field short-term mission arrangements. Field facilitators have management and communication responsibility for everything and everyone on the 'receiving-side' of a short-term mission (field administration, field set-up, field program support, field logistical support, and field follow-up). Field facilitators mutually design every short-term outreach in conjunction with the sending entity. Field facilitators are delineated first by their relationship to the sending entity, and second by their own personal culture of origin (nationality):

- *Relationship to Sending Entity*
  Field facilitators may be SE-contracted (one-time arrangements or for-hire situations); or SE-related (direct on-going relationships). 'Related' facilitators are normally employed by, or formally related to, the SE or the SE's other affiliated relationships.

- *Cultural Identity (Nationality)*
  Field Facilitators are grouped into one of these three sub-classifications: local/national people or organizations (same as intended

receptors' culture, different from goer-guests' culture); same-culture expatriate people or organizations (same as goer-guests' culture, different from intended receptors' culture); and other-culture expatriate people or organizations (different from goer-guests' culture, different from intended receptors' culture).

Intended Receptors (IR)

Intended receptors are the 'targeted' (a western marketing term[3]) intended receivers of the goer-guests' mission activity. With respect to all 777 million variations of short-term mission, we identify potential intended receptors within three subsets: human beings (people group or other human identity); aspects of God's creation (water, vegetation, the earth's minerals and other resources, animals, etc.); and aspects of human creation (corrupt civic or corporate structures, oppressive systems, etc.).

MISTM-Grid Usage

Even a cursory glance at the MISTM-Grid suggests certain ethical responsibility that short-term mission practitioners have perhaps not yet considered. The Grid also leaves itself open to a foray of ethically-based questions which may receive a variety of situation-dependent answers. That's because there are a vast number of short-term mission variations (777 million—cf. TABLE #3.1 in Chapter 3). Although answers may differ from one group to another, it's the ethical base of responsibility the Grid helps practitioners flush out.

We recognize that Grid terminology can be cumbersome at times. That's because we've attempted to include all 777 million short-term mission variations in its design. But when *you* use the Grid, go ahead and amend its terminology to fit your situation. For example, since the vast majority of short-term outreaches are team-based, most groups call their 'goer-guest leaders' *team leaders* (as a matter of fact, *team leader* is the term all three authors and our editor use within our respective groups).

Other groups may even need to expand their participant classifications on their Grid, especially on the host receiving side. For example, many of the fields where Adventures In Missions (AIM) teams work have well developed field structures. Within some of those field structures, AIM's President Seth Barnes points out that their field facilitators have their own cadre of supporters—field supporters which function on the receiving side in ways very similar to how the sending supporters function on the sending side.

Our response to these situations? Great!—go ahead and re-create your own version of the MISTM-Grid using your in-house terminology. Add more subsets of horizontal rows for your specific participant members. Make the tool actually work for *you*. Just make sure you retain the three primary rows of mega-participants (senders, goer-guests, and host receivers), and keep the pre-field, on-field, and post-field columns where they belong.[4]

In its current published format, we've created white oval 'fill-in-the-blank' spaces adjacent to certain participant trilogy members. That's so you can fill in actual names of actual people, which then helps you transfer from MISTM-Grid theory into user-friendly reality. (If you need extra copies of the MISTM-Grid the way we've designed it, or if you choose to create your own personalized Grid, kindly read and comply with Endnote #4 at the end of this chapter.)

MISTM-Grid Implications for the Short-Term Mission Practitioner

Many of the check-marked implications below are addressed in other chapters within this book:

✔ The Grid suggests that a sending entity does not merely have an ethical responsibility to follow-up with just those goer-guests it sends—but to somehow follow-up with field facilitators, intended receptors, and sending supporters as well.

✔ The Grid suggests that pre-field training for an upcoming outreach is not merely for goer-guests, but for sending supporters and field facilitators as well.

✔ The Grid suggests that every short-term mission will be different from another short-term mission, and that ethical responsibilities cannot be cookie cut from one to another.

✔ The Grid further implies that the goer-guest leaders are not the only leaders within the given short-term outreach. There will be other different leaders represented within the field facilitators, the intended receptors, and the sending entity. Therefore the Grid suggests that knowing who is in charge of whom at any given time is crucial to the short-term mission outreach's success.

MISTM-Grid Ethical Questions to Consider

Once you get a feel for the MISTM-Grid and import your own terminology into your own version, you'll find it worth your while to periodically sit down with the tool, and prayerfully let the Holy Spirit flush out ethical questions unique to your given short-term mission situation.

In the meantime, here are some questions you can begin processing through the cells of the MISTM-Grid:

Sending Supporters' Questions
1. What are my duties pre-field, on-field, and post-field?
2. If I need to report any problems or if my duties are not clear or if I need more information to better perform my duties, who is my primary sending entity contact person?
3. Who is responsible to let me know whether my support (prayer, financial, logistical, emotional, communication, re-entry) accomplished what I was led to believe it should accomplish?
4. What is my responsibility to other sending supporters?
5. What is my responsibility to the sending entity?
6. What is my responsibility to other goer-guests (other than the goer-guests I have already committed to support)?
7. What is my responsibility to the field facilitators?
8. What is my responsibility to the intended receptors?
9. What other ethical questions do the cells of the MISTM-Grid suggest?

Sending Entities' Questions
1. Are we the only sending entity involved?—or are we in partnership with another sending entity?
2. If we're in partnership with another sending entity, what our are responsibilities and their responsibilities with respect to:
   • The sending supporters? (pre-field?, on-field?, post-field?)
   • Each other as sending entities? (pre-field?, on-field?, post-field?)
   • Our goer-guest leaders and their goer-guest leaders? (pre-field?, on-field?, post-field?)
   • The goer-guests? (pre-field?, on-field?, post-field?)
   • The field facilitators? (pre-field?, on-field?, post-field?)
   • The intended receptors? (pre-field?, on-field?, post-field?)
3. Are we operating within a healthy, mutually-accountable partnership with the field (i.e., field facilitators)?
4. Has the given short-term mission outreach truly been mutually developed by ourselves and the host receivers?

5. Do we really understand the process trilogy? (cf. Chapter 5)
6. Do we really understand who all the participant trilogy members are? (cf. Chapter 6)
7. Do we really understand, and are we able to clearly articulate, our own philosophy of mission? (cf. Chapter 3, variable #7)
8. Is our philosophy of mission in relative alignment with our goer-guests? the field facilitators? all the leaders (pre-field, on-field, post-field)?
9. What other ethical questions do the cells of the MISTM-Grid suggest?

Goer-Guest Leaders' Questions

1. In which cells of the MISTM-Grid am I a leader? *the* leader?
2. In which cells of the MISTM-Grid am I a follower?
3. Who are the other leaders? in what cells am I on a 'peer' basis with other leaders? on a subordinated basis with other leaders?
4. Is my personal philosophy of mission in relative alignment with my sending entity? the field facilitators? all the leaders (pre-field, on-field, post-field)?
5. I understand this short-term mission has been mutually designed by both the sending entity and field facilitators. Am I willing to follow the 'game plan' they've laid out?
6. What will I do if I sense, during the actual outreach, that the Holy Spirit wants to amend the 'game plan' they've laid out?
7. What lasting post-field implications will my on-field leadership decisions make upon:
   - My sending supporters?
   - Other goer-guests' sending supporters?
   - My sending entity?
   - The other leaders?
   - The goer-guests?
   - The field facilitators?
   - The intended receptors?
8. What other ethical questions do the cells of the MISTM-Grid suggest?

Goer-Guest Followers' (i.e., Team Members') Questions

1. What is the real purpose of my upcoming short-term mission outreach?
2. Is my sending entity training me for that purpose?
3. What are my responsibilities with respect to:
   - My sending supporters? (pre-field?, on-field?, post-field?)

- Other goer-guests' sending supporters? (pre-field?, on-field?, post-field?)
- My sending entity? (pre-field?, on-field?, post-field?)
- My home church (if different from my sending entity)? (pre-field?, on-field?, post-field?)
- The sending entity agency my [church or school] is partnering with? (pre-field?, on-field?, post-field?)
- My leaders? (pre-field?, on-field?, post-field?)
- Other goer-guests? (pre-field?, on-field?, post-field?)
- The field facilitators? (pre-field?, on-field?, post-field?)
- The intended receptors? (pre-field?, on-field?, post-field?)

4. Is my church prepared to follow-up with me when I return home? (cf. the 'Post-Field' section of Chapter 5, especially pages 144–145)
5. What other ethical questions do the cells of the MISTM-Grid suggest?

Field Facilitators' Questions

1. Are we the only field facilitators involved in this upcoming short-term mission outreach?—or are we in partnership with another field facilitator?
2. If we're in partnership with another field facilitator, what our are responsibilities and their responsibilities with respect to:
   - The sending supporters? (pre-field?, on-field?, post-field?)
   - The sending entity? (pre-field?, on-field?, post-field?)
   - The incoming goer-guest leaders and our field-supplied leaders? (pre-field?, on-field?, post-field?)
   - The goer-guests? (pre-field?, on-field?, post-field?)
   - Each other as field facilitators? (pre-field?, on-field?, post-field?)
   - The intended receptors? (pre-field?, on-field?, post-field?)
3. Are we operating within a healthy, mutually-accountable partnership with the sending entity?
4. Has the given short-term mission outreach truly been mutually developed by ourselves and the sending entity?
5. Do we really understand the process trilogy? (cf. Chapter 5)
6. Do we really understand who all the participant trilogy members are? (cf. Chapter 6)
7. Do we really understand, and are we able to clearly articulate, our own philosophy of mission? (cf. Chapter 3, variable #7)
8. Is our philosophy of mission in relative alignment with the incoming

goer-guests? their sending entity? all the leaders (pre-field, on-field, post-field)?

9. Are we truly adequately trained as potentially excellent field facilitators? (cf. Chapter 3, variable #8)

10. What other ethical questions do the cells of the MISTM-Grid suggest?

Intended Receptors' Questions

1. Do the field facilitators really understand how they should be helping us? (pre-field?, on-field?, post-field?)

2. Does the sending entity really understand how they should be helping us? (pre-field?, on-field?, post-field?)

3. Is the partnership between the field facilitators and the sending entity really working? is our community better off because of their partnership?

4. Do we understand what is expected of our people during this short-term mission? (pre-field?, on-field?, post-field?)

5. What responsibilities might we have to other members of the participant trilogy? (pre-field?, on-field?, post-field?)

6. Will our community follow-up with the goer-guests after they return home?

7. Will we follow-up privately? or will we let the field facilitators know what we've asked of the goer-guests? will we let the sending entity know what we've asked of the goer-guests?

8. What other ethical questions do the cells of the MISTM-Grid suggest?

Summary

PLACING the Participant Trilogy on a Y-axis and the Process Trilogy on an X-axis gives us a matrix or grid of cells—cells which clearly relate to one another and which strongly suggest certain ethical responsibility all participants may have with other participants throughout the entire process of a short-term mission. The resulting MISTM-Grid can be readily used by any short-term mission participant to help flush out questions of responsibility, the well-thought-through and prayed-through answers of which can strongly improve the odds of creating maximum impact within that mission outreach.

Endnotes
Chapter 9

1. *(p. 183)* The Annual Fall Conference of the Fellowship of Short-Term Mission Leaders occurs every October for five days. The mission of FSTML is to seek ways to "bring God's glory to the nations by promoting increasingly effective short-term mission." For more information on the Annual FSTML Conference, go to www.FSTML.org.

2. *(p. 188)* Cf. Endnote #1 of Chapter 6.

3. *(p. 189)* Cf. Endnote #5 of Chapter 6.

4. *(p. 190)* **LIMITED INTERNAL-USE-ONLY COPYING PERMISSION GRANTED FOR THE MISTM-GRID**
    Permission is hereby granted to any owner of this book (whether the owner is an individual or an organization) to photocopy or reproduce by any other internal means, *limited to in-house use only*, and to subsequently reproduce and use in-house as many copies of the MISTM-Grid as needed over the course of the book owner's lifetime. Actual cost of making photocopies or reproductions may be passed on to, and collected from, the in-house recipients using the reproduced MISTM-Grid. But mark-up for any overhead or for any other reason whatsoever is strictly prohibited without obtaining express written permission from the publisher (STEM*Press*). All reproductions must further contain the original copyright mark (©) and related copyright information.

    LIMITED INTERNAL MODIFICATION AND SUBSEQUENT INTERNAL-USE-ONLY PERMISSION GRANTED FOR THE MISTM-GRID
    Permission is hereby granted to any owner of this book (whether the owner is an individual or an organization) to reasonably modify, or reasonably add to, the second column of PARTICIPANT TRILOGY names (but no permission is granted whatsoever to modify the first column of PARTICIPANT TRILOGY names of 'Senders,' 'Goer-Guests,' and 'Host Receivers,' nor to modify the PROCESS TRILOGY names of 'Pre-Field,' 'On-Field,' and 'Post-Field'), for the express purpose of creating a special in-house version of the MISTM-Grid that is unique to a given organization's needs. This release is *limited to in-house use only*. Actual cost of making subsequent photocopies or reproductions may be passed on to, and collected from, the in-house recipients using the modified MISTM-Grid. But mark-up for any modification or development costs, or for any overhead, or for any other reason whatsoever, is strictly prohibited without obtaining express written permission from the publisher (STEM*Press*). All such modifications and their subsequent reproductions must further contain the original copyright mark (©) and related copyright information, along with the statement "Permission Granted for MISTM-Grid Modification to _____ (name of your organization), pursuant to Chapter 9, Endnote #4, of the 'Maximum Impact Short-Term Mission' book published by STEM*Press*, © 2003, which book we legally own."

A BIBLICAL AND THEOLOGICAL BASIS

AVAILABLE DATA SOLIDLY CONFIRM THE NUMBER OF short-termer goer-guests are rapidly increasing (cf. Chapter 11). Therefore, the church, parachurch, and its missiologists of all Christian persuasions must honestly assess, "Is this growth of God . . . or is it of man?". Those involved in the present-day mission enterprise need not fear such a question, for if the short-term mission "undertaking is of men, it will fail; but if it is of God, [it] will not be able to [be stopped. Those opposing the plan] might even be found opposing God!" (Acts 5:38–39/RSV).

If short-term mission and its phenomenal growth is of God, then God's Holy Word will clearly show repetitive use of short-term mission throughout the Old and New Testaments. The Biblical use of short-term mission won't merely be an extrapolated footnote squeezed out from just a place or two.

If short-term mission does have a solid Biblical basis, then cognitive logic fabricated for or against the use of short-term mission is rendered mute. Instead, missiologists are now confronted with an even tougher job of re-thinking human resource deployment strategies for some of the lofty goals yet to be completed. The old paradigm that "such things cannot be accomplished by [short-termers],"[1] cited by an career missionary working in Nigeria, may need to be reconsidered.

Is short-term mission a Biblical strategy of missiological significance in both the Old and New Testament? If you've already read Chapter 1 (God's Fools), you know our answer. In that chapter we argued—and Biblically defend—God's preferred choice over and over again to send average, common, lay non-professionals into the world with His Good News. (If you haven't yet read Chapter 1 and you're looking for the Biblical and theological basis for short-term mission, you'll need to go back and start there before studying Chapter 10.)

Jesus got it. He opened up His public ministry in Matthew 5 by telling not just the 12 disciples, but by telling a great crowd of 'average' people they were *already* the salt of the earth and *already* the light of the world. (Most of those folks must have been fairly common, average people, because most of them didn't show up in Scripture ever again.)

The Apostle Paul caught hold of God's 'average-man' strategy: "God chose what is foolish in the world ... God chose what is weak in the world ... God chose what is low and despised in the world ..." (I Corinthians 1:27).

Even bull-headed Peter figured out this one. He fused Exodus 19:6 into a letter he wrote to Jewish exiles (I Peter 2:9): "But you are a royal priesthood, a holy nation, God's own people, that you may declare the wonderful deeds of Him who called you out of darkness into His marvelous light."

This doctrine we now call 'priesthood of all believers' is a dangerous one. If we're to accept it (and all Protestant traditions do), then there's no other conclusion we can come to other than God wants all His redeemed people sent forth as 'priests'—ministers of *His* Holy Name, *His* Holy Kingdom, *His* Holy Righteousness, *His* Holy Justice, *His* Holy Son. No worldwide strategy exists today to comply with this doctrine—except the menacing, chancy tactic we call short-term mission.

Theologically, when we work from that well-grounded foundational knowledge (i.e., God always calls *average* people, and *every* believer is a priest to God), the proof-texting passages we're about to present in this chapter then cement themselves firmly on top. The resulting structure becomes stable and very dependable for use.

As we conclude this chapter, we'll do so by suggesting Scripture holds at least five other theological bases of use and purpose for short-term mission. As He has always done, God is still accomplishing much more than just 'mission' alone during a short-term *mission*.

Examples of Biblical Short-Term Mission

A SHORT period of cross-cultural on-field ministry time (i.e., a 'temporary' engagement) is the obvious angle to pursue when citing Biblical proof-texts to make the case for short-term mission. Temporary suggests a guest. Temporary suggests a sojourner. Temporary suggests not a one-way ticket, but a round-trip ticket. Temporary suggests you won't build a new house wherever it is you're going. Temporary means you're headed back somewhere else (your home) when your assignment is done.

In the following examples take note especially of the temporary sojourn, as well as other elements from our definition (cf. Chapter 4) and defining variables (cf. Chapter 3). Remember—these proof-texts sit on top of the deeper theological foundation we laid in Chapter 1.

OLD TESTAMENT EXAMPLES

We've chosen nine Old Testament examples where God used a temporary short-term endeavor to accomplish His mission.

✔ *Three Men—The LORD and Two Angels* *
Genesis 18:1–19:29
LENGTH OF MISSION: *16–20 hours*
Three heavenly visitors appeared to Abraham "in the heat of the day" (Genesis 18:1/RSV), about two o'clock one afternoon. Following a hearty meal, one of the men, the LORD, promised a son to Abraham and Sarah next year. Shortly thereafter He revealed to Abraham what He was about to do to Sodom and Gomorrah, while the other two men left for the first of those cities.

The two angels (Genesis 19:1) arrived at Sodom where Lot brought them to the protection of his house. After another big meal, but before retir-

---

* Passages in this chapter marked with an asterisk were first brought to our attention (Peterson and Sneed) during the October 2000 Annual Conference of the Fellowship of Short-Term Mission Leaders, as the direct result of programmed small group discussions during that conference.

ing to bed, all the men of the city showed up, clamoring to have sex with Lot's guests. As the men of Sodom pressed hard against Lot they nearly broke down his door. His two short-term guests rescued Lot and "struck with blindness the men who were at the door of the house, both small and great, so that they wearied for themselves groping for the door" (Genesis 19:10–11/RSV).

Early the next morning the angels urged Lot to grab his family and flee. By the time the sun was up, Lot and his two daughters were in the safety of another city. At that point—less than 24 hours after first appearing to Abraham—the LORD wiped out Sodom and Gomorrah including all their inhabitants and everything that grew on the ground.

The three visitors from heaven had just accomplished a short-term mission. They weren't members of the local receiving culture. They were cross-cultural goer-guests, first to Abraham (near the Oaks of Mamre) who hosted them with a fine meal, then to Lot (in Sodom) who hosted them with another feast and a safe place to sleep. While on this short-term outreach the goer-guests gave an old infertile couple a son and foretold tomorrow's destructive events. They also kept the relatives safe from the effects of grave wickedness (by disabling the enemy), and safe from the all-consuming effects of God's cleansing destruction. Quite a lot accomplished in this temporary mission of no more than 20 hours in length.

✔ Moses and the Egyptian Royal Court
Exodus 3–12

LENGTH OF MISSION: *Less than 1 year*

Theologians rightly see Moses as the 'great deliverer' of two to three million Jews enslaved in back-breaking bondage to a foreign power. Certainly that is true. Yet Moses was also a 'great missionary'—a great *short-term* missionary.

Moses received his call into full time ministry late in life. He stuck with that call 40 years—long-term by most definitions. But Donald Kitchen points out God launched his late-life career by way of a one-year short-term mission:

> "Moses' ministry in Egypt began when he was 80 years old and was
> less than a year's duration in that place. Furthermore he knew
> beforehand that he was going for a specialized 'short-term' ministry
> to Egypt and would return to Midian afterwards, [bringing with him]
> the people God had sent him to deliver [in order that together they
> might] 'serve God on this mount' (Exodus 3:12)."[2]

200

Moses encountered great difficulty and considerable resistance during his short-term mission to Egypt. Yet God worked through him in a way He has through no other human being. The short-termer Moses clearly discharged mission (cf. Chapter 2). He performed miracle after miracle before his intended receptors (the Egyptian people). He gave irrefutable testimony to the Great "I AM" before Pharaoh and his court. Although Pharaoh's heart grew hard, Egypt's great ruler eventually released the nation of Israel into Moses' hands—allowing the short-termer to successfully complete his 'great delivery' assignment within the year.

But during that same year, the Hebrew Moses also completed a *cross-cultural* 'great missionary' task. Within the span of that year he became known as "very great in the land of Egypt, in the sight of Pharaoh's servants and in the sight of the people" (Exodus 11:3B/RSV). God's words which he spoke, and God's miracles which he performed caused God's name to "be declared throughout all the earth" (Exodus 9:16/RSV; cf. Exodus 7:5, 7:17, 9:29, 10:2). Some of the royal court's servants actually learned to "fear the word of the LORD" (Exodus 9:20–21). There were even moments during Moses' short-term when Pharaoh temporarily yielded to God: "Entreat the LORD [to take away this plague]" (cf. Exodus 8:8, 8:28, 9:28/RSV). And there were yet other moments when Pharaoh shockingly confessed his sin: "I have sinned this time; the LORD is in the right, and I and my people are in the wrong" (Exodus 9:27/RSV; cf. Exodus 10:16–17).

All this cross-cultural work took place in less than a year. And its radical, life-altering outcomes back then still remain the continuing testimonies of God's incredible power today. Moses was an *effective* short-term missionary.

✔ *Jewish Spies and Their Short-Term Fact Finding Missions*
On two different occasions before entering the promised land, Israel sent out spies on short-term intelligence-gathering missions. The first one was largely a flop. The second one succeeded.

The Twelve-Man Team
Numbers 13–14
LENGTH OF MISSION: *40 days*
In Chapter 2, we briefly noted the 12 spies God sent via Moses (cf. Numbers 13:1–2, 16–17). At the time of this short-term deployment, these men were encamped with the entire Israeli nation at Kadesh in the dry Desert of Paran. They temporarily left Kadesh and went cross-culturally for 40 days (Numbers

13:25) throughout the fruitful hill country of Canaan, inhabited by the Anak giants, the Hittites, Jebusites, Canaanites, and the Amorites.

Their mission was to learn what they could about the land God was giving them—its people (their strength, their numbers, their quality of housing), the land itself (its fruit, whether it produced wood). An accurate report of these conditions would have enabled Moses and his military leaders to strategize an easy take-over and wipe out the sin from that land. But not unlike some short-term outreaches today, ten of the short-termers infused their own godless subjectivity into what they had experienced. When they did post-field debriefing with Moses and the people, they mixed factual findings with their own godless fear and gave "an evil report" (cf. Numbers 13:27–29, 13:32, 14:36–37). Only Joshua and Caleb held steadfast during the debriefing, reporting the message God wanted all spies to have reported (cf. Numbers 13:30, 14:6–9, 14:30).

Not all short-term mission endeavors work out the way God intends. But God *wanted* it to work out. He set it up. He commissioned it through Moses. It was swift, it was cross-cultural, it was temporary. It was short-term mission.

The Two-Man Team
Joshua 2:1–24
LENGTH OF MISSION: *5 days*
Not at all unlike initial explorations often required to begin work in a new area or within one of today's unengaged people groups, the Israelite commander Joshua ordered two of his men to leave Shittim and go spy out Jericho. A relatively easy one-day journey for two young men (cf. Joshua 6:22–23), about 15 miles on foot, the spies were probably deployed right away (perhaps less than a day's notice? perhaps less than an hour's notice?—either way it was a very swift deployment). Although Scripture doesn't tell us, it's likely they departed early in the morning and arrived inside the city of Jericho that same night ("...certain men of Israel have come here *tonight*"—Joshua 2:2; emphasis ours).

Regardless of how long it took to pre-field train and deploy them, and regardless of whether they arrived the same day or not, their mission was probably a five-day short-term mission—including round trip travel time. The lodge-keeper Rahab hid them the night of their arrival (Joshua 2:6), then secretly let them escape the same evening (Joshua 2:8–15). She instructed them to hide outside in the safety of the hills for three days while their pursuers searched for them along the roadway areas. After that it would be safe for the men to return back home (Joshua 2:16–21). So the two spies hid in the hills for three days, then returned home on what was probably the fifth and final day of their mission (Joshua 2:22–23). Joshua—who himself was one of the earlier spies debriefed by Moses—now debriefed these two new spies (Joshua 2:23) and learned of Israel's impending success: "Truly the LORD has given all the land into our hands; and moreover all the inhabitants of the land are fainthearted because of us."

These young short-termers were successful. They got going right away. They collected the right intelligence. They reported the right intelligence on their return (which no doubt strengthened the resolve of Israel to move forward into their promised land). And they did it all in less than a week.

Oh, and one other thing. They saved a prostitute and her family—a woman who wound up being the great-great grandmother of King David and an ancestor to Jesus of Nazareth. Their five day short-term generated some pretty significant long-term results.

✔ Samuel's Repetitive Short-Term Endeavors
I Samuel 7:15–17
LENGTH OF MISSION: *an average of 3 months per city*
Samuel was a busy man—prophet, priest, and judge. Although he made his home in Ramah in Benjamin (northwest of the Dead Sea), God deployed him away from his home every year on a three-city tour. "Samuel judged Israel all the days of his life. And he went on a circuit year by year to Bethel, Gilgal, and Mizpah; and he judged Israel in all these places. Then he would come back to Ramah, for his home was there, and there also he administered justice to Israel" (I Samuel 7:15–17/RSV).

Although Samuel was clearly a full-time professional in ministry (cf. I Samuel 3:19–21), and remained within the context of his own culture, he still used several short-term mission strategies. His mission was God-commanded, temporary to three of the cities, and repetitive to all four cities.

✔ Elijah and The Widow of Zarephath
I Kings 17
LENGTH OF MISSION: *3 years*
A great miracle-working prophet from the northern kingdom of Israel, Elijah's ministry took place nine centuries before Christ. His home town of Tishbe was east of the Jordon River, although most of his work occurred west of the river. God empowered Elijah to battle Ahab, one of the most evil kings of Israel. Ahab had allowed his Phonecian wife Jezebel to lead Israel in idolatry—following her god Baal and Baal's consort, the goddess Asherah.

It was on this royal pagan stage that Elijah made his entrance. He announced to Ahab that Israel would suffer a severe drought until Elijah said otherwise. At that point God told Elijah to hide east of the Jordon, where God appointed ravens to bring him daily food. When the local water source dried up because of the drought, God sent the prophet cross-culturally to Zarephath. Zarephath was in Phonecia (present-day Lebanon), about 150 miles north of Jerusalem. Phonecia was the home of the fertility idol-god Baal.

In Zarephath God had appointed a widow to feed Elijah. But the drought was affecting this region as well, for when Elijah found her and asked for a little water and a morsel of bread, she told him all she had was "only a handful of meal in a jar, and a little oil in a cruse; and now, I am gathering a couple of sticks, that I may go in and prepare it for myself and my son, that we may eat it, and die" (I Kings 17:12/RSV). In the midst of her devastating situation, Elijah still told her to feed him first, then herself and her son—promising the widow that God would not allow her jar of meal to be spent nor her cruse of oil to fail until the day God restores the rain. The widow went and did as Elijah said, and the meal and oil continued to last as the prophet had promised.

Eventually the widow's son got sick and died. Elijah took the boy to the room where he stayed and cried to the LORD for the child's life back. God "hearkened to the voice of Elijah; and the soul of the child came into him again, and he revived" (I Kings 17:22/RSV). The elated boy's mother responded, "Now I know you are a man of God, and that the word of the LORD in your mouth is truth" (I Kings 17:24/RSV). Finally in the third year (cf. I Kings 18:1), God told Elijah to return to King Ahab and announce the return of rain.

Was Elijah hiding from King Ahab? Or was he also doing a three-year short-term mission to the pagan nation of Phonecia? By the word of the LORD through the mouth of Elijah, his host family fed and housed him the entire time. When a young family member died, God hearkened to Elijah's request for a resurrection. Before Elijah's short-term was up, his Phonecian receiving host (from the pagan nation) acknowledged the reality of God and the truth of His word. This was a successful three-year short-term mission.

✔ Elisha and the Shunammite Family *
II Kings 4:8–37
LENGTH OF MISSION: *repetitive sojourns*
Elijah and the sons of the prophets spent a fair amount of time in Jericho and Gilgal (just a few miles north of the Dead Sea) and at Bethel (about 12 miles north of Jerusalem (cf. II Kings 2:3, 2:5, 4:38). Yet Elisha was often farther

north where he frequently spent time in the town of Shunem (60 miles north of Jerusalem) with a wealthy family.

The woman of the household fed Elisha "whenever he passed that way" (II Kings 4:8), and convinced her husband they should build another room on top of their home and furnish it for Elisha because he came that way so often (cf. II Kings 4:9–10). On one of his repetitive short-term visits, he blessed the infertile couple with the promise of a child.

Several years later this child developed a severe headache and eventually died. The Shunammite woman saddled her donkey and pressed on as fast as that slow animal would carry her on the 25–30 mile trip east to Mount Carmel to find Elisha. Elisha returned with her, and went up into his room where the woman had placed her dead child. Elisha prayed to the Lord (II Kings 4:33), then pressed his body against the child's (twice), and the boy was resurrected.

Continual, repetitive short-term visits to the family in Shunem. Each time his host family refreshed the prophet on his way to or from somewhere else. And on two of those short-term missions, the miracle-working prophet blessed his host family with the marvel of bona fide miracles.

✔ Nehemiah and a Short-Term Construction Mission
Nehemiah 2–10

LENGTH OF MISSION: *52 days*

Twenty years into the reign of Babylonian King Artaxerxes (son of Queen Esther's husband Ahasuerus—also known as Xerxes), his Jewish wine bearer Nehemiah temporarily relinquished a prestigious position in the Persian court to serve his father's people back in Jerusalem (cf. Nehemiah 2:1–5). Wycliffe's Bible Commentary provides the situational context which may have helped launch Nehemiah's short-term, circa 445 B.C.:

> "One of the by-products of the revival under Ezra seems to have been an effort on the part of the Jews to rebuild the walls of Jerusalem. This in turn provoked the wrath of Rehum and Shimshai, who wrote an accusation against them to Artexerxes (Ezra 4:7–16). The king commanded the work to cease ...
>
> "... upon receiving this decree from the king, [Rehum and Shimshai] 'made them cease by force and power,' presumably breaking down the wall that had been started and burning the gates (Ezra 4:23; Nehemiah 1:3). It was the news of this fresh disaster that shocked Nehemiah and brought him to his knees before God."[3]

That prayer (i.e., on his knees before God) apparently gave Nehemiah his strategy, and also gave him favor with the King (cf. Nehemiah 2:4–6). Upon arrival in Jerusalem, "Nehemiah immediately made a tour of Jerusalem by night to inspect and appraise the conditions. Immediately he organized the people who responded enthusiastically in rebuilding the walls of the city."[4]

Fifty-two days after commencing the work, Jerusalem's wall stood complete (Nehemiah 6:15)—an astounding, highly successful two-month short-term mission. Shortly thereafter Nehemiah put his brother in charge (Nehemiah 7:1–2), presumably so he could return to his duties in Babylon (cf. Nehemiah 2:1, 2:6, 13:6). Although Nehemiah spent more than two months' time working in and cleansing "Jerusalem, and the province, of various evils that had crept in during his absence since 432 B.C. ...,"[5] his short-term cross-cultural construction project was indeed a success—such a success that all Israel gathered to hear Ezra read the law, to worship, to hear a Godly sermon, and to sign their agreement to follow God's ways (Nehemiah 8:1–10:39).

Some may content that this was not a genuine short-term mission since Nehemiah led his construction project back to his country of origin. But note that our definition of short-term revolves around a *temporary* deployment. Nehemiah did not plant permanent stakes for himself when he came into Jerusalem. Instead, when he completed the job he returned back to his then-current home and back to his full-time job in Babylon as he had earlier promised King Artaxerxes he would (Nehemiah 2:6).

✔ *Jonah and Nineveh*
Jonah 1–4
LENGTH OF MISSION: *2–40 days*

Sunday School has programmed most of us to think about the fish story whenever someone mentions the name Jonah. Unfortunately that miraculous three-day survival inside the whale often overshadows the other bedrock message of the story. Jonah, son of Amittai, is a story about a fool God sent out to do mission—short-term mission (only a real fool dares flee from the presence of the Lord by paying someone else to ship him the other direction).

Jonah, a Northern Kingdom Prophet, was a Jew from Gath-hepher (II Kings 14:25/RSV) which we know as Galilee. During the reign of Jeroboam II (the son of Joash), about 780–750 B.C., God sent Jonah cross-culturally to the wicked Gentile city of Nineveh. Nineveh was located on the east bank of the Tigris River in Assyria, about 500 miles northeast of Israel. This "great city"

(Jonah 1:2/RSV) built by Nimrod (Genesis 10:8–12) may have had a surrounding metropolis of more than 600,000 people, being 90 miles in breadth.[6] For most Christian mission boards, Jonah's assignment would certainly be classified as cross-cultural frontier mission work to an unengaged, unchurched, unreached people group.

Since God had decreed destruction of Nineveh in 40 days (Jonah 3:4B), it is likely Jonah spent no more than 40 days in the city (that's short-term). It is even more likely he spent just two days in the city, going in one day's journey to cry out God's message (Jonah 3.4A), then perhaps leaving the following day (that's *very* short-term).

Whether his visit was two days, 40 days, or something in between, Jonah's sojourn was a short-term cross-cultural proclamation mission. The temporary engagement by this Jewish man in an Assyrian culture was not done out of his deep love and compassion for the lost, unsaved, wicked foreigners (Jonah 3:10–4:1). Yet his two day physical presence and his spoken word caused the people of Nineveh to repent and believe God (Jonah 3.5, 8–10). For the time being God withheld judgement. Though God did destroy Nineveh about 150 years later (circa 612 B.C.) by allowing the Chaldeans entrance into the city through a breach in the wall caused by the overflowing Tigris River, Jesus Himself implies the eternal success of Jonah's cross-cultural short-term mission stating, "the men of Nineveh will arise at the judgment with this generation and condemn it; *for they repented at the preaching of Jonah* ..." (Matthew 12:41/RSV; italics ours).

NEW TESTAMENT EXAMPLES

Explicit, decisive examples of short-term mission saturate the book of Acts, and are also found in much of the remaining portions of the New Testament as well.

✔ *The Wise Men* *
Matthew 2:1–12
LENGTH OF MISSION: *a few days in Jerusalem and Bethlehem*
When did the Magi visit Jesus, bringing their humble worship of the Infant King and their financial support to the Child's otherwise impoverished family? About 4 B.C. (the definitive date of King Herod's death), but most probably in the period of time when Jesus was at least 40 days old (after Mary's purification—cf. Luke 2:22, Leviticus 12:1–4), but not older than two years (Matthew 2:16).

The term 'wise men' at this time generally denoted the priestly caste among Persians and Babylonians—an eastern land where many Jews still lived, giving rise to the probability that the wise men may have been familiar with Jewish Scripture and knew of the forthcoming Messianic King. Because of their long journey (600 to more than 1,000 miles) through desert and other places filled with bandits, and because of the wealth they were transporting, their entourage was very likely many, many more than just three men our Christmas pageants erroneously portray (Scripture never says anything about just *three wise men*—only *three gifts*). Their entourage would obviously have aroused all of Jerusalem when they appeared, which is what happened (Matthew 2:3).[7]

When Herod heard of their arrival and their quest for *another* King, Herod went into action immediately. After completing his initial research and learning that the Christ was to be born in Bethlehem, Herod now summoned the wise men and learned the star had first appeared two years ago (Matthew 2:7,16). Herod immediately ordered them to go find the other King. As soon as the wise men went on their way, the star reappeared and directed them not to the manger scene—but rather to "the house" (Matthew 2:11/KJV) where Mary and Joseph had relocated. After worshipping the Child, and giving their gifts (which no doubt financed the family's flight into Egypt), the wise men returned back home.

The wise men were *temporary* short-term missionaries to Jerusalem and Bethlehem. They brought worship, they brought financial support, and they indirectly let all of Jerusalem know the New King had arrived.

✔ Jesus and the Samaritan Woman at the Well
John 4:3–43

LENGTH OF MISSION: *2 days*

In about 28 A.D. Jesus and his disciples headed north from Judea to Galilee, probably a two-day journey on foot. The most direct route took them through the racial hotbed of Samaria. Midway through their trip Jesus' earthly body had had it; furthermore it was time for a lunch break (cf. John 4:6 in the KJV, RSV, or NIV—the "sixth hour" meant noon). The watering hole just a couple miles outside of Sychar had been dug by Jacob centuries earlier, and would serve as a great stop for rejuvenation—even though they might have to mingle with the Samaritans. Sure enough, here comes a thirsty local.

Four theologians help us grasp this prejudiced background, making Jesus' tender, probing encounter with the thirsty local women even more spectacular:

- The Wycliffe Bible Commentary reveals Jewish conventional wisdom at the time: "Samaria ... [was] a territory to be avoided if possible by Jews."[8]
- Halley tells us, "Samaritans of an alien race, had been planted there by the Assyrians, 700 years before."[9]
- Bryant's *Today's Dictionary of the Bible* calls the nearby Samaritans "strangers," explaining they were "mixed inhabitants whom the king of Assyria brought from Babylon and other places." Bryant notes "these strangers (cf. Luke 17:18) amalgamated with the Jews still remaining in the land ...".[10]
- Even within this passage the writer John adamantly states, "for Jews have no dealings with Samaritans" (John 4:9B/RSV).

In spite of the prevailing cultural bias and racially-motivated hate between the Jews and Samaritans, Jesus' penetrating, yet loving, discourse with the non-Jewish woman not only caused her to believe (cf. John 4:29), but on the spot, converted this adulterer into an evangelist (cf. John 4:39).

She even left her beverage behind (cf. John 4:28) and quickly made the two mile trip back to town. So effective was her first-time witness, that fellow villagers now dropped what they were doing and made the two mile trip back to the well (cf. John 4:30). Now by invitation, Jesus spoke with other villagers, and many more believed because of His word. The villagers confessed, "we know that this is indeed the Savior of the world" (John 4:42B/RSV).

This Sychar revival, initiated by a traveling cross-cultural visitor, occurred within the short-term context of just two days (cf. John 4:40,43). On the spot he trained a local to help. When his own buddies suggested he take a break from that training and grab a bite to eat, he chided them "[hey guys,] open your eyes and look at the fields! They are ripe for harvest ... for eternal life" (John 4:35–36/NIV).

Deviating from His original plan, Jesus temporarily, intentionally engaged Himself in cross-cultural mission—and was successful—in the whopping span of just 48 hours. Are you ready for this? ... Jesus was a short-term missionary.

✔ *The Apostle Paul*
Acts and Several Other NT Books
Few New Testament characters rival the Apostle Paul. He is considered by many to be the premier apostle, preacher, writer, and missionary of the First Century. Some even hold Paul as the greatest missionary ever. But to those

who champion Paul as an ideal example of the commitment a real missionary should have, Donald Kitchen avidly points out:

> "Paul ... never spent a full 'four-year term' in any place but was constantly changing his field of ministry. His longest stay in any one place was two years (at Ephesus). Many of his ministries were accomplished in time periods that today would be considered as only a brief visit to the mission field. Paul, however, was used of God to plant churches in four different provinces of the Empire, spanning two continents in less than ten years."[11]

When discussing China missionary Roland Allen's writings, Lesslie Newbigin adamantly agrees concerning Paul's astonishing success: "Paul achieved [more] in ten years of work [than] what modern missions had ... achieve[d] in a century".[12] Although he cites four insightful points for Allen's claim, the first point corroborates with our contention that Paul was a short-term missionary: "When, as the result of preaching the Gospel, a Christian community has come into being, Paul entrusts the whole responsibility of the local leadership and *moves on* (italics ours).[13]

Paul's ambition was not to start up a mission station. Rather, his ambition was "to preach the Gospel where Christ was not known so ... those who have not heard [about Christ] will understand" (Romans 15:20–21/NIV). Charles Mellis adamantly agrees:

> "Paul & Co. ... knew what their function was: *to progressively move on* and preach Christ where he was not yet named; or, in modern parlance, to plant churches—not to develop and develop and develop and develop them! Maybe if we were really clear on this ... we'd have less problem ... When the former hangs around after the latter is clearly established ... tensions are inevitable" (italics ours).[14]

Harold Cook concurs: "our mission 'stations' are rightly named, for the missionaries in them often tend to become quite stationary."[15] Cook takes the issue deeper yet, deftly fusing the short-term paradigm within context of a longer-term commitment:

> "Missionary work, though it may occupy a missionary's lifetime, is

essentially temporary in nature. The missionary always looks forward to the time when this part or that, or even the whole work will be completed. What does this mean to the missionary? It means that if he is a capable worker, one of two things will happen. Sooner or later he will have to change his location, as each job is completed; or he will have to have the mobility within himself to change his type of work as the old needs are filled and new ones present themselves. In either case he needs to be mobile."[16]

Although Paul had the full commitment of a long-term career missionary, Paul's strategy—a successful strategy as indicated by Kitchen, Allen, Newbigin, Mellis, and Cook above—was clearly short-term.

Paul's Missionary Journeys: Was it Three—Or Was it Seven?[17]
Earlier we briefly challenged the prevailing theological assumption that Paul made just three missionary trips. But even when we examine just these three, we note that all three completed round trips were still *temporary* outreaches. They were short-term missions ranging from two years (first-'recognized' outreach) to four years (third-'recognized' outreach). But it's crucial to note that Paul's *maximum* stay in any one host location was two years and three months (Ephesus, during his third-'recognized' outreach—cf. Acts 19:8–10). On-site stays in other host locations were as short as just a few days, and even just a few hours while in pass-through locations.

As we define 'mission' (cf Chapter 2—Defining 'Mission') and as we define 'short-term' (cf. Chapter 3—Defining 'Short-Term' Mission), here now are Paul's seven short-term outreaches:

1. **FROM JERUSALEM TO DAMASCUS AND ARABIA TO JERUSALEM**
   LENGTH OF MISSION: *3 years*
   DATES OF MISSION: C. 37–40 A.D.
   BIBLE REFERENCE: Acts 9:1–31 (cf. Galatians 1:17–18)
   ACCOMPANYING GOER-GUESTS: "his disciples" (Acts 9:25/RSV)
   SENT OUT FROM: Jerusalem
   MILES TRAVELED: 150+
   HOST RECEIVING LOCATIONS: 4
      Damascas, Arabia, Damascas, Jerusalem.
   RECEIVING FIELD FACILITATORS: Ananias and other disciples in Damascas; Barnabas in Jerusalem.

GIVING/SOWING ACTIVITY AND RESULTS:

- *Damascas* "in the synagogues immediately [Paul] proclaimed Jesus" and eventually "confounded the Jews who lived in Damascus by proving that Jesus was the Christ" (Acts 9:20–22/RSV).
- *Arabia* unknown (but assumed missionary activity—cf. Galatians 1:17–18).
- *Damascas* assumed continued missionary activity.
- *Jerusalem* Paul "preached fearlessly in the name of Jesus;" and the churches were "strengthened; and ... grew in numbers, living in the fear of the Lord" (Acts 9:28, 9:31/NIV).

DEBRIEFING AND FOLLOW-UP: Barnabas took Paul to the apostles in Jerusalem where Paul "declared to them how on the road he had seen the Lord, who spoke to him, and how at Damascus he had preached boldly in the name of Jesus" (Acts 9:27/RSV.

OBSERVATIONS:

1. Although Paul (Saul at the time) was sent out by the high priest in Jerusalem to persecute the Christians in Damascus, we contend the Sovereign Lord was behind this, knowing full well of Paul's forthcoming conversion, and of Paul's impending evangelistic missionary activity.

2. Commensurate with our short-term mission definition, Paul 'swiftly' began preaching after his conversion.

3. "The word 'Arabia' is misleading to the modern mind. In Paul's day one was in Arabia as soon as he got out of the bailiwick of Damascus."[18] Paul's work in Arabia can be compared to American Christians living near the U.S./Mexican boarder, and traveling into Mexico on a short-term mission.

4. Paul left Damascus for Jerusalem because of a murder plot hatched against him; he stayed with Peter for 15 days (Galatians 1:18). Paul also left Jerusalem for his home city of Tarsus for the same reason (Acts 9:29–30).

2. **FROM JERUSALEM / TARSUS TO ANTIOCH TO JERUSALEM (RELIEF AND HUMANITARIAN AID) TO ANTIOCH**
LENGTH OF MISSION: *1–2 years*
DATES OF MISSION: C. 43–44 A.D.

BIBLE REFERENCE: Acts 11:25–30; 12:25
ACCOMPANYING GOER-GUESTS: Barnabas, John Mark
SENT OUT FROM: Jerusalem (Barnabas) and Tarsus (Paul)
MILES TRAVELED: 1,125+
* Jerusalem–Tarsus: 380 (65 by land, 315 by sea);
* Tarsus–Antioch–Jerusalem–Antioch: 745 (655 by land, 90 by sea)
HOST RECEIVING LOCATIONS: 2
   Antioch in Syria, Jerusalem
RECEIVING FIELD FACILITATORS: the church in Antioch;
   and the elders in Jerusalem.
GIVING/SOWING ACTIVITY AND RESULTS:
* *Antioch* Barnabas and Paul discipled (taught) a "large company of people" at the church for an entire year; for the first time the disciples were called Christians (Acts 11:26/RSV).
* *Jerusalem* Barnabas and Paul provided relief and humanitarian assistance from the church at Antioch to the brethren living in Judea; Barnabas and Paul "fulfilled their mission" (Acts 12:25/RSV).
DEBRIEFING AND FOLLOW-UP: Barnabas and Paul returned from Jerusalem to the church at Antioch (where it is logical to assume they debriefed their Jerusalem relief efforts).
OBSERVATIONS:
1. Barnabas was actually the leader of this short-term outreach, with Paul (Saul) as the accompanying goer-guest (cf. Acts 11:25, 11:30).
2. Both men went to Tarsus from Jerusalem—Paul in c. 40 A.D., and Barnabas in c. 43 A.D. in search of Paul.
3. While in Tarsus, Paul may have done short-term outreaches into Syria and Cilicia (cf. Galatians 1:21).
4. John Mark accompanied Barnabas and Paul on their return to Antioch (Acts 12:25).

3.   FIRST-'RECOGNIZED' MISSION OUTREACH
LENGTH OF MISSION: *2 years*
DATES OF MISSION: C. 46–48 A.D.
BIBLE REFERENCE: Acts 13–14
ACCOMPANYING GOER-GUESTS: Barnabas, John Mark
SENT OUT FROM: Antioch
MILES TRAVELED: 1,200+ (by land)

HOST RECEIVING LOCATIONS: 10

Salamis in Cyprus, Paphos, Pisidian Antioch, Iconium, Lystra in Lycaonia, Derbe in Lycaonia, Lystra in Lycaonia, Iconium, Pisidian Antioch, and Perga in Pamphylia.

GIVING/SOWING ACTIVITY AND RESULTS:

- *Salamis* Paul and Barnabas preached; John Mark observed and helped (Acts 13:5).
- *Paphos* Paul and Barnabas preached; Paul used spiritual warfare and manifestational gifts (he cursed a Jewish sorcerer who was hindering their work with temporary blindness); the Roman proconsul was converted (Acts 13:6–12).
- *Antioch* Paul preached on two consecutive Sabbaths; many were converted and briefly discipled by Paul and Barnabas for just one week; Paul and Barnabas now directed their ministry to the Gentiles (Acts 13:14–52).
- *Iconium* Paul and Barnabas preached and performed manifestational gifts; a "great company believed" (Acts 14:15/RSV).
- *Lystra* Paul and Barnabas preached; Paul performed a manifestational gift; the Jews stoned Paul (Acts 14:6–20).
- *Derbe* Paul and Barnabas preached and "made many disciples". (Acts 14:20–21/RSV).
- *Lystra, Iconium, Antioch* Paul and Barnabas made a repeat short-term back to these cities to disciple the new believers and appoint elders for them (Acts 14:21–23).
- *Perga* Paul and Barnabas preached (Acts 14:24–25).

DEBRIEFING AND FOLLOW-UP: When Paul and Barnabas arrived back at Antioch, "they gathered the church together and reported all that God had done through them and how He had opened the door of faith to the Gentiles. And they stayed there a long time with the disciples" (Acts 14:27–28/NIV).

OBSERVATIONS:

1. Because the entire mission journey was just two years, and because the *majority* of that time would have been spent in travel, the average stay in any of the host locations was probably measured by days, weeks, or months at most (note how Jesus' own disciple Luke considered their outreach at Iconium to be a "long time"—cf. Acts 14:3/RSV—even though it was still very short-term!).

2. Paul and Barnabas practiced the 'repetitive deployment' aspect of short-term mission during this two-year journey. They returned to three of their earlier host cities (Lystra, Iconium, and Antioch) to continue their short-term discipleship efforts. They also returned to Perga where they had earlier just passed through; this time they "preached the word" (Acts 14:25/NIV).
3. John Mark returned to Jerusalem fairly soon, after their short-term outreach at the second host location. Paul and Barnabas completed the remaining eight.

4. FROM ANTIOCH THROUGH PHOENICIA AND SAMARIA TO THE JERUSALEM COUNCIL TO ANTIOCH

LENGTH OF MISSION: *several days to a few weeks*

DATES OF MISSION: C. 49 A.D.

BIBLE REFERENCE: Acts 15:2–35

ACCOMPANYING GOER-GUESTS: Barnabas and others; and Judas Barsabbas and Silas.

SENT OUT FROM: Antioch

MILES TRAVELED: 640+

HOST RECEIVING LOCATIONS: 3
Phoenicia, Samaria, and Jerusalem.

RECEIVING FIELD FACILITATORS: the church and the apostles in Jerusalem.

GIVING/SOWING ACTIVITY AND RESULTS:

*   *Phoenicia, Samaria* Paul, Barnabas, and others from Antioch did pass-through discipleship, encouraging the brethren and giving them joy concerning the conversion of the Gentiles (Acts 15:3).
*   *Jerusalem* At the council meeting of church leaders, the short-termers reported to the church, the apostles, and the elders all that God had done; some believers (who were Pharisees) still contended the Gentiles needed to be circumcised. After the apostles, elders, and short-termers had much discussion and debate, they resolved the issue and sent their written report back to Antioch via the short-termers (now including Judas and Silas).

DEBRIEFING AND FOLLOW-UP: The entire band of short-termers "gathered the congregation together [in Antioch and] delivered the letter [from the church in Jerusalem]. And when they read it, they rejoiced" (Acts 15:30–31).

OBSERVATION:

- Judas Barsabbas and Silas did their own 640 mile short-term. Accompanying the original goer-guests back to Antioch, they "spent some time" and "exhorted the brethren with many words and strengthened them" before being "sent off in peace by the brethren to those who had sent them" (Acts 15:32–34/RSV).

5. **SECOND-'RECOGNIZED' MISSION OUTREACH**

LENGTH OF MISSION: *2¹/₂ to 3 years*

DATES OF MISSION: C. 49–52 A.D.

BIBLE REFERENCE: Acts 15:36–18:22

ACCOMPANYING GOER-GUESTS: Silas, Timothy, Luke, Aquila and Priscilla

SENT OUT FROM: Antioch

MILES TRAVELED: 2,700+ (1,290 by sea, 1,410 by land)

HOST RECEIVING LOCATIONS: 14+
Syria, Cilicia, Derbe, Lystra, [Iconium?, Antioch?, others?], Phrygia, Galatia, Troas, Macedonia (Philippi, Thessalonica, Berea), Achaia [Greece] (Athens, Corinth, Cenchrea), and Ephesus.

RECEIVING HOST FIELD FACILITATORS: Lydia, Jason, Aquila and Priscilla

GIVING/SOWING ACTIVITY AND RESULTS:

- *Syria, Cilicia* Paul and Silas discipled believers (Acts 15:41).
- *Derbe, Lystra, and other cities* Paul and Silas (and Timothy) discipled believers in the churches (Acts 16:1-5).
- *Phrygia, Galatia* Paul, Silas, and Timothy probably discipled local converts (Acts 16:6; cf. Acts 18:23).
- *Troas* Paul received supernatural instructions to go to Macedonia (Acts 16:8–10).
- *Philippi* The short-termers remained here "several days;" they spoke with the women (Lydia and her household were converted and baptized); Paul used spiritual warfare and manifestational gifts (he delivered a slave girl from the spirit of divination); Paul and Silas were miraculously delivered from jail which led to the jailer and his household being converted and baptized; they briefly discipled (strengthened and encouraged) the brethren (Acts 16:12–40/NIV).

- *Thessalonica* Paul preached from the Scriptures on three Sabbaths; some Jews, some prominent women, and many Greeks "joined Paul and Silas" (Acts 17:1–9/NIV).
- *Berea* Paul preached at the Jewish synagogue; many Jews, Greek men, and prominent Greek women believed (Acts 17:10–14).
- *Athens* Paul preached ("reasoned") in the synagogue with Jews and God-fearing Greeks, and daily in the marketplace to "those who happened to be there;" "a few" became followers before Paul left (Acts 17:15–34/NIV).
- *Corinth* Paul preached, reasoned, and taught the Word of God every sabbath for a year and a half; many Corinthians including the synagogue ruler believed and were baptized; because of continued Jewish opposition and abuse, Paul declared, "Your blood be on your own heads! ... From now on I will go to the Gentiles" (Acts 18:1–17/NIV).
- *Cenchrea* Paul fulfilled a vow (Acts 18:18).
- *Ephesus* Paul preached in the synagogue and promised to return on another short-term if it was God's will (Acts 18:19–21).

DEBRIEFING AND FOLLOW-UP: "When he landed at Caesarea, he went up and greeted the church and then went down to Antioch [where he spent] some time in Antioch" (Acts 18:22–23/NIV).

OBSERVATIONS:

1. Paul's primary intended activity of this second-'recognized' short-term was to "return and visit the brethren in every city where we proclaimed the word of the Lord, and see how they are;" Paul was employing the repetitive deployment strategy which identifies a short-term mission (Acts 15:36/RSV).
2. Timothy joined up with Paul and Silas at the forth host location.
3. Luke appears to have joined this band of short-term missionaries in Troas and Philippi, because the pronoun used in the Biblical narrative temporarily switches from "they" to "we/us" (cf. Acts 16:8–17).
4. Silas and Timothy remained a short time longer in Berea while Paul went on ahead of them to Athens. Paul began preaching in Athens even before his companions arrived (cf. Acts 17:14–17); Silas and Timothy met up with Paul in Corinth (cf. Acts 18:5).

5. Aquila and Priscilla accompanied Paul from Corinth to Cenchrea to Ephesus (cf. Acts 18:18–19).

6. THIRD-'RECOGNIZED' MISSION OUTREACH

LENGTH OF MISSION: *4 years*

DATES OF MISSION: C. 53–57 A.D.

BIBLE REFERENCE: Acts 18:23–21:16

ACCOMPANYING GOER-GUESTS: Luke, Erastus, Sopater, Aristarchus, Secundus, Gaius, Timothy, Tychicus, Trophimus, unnamed disciples from Caesarea.

SENT OUT FROM: Antioch

MILES TRAVELED: 2,500+ (1,190 by sea, 1,325 by land)

HOST RECEIVING LOCATIONS: 12
Galatia, Phrygia, Ephesus, Macedonia, Greece, Macedonia, Troas, Miletus, Tyre, Ptolemais, Caesarea, and Jerusalem.

RECEIVING FIELD FACILITATORS: unnamed disciples and believers in many locations; and Philip in Caesarea, Mnason in Jerusalem.

GIVING/SOWING ACTIVITY AND RESULTS:

- *Galatia, Phrygia* Paul discipled the believers as he traveled incessantly throughout this region (Acts 18:23).
- *Ephesus* This was Paul's longest short-term outreach; "the word of the Lord spread widely and grew in power" as Paul preached boldly for three months in the synagogue, and with his disciples provided another two years' worth of daily discussions in the lecture hall of Tyannus "so that all the Jews and Greeks ... heard the word of the Lord;" Paul used spiritual warfare and substantial manifestational gifts so that "their illnesses were cured and the evil spirits left them;" many also publicly confessed their evil deeds (Acts 19:1–20:1/NIV).
- *Macedonia* Paul discipled believers in this region by "speaking many words of encouragement to the people" (Acts 20:1–2/NIV).
- *Greece* Paul spent three months in Greece; Scripture doesn't indicate what, if any, ministry Paul did here—although we assume he did do some sort of ministry because "the Jews made a plot against him" (Acts 20:2–3/NIV). Corinth appears to be one of his stops in Greece (cf. II Corinthians 12:14, 13:1).

- *Macedonia* Paul had to change plans and re-route his travel back through Macedonia; Sopater, Aristarchus, Secundus, Gaius, Timothy, Tychicus, and Trophimus accompanied Paul; we assume there may have been personal ministry and personal debriefing among these goer-guests during their brief time passing through Macedonia (Acts 20:4).
- *Troas* Paul and his companions stayed here seven days; Paul preached and performed a manifestational gift (Acts 20:6–12).
- *Miletus* Paul made one final discipleship effort with the elders at Ephesus who came the 20-mile distance at Paul's request while he was in Miletus (Acts 20:15–38).
- *Tyre* The short-termers spent seven days with the disciples here and bade good-bye to Paul (Acts 21:3–6).
- *Ptolemais* The short-termers stayed one day with the brothers (Acts 21:7).
- *Caesarea* This appears to be primarily a rest stop and preparation for Paul's journey to Jerusalem in spite of warnings not to go (Acts 21:8–15).
- *Jerusalem* Paul's arrival in Jerusalem was first marked by a debriefing session (cf. below) with the brothers, James, and the elders. Then the following week Paul was arrested (Acts 21:17–33). Titus may have been on the portion of this short-term to Jerusalem—cf. Galatians 2:1–5).[19]

DEBRIEFING AND FOLLOW-UP: "Paul ... reported in detail [to James, the elders, and others] what God had done among the Gentiles through his ministry. When they heard this, they praised God" (Acts 21:18–20/NIV).

OBSERVATIONS:

1. Paul's time in Galatia and Phyrgia no doubt included many repeat short-term visits to churches and believers he had ministered to on his earlier short-term outreaches.
2. Toward the end of his 2¼-year short-term in Ephesus, Paul determined to go to Jerusalem by way of Macedonia and Achaia (opposite direction of Jerusalem); at that point he sent Timothy and Erastus on ahead of him to Macedonia (cf. Acts 19:21–22).
3. In several of his mini short-term side trips while on their return to Jerusalem, Paul and his short-term mission companions simply stayed with local believers. Scripture gives no indication of

what ministry took place in several of those instances. We assume that some form of discipleship (mutual encouragement, mutual prayers) and hospitality took place, in addition to personal ministry, post-field debriefing of previous short-term endeavors, planning for the future, personal rest and relaxation—and simply *being* with each other in fellowship. But this is just a guess (and we think a pretty good one at that).

7. **FROM JERUSALEM TO ROME (AND SPAIN AND BEYOND?)**
   LENGTH OF MISSION: *2¹/₂-years; and beyond?*
   DATES OF MISSION: C. 59–62 A.D.
   BIBLE REFERENCE: Acts 21:17–28:31
   ACCOMPANYING GOER-GUESTS: Luke, Aristarchus, various Roman soldiers/guards including the centurion Julius, brothers from Rome, Titus
   SENT OUT FROM: Jerusalem
   MILES TRAVELED: 2,130+ (1,920 by sea, 210 by land)
   HOST RECEIVING LOCATIONS: 10+
      Jerusalem, Caesarea, Sidon, two ships sailing the Mediterranean (one from Adramyttium, another from Alexandria with the twin-god figurehead of Castor and Pollux), Malta, Puteoli, the Forum of Appius, Three Taverns, Rome, (Spain? Crete? Nicopolis?).
   RECEIVING FIELD FACILITATORS: Mnason in Jerusalem; Governor Felix and Paul's friends in Caesarea; the centurion Julius throughout the journey; Paul's friends in Sidon, the islanders of Malta including the chief official Publius.
   GIVING/SOWING ACTIVITY AND RESULTS:
   - *Jerusalem* Paul gave his testimony to the crowd while standing in front of the barracks before being imprisoned (Acts 21:37–22:24). The next day Paul gave a brief verbal witness to Ananias (high priest) and the Sanhedrin (Acts 22:30–23:10). The next night the Lord instructed Paul to go to Rome (Acts 23:11).
   - *Caesarea* Paul spoke about Jesus Christ to Felix, Ananias the high priest, Tertullus the lawyer, the assembled Jews and other government officials present before Felix (Acts 23:23–24:26). Paul proclaimed that Jesus was alive to Felix's successor, Porcius Festus (cf. Acts 24:27,19), and again in much more detail to Festus, King Agrippa, Bernice, high ranking officers, and leading

men of Caesarea (Acts 25:22–26:29).

- *Sidon* This time on the receiving end, "Julius, in kindness to Paul, allowed him to go to his friends so they might provide for his needs (Acts 27:3/NIV).

- *Sailing the Mediterranean* While south of the island of Crete, Paul discerned impending danger and made safety recommendations, but the others did not follow his advice (cf. Acts 27:9–12, 27:21). Mid-journey and mid-storm, Paul testified of the mission God had given him and of his faith in God, and that none of the 276 would be lost in the storm (Acts 27:21–26). Two weeks later Paul again gave public testimony to God and encouraged all on board to eat, which they did (Acts 27:33–38).

- *Malta* "The islanders showed us unusual kindness. They built a fire and welcomed us because it was raining and cold" (Acts 28:2/NIV), and "Publius, the chief official of the island … welcomed us to his home for three days and entertained us hospitably" (Acts 28:7/NIV). Paul miraculously healed Publius' sick father, and "the rest of the sick on the island came and were cured" (Acts 28:9/NIV). In a true short-term mission serendipitous 'reciprocity of give and take,' the islanders then furnished them with the supplies they needed before sailing onto Rome.

- *Puteoli, the Forum of Appius, Three Taverns* The brothers at Puteoli invited Paul and his companions to spend a week. Other brothers from Rome caught up with the short-termers at the Forum of Appius and at Three Taverns, which encouraged Paul in his mission (Acts 28:13–16).

- *Rome* Paul finally arrived at the world capital of Rome. He rented a house and very early in his stay the local leaders of the Jews and others "came in large numbers to his home. From morning till evening he explained the kingdom of God and Jesus, using the Law of Moses and the Prophets. Some were convinced, but others would not believe (Acts 28:23–24). Paul's response was "Therefore I want you to know that God's salvation has been sent to the Gentiles, and they will listen!" (Acts 28:28/NIV). Then "For two whole years Paul stayed there in his own rented house and welcomed all who came to see him. Boldly and without hesitation he preached the kingdom of God and taught about the Lord Jesus Christ" (Acts 28:30–31/NIV).

- *Spain?* When Paul wrote the Romans from Corinth, he promised to visit the Romans "when I go to Spain" (Acts 15:24/NIV). Clement of Rome (c. 95 A.D.) may have known Paul personally, and seems to think Paul went to Spain after surviving his legal trial in Rome[20]—but this of course, cannot be Scripturally verified.

- *Crete? Nicopolis?* The Pastoral Epistles (I Timothy, II Timothy, Titus) give some indication that Paul had other missionary activity.[21] Paul implied that he was in Crete (Titus 1:5), and encouraged Titus to join him for the winter at Nicopolis (Titus 3:12). Because the Pastoral Epistles were written *after* arriving in Rome (between the years of about 63–67 A.D.), they seem to suggest additional missionary activity.

DEBRIEFING AND FOLLOW-UP: No debriefing is specified in Scripture. However while in Rome for two years, Paul had ample time to report to friends and colleagues on his two and a half year journey to get there.

OBSERVATIONS:

1. Paul spent more than two years under guard (with some limited freedom) in Caesarea (cf. Acts 24:23,27).

2. Aristarchus, a Macedonian from Thessalonica, joined Paul as they left Caesarea (Acts 27:2).

3. Brothers from Rome joined Paul on the final leg of his journey into Rome (Acts 28:15–16).

4. Titus appears to have traveled with Paul at some point after leaving Rome (cf. Titus 1:5), and as mentioned may have joined Paul in Nicopolis (cf. Titus 3:12).

✔ *The Church Adventitiously Sends its First Short-Term Missionaries*
Acts 8:1–40

"On that day (c. 37 A.D.) a great persecution broke out against the church at Jerusalem, and *all* except the apostles were scattered ... those who had been scattered preached the word wherever they went (Acts 8:1,4/NIV, emphasis ours).

OBSERVATIONS:

1. The *professionals* stayed behind (for the time being). The *non*-professionals went out, and went out *swiftly* after Stephen's death.

2. These short-term *non*-professional missionaries preached the Word

wherever they went. Scripture lists some of those host receiving locations, and does so using language that suggests *temporary* involvement in those locations (rather than a permanent move and permanent stay):

- "throughout" Judea and Samaria (Acts 8:1/NIV)
- they "traveled as far as" Phoenicia, Cyprus, and Antioch (Acts 11:19/NIV)
- "men from Cyprus and Cyrene went" to Antioch (Acts 11:20/NIV)

GIVING/SOWING ACTIVITY AND RESULTS:

1. "Those who had been scattered preached the word wherever they went" (Acts 8:4/NIV).
2. "...telling them the Good News about the Lord Jesus. The Lord's hand was with them, and a great number of people believed and turned to the Lord" (Acts 11:20–21/NIV).

✔ *Philip the Evangelist*
Acts 8:5–13, 26–40

LENGTH OF MISSION:

- Samaria: *temporary*
- Desert Road: *a few hours*
- Azotus, et al: *a few days*
- Caesarea: *permanent*

Philip was one of seven chosen in Acts 6 to "wait on tables" (c. 33 or 34 A.D.) when early church growth was exploding. Philip was also one of those deployed *swiftly* as a result of the persecution. In about 37 A.D., he first spent an unspecified period of time roughly 40 miles north of Jerusalem in an unnamed city in Samaria (probably Sebaste, rebuilt by Herod as a Hellenistic city[22]). His short-term mission activity consisted of preaching and evangelism, and of performing incredible miracles: "With shrieks, evil spirits came out of many, and many paralytics and cripples were healed. So there was great joy in that city" (Acts 8:7–8/NIV). During a portion of this outreach, Philip worked with Peter and John who themselves had come to this same city on an even shorter short-term (Acts 8:14–25).

Philip's second short-term occurred the same year (c. 37 A.D.) and began on the back of his first. It began by departing this Samaritan city, heading south (following instructions from an angel of the Lord) to a desert road southwest of Jerusalem (Acts 8:26), continuing northwest to Azotus, then bearing northward to several other towns near the Mediterranean coast (Acts 8:40), finally winding up in Caesarea.

While on the desert road Philip met up with an Ethiopian official and—in what appears to be the *temporary* span of merely a few hours at most—successfully evangelized the already-seeking Ethiopian, baptizing him as a believer in Christ. Disappearing at that point, Philip appeared in Azotus and "traveled about, preaching the Gospel in all the towns until he reached Caesarea" (Acts 8:40/NIV). Some of those towns receiving Philip's *temporary* short-term 'pass-through' ministry may very well have included Lydda and Joppa. It then appears Philip settled down and raised four daughters in Caesarea, where 20 years later he hosted Paul on Paul's journey to Jerusalem during the last leg of his sixth short-term outreach in about 57 or 58 A.D. (Acts 21:8-9).

✔ Barnabas, Son of Encouragement
Acts 4–15

BARNABAS' 1ST SHORT-TERM: *Antioch* (c. 41 A.D.)

BARNABAS' 2ND SHORT-TERM: *Tarsus; and Antioch and Jerusalem with Paul on Paul's second short-term* (c. 43–44 A.D.)

BARNABAS' 3RD SHORT-TERM: *with Paul on Paul's third short-term* (c. 46–48 A.D.)

BARNABAS' 4TH SHORT-TERM: *with Paul on Paul's fourth short-term* (c. 49 A.D.)

BARNABAS' 5TH SHORT-TERM: *with John Mark to Cyprus* (c. 50 A.D.)

Barnabas (originally Joseph, a Levite from Cyprus), cashed out of his for-profit business and joined the early Jerusalem church in Acts 4 by donating all his proceeds to the church's common purse in about 31 or 32 A.D. The disciple Barnabas was gifted as a prophet (Acts 13:1) and apostle (Acts 14:14), and the early church used a short-term mission strategy to extend the impact of Barnabas' spiritual gifts.

Originally, Barnabas was the only disciple in Jerusalem who had the courage and faith to receive the radically converted Saul (Paul), opening the door for him to meet with the other apostles in about 40 A.D. (Acts 9:26-28).

When "men from Cyprus and Cyrene went to Antioch and began to speak to the Greeks ... about the Lord Jesus ... and a great number of people believed and turned to the Lord" (Acts 11:20-21/NIV), the Jerusalem church sent their "good man" (NIV) Barnabas on a short-term to Antioch to encourage and disciple these new converts in about 41 or 42 A.D. (Acts 11:22-24).

Roughly one to two years later (c. 43 A.D.), Barnabas—Son of Encouragement—left Antioch and sought out Paul in Tarsus. In Tarsus he encouraged Paul to join his short-term ministry back in Antioch. A year later, the Antioch church selected Barnabas and Paul for a humanitarian aid and relief short-term to the church in Jerusalem. In these instances, Scripture mentions Barnabas' name first, suggesting that he was probably the leader of their short-term mission efforts (Acts 11:25–30).

Other short-term endeavors undertaken by Barnabas include teaming up with Paul on Paul's third and fourth short-terms (cf. above). Then in an apparent role reversal, Paul now initiated a fifth short-term (cf. above), inviting Barnabas to join him (Acts 15:36). When Barnabas insisted on taking John Mark against the recommendation of Paul, their unresolved contention sent Paul and Silas north (Paul's fifth short-term), and sent Barnabas and John Mark west on what appears to be their own short-term outreach to Barnabas' home island of Cyprus (about 49 or 50 A.D.).

✔ *The Apostle Peter*
Acts 8:14–11:2

PETER'S 1ST SHORT-TERM: *Samaria* (c. 37 A.D.)
PETER'S 2ND SHORT-TERM: *Lydda, Joppa, Caesarea* (c. 40 A.D.)

Peter was the key anchor Apostle in Jerusalem—the man who initiated the replacement of Judas, the man who spoke out boldly in public on numerous occasions, the man in whom the Spirit of God abode so strongly that even his shadow could heal. Peter was the man who told the Sanhedrin, "We must obey God rather than men!" (Acts 5:29/NIV). For roughly the first seven years (about 30–37 A.D.), the first seven chapters of the book of Acts center in on Peter and his incredible ministry that took place in Jerusalem. But during the next four years Peter ventured out on at least two short-term mission outreaches.

With God working through the short-termer Philip in Samaria (cf. above), baptizing new believers and performing miracles, "the apostles in Jerusalem heard that Samaria had accepted the word of God," and they sent Peter and John to "pray for them that they might receive the Holy Spirit, because the Holy Spirit had not yet come upon any of them" (Acts 8:14–16/NIV). It appears this was a very *temporary* assignment for Peter and John, for "when they had testified and proclaimed the word of the Lord, Peter and John returned to Jerusalem" (Acts 8:25). And they didn't just rush back nonstop. Rather, they continued in the context of their short-term mission, preaching the Gospel in other Samaritan villages on their way back home (Acts 8:25).

About three years later we once again find Peter away from Jerusalem, traveling about the country (Acts 9:32). While making a short-term stop in Lydda, he healed the bedridden paralytic Aneneas—the impact of which caused all the onlookers from Lydda and nearby Sharon to turn to the Lord (Acts 9:32–25). Nearby Joppa was another of Peter's visits during this short-term outreach. Here he resurrected the disciple Tabitha (Dorcas). This, too, caused many people in Joppa to believe in the Lord. Although he stayed "some time with a tanner named Simon" (Acts 9:43), it was still a *temporary* outreach of probably less than one year.

During this same short-term mission, Peter made yet another *temporary* sojourn ("a few days" in Acts 10:48/NIV), this time to Caesarea by invitation from the Roman centurion Cornelius as a result of Cornelius' vision. While Peter himself was pondering his own separate vision (not yet realizing it was directly related to the forthcoming events), Cornelius' men arrived in Joppa to escort Peter and six other short-termers (cf. Acts 11:12) to Caesarea. When Peter arrived, his ministry was so successful that Cornelius, his relatives, and close friends received the gift of the Holy Spirit and were subsequently baptized as believers. Newbigin reminds us not only of the [short-term mission] success of Peter's ministry to the foreigner Cornelius, but also "of the conversion of Peter and of the church."[23] This last stop on Peter's short-term mission resulted not only in the fantastic conversion of Cornelius and his Gentile household of "uncircumcised pagans,"[24] but it played a key, significant role in the broadened vision for mission of the early church.

✔ Tychicus*

Acts, Ephesians, Colossians, II Timothy, Titus

TYCHICUS' 1ST SHORT-TERM: *Macedonia* (C. 47 A.D.)

TYCHICUS' 2ND SHORT-TERM: *Ephesus, Corinth* (C. 61 A.D.)

Tychicus was one of seven men in about 47 A.D. that accompanied Paul as Paul began the return segment of his sixth short-term mission (Acts 20:4). About 14 years later while under house arrest imprisonment in Rome (C. 61 A.D.), we find Paul sending Tychicus on short-term visits to the churches at Ephesus and Colosse (Ephesians 6:21–22, Colossians 4:7–8) to inform both churches how Paul and his colleagues were doing, and to encourage the believers in those churches. In II Timothy 4:12, Paul confirms that he had already sent Tychicus to Ephesus. And, Onesimus may have done this entire short-term with Tychicus (cf. Colossians 4:9). Tychicus may have done a third short-term as well: after Paul's release from prison, Paul wrote Titus (C. 64 or 65 A.D.) with definitive plans of sending either Artemas or Tychicus on a short-term to Titus (Titus 4:12) who himself was on a short-term mission to the island of Crete.

✔ *Titus* *

II Corinthians, Galatians, II Timothy, Titus

TITUS' 1ST SHORT-TERM: *Corinth* (c. 53 A.D.)
TITUS' 2ND SHORT-TERM: *Macedonia* (c. 55 A.D.)
TITUS' 3RD SHORT-TERM: *Jerusalem* (c. 55 A.D.)
TITUS' 4TH SHORT-TERM: *Corinth* (c. 56 A.D.)
TITUS' 1ST LONG-TERM: *Crete* (c. 59–65 A.D.)
TITUS' 5TH SHORT-TERM: *Dalmatia* (c. 66 A.D.)

Titus was *swiftly* and *repetitively* deployed as a short-term missionary on at least five distinct short-term outreaches.

When Paul arrived in Macedonia about 55 A.D. during his sixth short-term mission[25] (probably the same time he wrote this letter to the Corinthians), Paul was weary and downcast. But Titus, a Greek, showed up on his own separate short-term mission to Macedonia, bringing comfort and encouragement to Paul and his other goer-guest companions (II Corinthians 7:5–7). This comfort and encouragement came as a result of Titus' earlier short-term assignment to Corinth, where he (and at least one other companion—cf. II Corinthians 12:18) had been sent by Paul (II Corinthians 7:13–16), probably sometime after Paul's year and a half short-term outreach to the Corinthians in about 51–52 A.D. During Titus' first short-term to Corinth, Titus encouraged the Corinthians to be givers (II Corinthians 8:6); his Corinthian colleagues were great host receivers, and refreshed Titus during his stay (II Corinthians 7:13–16). Now it was time to complete the collection of this gift, so Paul made plans to send Titus (and others) back to Corinth (II Corinthians 8:1–24). This would have been Titus' second short-term mission to that city, which likely took place either prior to, or shortly after, Titus' short-term to Jerusalem with Paul (cf. below).

Titus also did a short-term to Jerusalem with Paul on the last leg of Paul's sixth short-term, sometime around 54 A.D. (maybe as late as 57 A.D.).[26]

In Titus 1:8, Paul makes a reference to leaving Titus in Crete. Could this have been on Paul's seventh short-term on his way to Rome (cf. Acts 27:3–8), in about 59 A.D.? Whatever the date, Titus had what appears to be *longer*-term ministry of perhaps four to six years in Crete to help lead the troubled church on this island (cf. Titus 1–3). Titus appears to have remained in Crete at least until about 63–65 A.D., the date-range assigned to Paul's letter to Titus.

Just a year or so later, Titus went on another short-term, this time to Dalmatia—a mountainous country on the eastern shore of the Adriatic, part of the Roman province of Illyricum.[27] Titus did his outreach to Dalmatia (II Timothy 4:10) likely during the time Paul wrote this letter to Timothy (c. 66 or 67 A.D. during Paul's second Roman imprisonment).

✔ Apollos
Acts, I Corinthians, Titus
APOLLOS' 1ST SHORT-TERM: *Ephesus, Corinth* (c. 54 A.D.)

APOLLOS' 2ND SHORT-TERM: *Corinth* (c. 56 A.D.?)

APOLLOS' 3RD SHORT-TERM: *Crete* (c. 65 A.D.)

In c. 54 A.D. Apollos (a Jew) arrived in Ephesus on a short-term mission. Apollos was a native of Alexandria (on Egypt's Mediterranean shoreline)—the grand city founded by Alexander the Great (c. 333 B.C.) where tradition says 70 learned men translated the Hebrew Bible into Greek during the third and second century B.C. (the SEPTUAGINT). Alexandria, known for its famous library of 700,000 books, was the cultural backdrop of intellect that allowed Apollos to be "a learned man, with a thorough knowledge of the Scriptures" (Acts 18:24/NIV). While in Ephesus "he spoke with great fervor, and taught about Jesus accurately" (Acts 18:25/NIV), although the local receiving hosts Priscilla and Aquila had to bring him up to speed in the most recent developments concerning "the way." Shortly thereafter Apollos wanted to go to Achaia (southern Greece). The brothers at Ephesus supported Apollo in this, and wrote to the disciples there to welcome him. As a result, Apollos wound up on a short-term to Corinth (Acts 19:1). Later, when Paul wrote his first letter to the Corinthians (c. 54 or 55 A.D.), he closes his letter by mentioning that he has strongly encouraged Apollos to return to Corinth on a *repetitive* short-term mission (I Corinthians 16:12), and that Apollos has indicated he would go when the opportunity availed itself (c. 56 A.D.?). It appears Apollos did yet another short-term—a visit to Titus on the island of Crete about 65 A.D. as well (Titus 3:13).

✔ The Women
Matthew, Mark, Luke
LENGTH OF MISSION: *less than 3 years*

Women were key, significant short-term mission participants in the Gospels—both as sending supporters, and as goer-guests. Mary Magdalene, Joanna (wife of Cuza who managed Herod's household), and Susanna (cf. Luke 8:1–3); Mary (the mother of James and Joses), the mother of James and John (sons of Zebedee), Salome, and "many other women" (cf. Mark 15:40–41/NIV and Matthew 27:55–56). Scripture is clear about the crucial role these women played as short-term mission participants. They helped support Jesus and the disciples out of their own means, often traveling with Him wherever He went.

✔ Jesus Sends Out the Short-Termers
Luke 9, Luke 10

Jesus began his Holy Spirit-anointed earthly ministry in about 28 A.D. Within about a year (c. 29 A.D.), He began sending out teams of short-term goer-guests. These folks were far from fully trained (Jesus still had another two years' worth of mentoring to do with them, prior to turning over His work to them). Even so, consider how they were sent out:

- *God-commanded* (Jesus Himself gave them power and authority)
- *Repetitively Deployed* (Jesus sent out not one, but two separate teams)
- *Swiftly Deployed* (the goer-guests probably had less than a year's worth of training, if that much)
- *Temporarily Deployed* (they were probably on-field for just a few weeks at most)
- *As Non-professionals* (although the first team eventually became full time professionals, so little is known about the second team, that we assume most were common, average, 'fools' for Christ)

Jesus Sends out the Team of Twelve
Luke 9:1–10; cf Mark 6:7–31

Here were 12 men—some uneducated, brash, common, one who was a devil (John 6:70), and another who was possessed at least once by Satan (Matthew 16:23). Far from being perfect candidates for full time ministry, Jesus nonetheless used a type of short-term mission experience in order to further these men's training and practical ministry skills. But this wasn't merely a training event only!—for their specific charge (their God-commanded intended activity) was to drive out demons, heal the sick, and preach the Gospel.

Note the following observations of the Twelve's short-term outreach, which short-term practitioners should consider applying to today's endeavors:

- They were sent, commissioned by a Godly authority (Luke 9:1–2)
- They went out in groups [in pairs] (Mark 6:7)
- They were given pre-field instructions and training (Luke 9:2–5)
- They achieved measurable, Kingdom-expanding results (Mark 6:13)
- They received post-field debriefing and follow-up (Luke 9:10)

Jesus sends out the Team of Seventy (KJV, RSV)
Luke 10:1–19

It worked with the 12. Now it was time for the 70 (72 in the NIV). This time Jesus used an even larger group of potential ministry candidates, most of whom we have no information about whatsoever (our guess is that this time around, some were probably women). And just like the 12, the 70 weren't sent merely on a training exercise, but were sent in *MISSIO DEI*, to prepare the villages for Jesus' eventual coming. They were also sent to preach the Kingdom of God, heal the sick, and subject the demons to Jesus' Name. This group does *not* appear to have included the original 12 ("After this the Lord appointed seventy *others*"—cf. Luke 10:1/RSV, emphasis ours). They appear to be your run-of-the-mill, average people. And they achieved whomping success (Luke 10:17–20).

The following observations for the short-term mission of the Seventy are identical to the Twelve:

- They were sent, commissioned by a Godly authority (Luke 10:1)
- They went out in groups [in pairs] (Luke 10:1)
- They were given pre-field instructions and training (Luke 10:2–12)
- They achieved measurable, Kingdom-expanding results (Luke 10:17)
- They received post-field debriefing and follow-up (Luke 10:17–19)

✔ *The Seven Great Commission Passages*
Matthew, Mark, Luke, John, Acts

None of the seven so-called "Great Commission" texts give, either explicitly or implicitly, a recommended length of measurable time or a fixed length of service with which to comply. The popular understanding is, of course, that they are applicable to all Christians at all times. But the specific point is this: the Great Commission passages, taken in their plain sense, do not prohibit— nor do they show lack of endorsement for—short-term mission. A brief comment to support our view will follow each passage.

1. *Matthew 24:14/RSV*
   "And this Gospel of the kingdom will be preached throughout the whole world, as a testimony to all nations; and then the end will come."

The methodology implied in Matthew 24 is simply preaching throughout the whole world. Short-term mission—indeed any classification of mission—is capable of doing this. The text implies no emphasis whatsoever for any recommended length of time. To claim this passage endorses only 'long-term career' strategies would be objectionable exegesis at best.

2. *Matthew 28:19–20/RSV*
    "Go therefore and make disciples of all nations, baptizing them in the Name of the Father and of the Son and of the Holy Spirit, teaching them to observe all that I have commanded you . . . ".

Matthew 28 is the most-recognizable of the Great Commission texts. It does seem to suggest a longer-term commitment because of the time required to adequately (a highly-subjective term) disciple and teach. Even so, discipleship and teaching can occur over a period of time with a variety of different instructors—much like Western elementary education which assigns one teacher to one class for one year. Logically, it follows that a given short-termer could likewise disciple and teach (in compliance with Matthew 28) in a mission setting for just one year, while another short-termer assumes the instructor role in the subsequent year, and so on. Although benefits of an over-arching long-term plan are obvious, the point is this: a short-term missionary can intentionally and temporarily engage in the task of Matthew 28, and do it in full compliance with this Biblical text.

3. *Mark 13:10/RSV*
    "And the Gospel must first be preached to all nations."

In the RSV, this is the shortest rendition of the seven Great Commission texts (John 20:21 is one word longer). How much more clear can Jesus make it? Before the end of the world comes, the Gospel must first be preached to *all* nations. It seems to us that anyone concerned with preaching the Gospel to all nations would use any reasonable methodology at their disposal—including short-term and long-term strategies suitable to the given field.

4. *Mark 16:15–16/RSV*
    "Go into all the world and preach the Gospel to the whole creation. He who believes and is baptized will be saved; but he who does not believe will be condemned."

Although some Biblical scholars question the authenticity of this text, there is nothing in this passage which is not fully supported elsewhere in canonical Scripture. The methodology given is worth examining, in light of the short-term mission paradigm. The passage instructs believers to: (1) go everywhere, and (2) preach. Nothing is complicated about these instructions, unless the old paradigmatic view overshadows the pure simplicity of Jesus' command. Short-term mission can readily comply with this passage, for short-termer goer-guests can (1) go virtually anywhere in the world, and short-termers can (2) preach the Gospel in word and deed to the whole of creation (mankind, and other objects of God's creation). This text asks nothing more.

5.   *Luke 24:47/RSV*
"*. . . repentance and forgiveness of sins should be preached in His Name to all nations, beginning from Jerusalem.*

The methodology implied is simply preaching everywhere, with an emphasis on repentance and forgiveness. Short-term missions is capable of doing this. There is no long-term confine placed on this passage of Scripture.

6.   *John 20:21/RSV*
"*. . . As the Father has sent Me, even so I send you.*"

Jesus itinerated in a variety of places throughout his three-year ministry, moving about from village to village. He did this according to God's plan (cf John 12:49, John 14:31). Jesus, while active in ministry, had no permanent base of operation, no headquarters, not even a regular bed to guarantee a good night's sleep (Luke 9:58). In full compliance and total obedience with the commands of God, Jesus did not plant Himself exclusively in one locale. One application of John 20:21 would suggest our style of ministry should be the same. This passage seems to fully encourage the fluid, non-anchored mobility commonly associated with short-term mission, which was clearly demonstrated by the New Testament short-termers we discussed above. In fact this passage seems to caution any long-term missionary from ever sinking roots into a given spot, for once the people of God have a place to lay their heads, it becomes increasingly more difficult to follow Jesus (Luke 9:57–62).

7.   *Acts 1:8/RSV*
"*But you shall receive power when the Holy Spirit has come upon you; and you shall be My witnesses in Jerusalem and in all Judea and Samaria and to the end of the earth.*"

Short-term mission goer-guests—like any other classification of mission-aries—are candidates for 'receiving the power of the Holy Spirit,' and therefore are capable of being witnesses. According to this passage, becoming a witness for Jesus has nothing to do with schooling, breeding, personal family history, or any other 'law' some missiologists try to lay on the back of other people. It has only to do with receiving the power of the Holy Spirit. Clearly this text shows it is the Holy Spirit who empowers God's people for mission. The Holy Spirit, plus nothing, equals power to witness for Jesus. Each living person can potentially receive God's Spirit, and therefore intentionally engage in mission—whether for a week, a year, or a lifetime.

Additional Theological Rationale for Short-Term Mission

THE primary purpose for short-term mission *must* be 'Christian mission' as we have attempted to define 'Christian mission' in Chapter 2 (and throughout all of this book). The principle outcome of short-term mission should *not* be engineered primarily for the goer-guests, but always for the benefit of intended receptors.

Yet it's interesting to note that as God's people engage in God's task, that serendipitous blessings accrue to the goer-guests involved in that task (cf Chapter 7—The Reciprocity of Give 'n Take). These Biblically-based blessings should not be taken lightly. Nor should they be the primary, let alone the only, purpose for engaging in short-term mission. But because they do so often occur, and because there is a Biblical basis for such occurrences, prudence dictates we plan for receiving these blessings as well, and plan for their multiplied use within God's Kingdom.

These common, serendipitous occurrences are what we identify as 'additional theological rationale' as we make our case for short-term mission.[28]

Additional Rationale #1
GIFT DISCOVERY

God has gifted each of His children in different ways for building up the body of Christ. Paul expresses this clearly in letters to the Corinthians and Ephesians. However, each person's gifts may not be immediately obvious even to the individual. One of the benefits of short-term mission is the exposure goer-guests are given to ministry in a cross-cultural environment. Within such a context, they often take part in ministry outside of their daily routine. God may use such a situation to bring to the surface specific gifts and abilities of which these short-term missionaries were previously unaware. He may also provide an awareness that there exist ministry opportunities, even yet unknown, for which the goer-guests may be gifted (and for which they may actually enjoy).

This sort of serendipitous discovery seems to have a strong Biblical basis with the disciples on the occasions when the 12 and the 70 were on their short-term mission assignments (cf. above). When the 70 returned, they expressed excitement over the fact the demons had submitted to them in Christ's name (Luke 10:17). It seems that while they had witnessed Jesus exhibiting such authority and power, they had not experienced it personally. Jesus used the disciples' short-term experience to uncover gifts and reveal to them aspects of ministry which they had only experienced second-hand before. Could God not desire to continue using short-term mission experiences in a similar way today?

In our nicely-programmed church services and other 'controlled' ministry activities occurring in our 'normal' lives, we may not be given opportunity to hands-on explore the talents and gifts God has given us. Yet short-term mission readily provides that opportunity.

Additional Rationale #2
TRAINING

Aside from the aspect of revealing gifts, Jesus, as well as Paul, used short-term mission outreaches for training and preparation for future involvement in ministry. Jesus' disciples and Paul's co-workers were active in ministry while simultaneously in the process of being trained. Seminaries and Christian schools should take note: this type of cooperative training model has potential for offering the best training for Christian ministry. The balance of Biblical study and theological training within a hands-on mission environment offers the best of both worlds for future missionaries, pastors, church leaders—and for the common, average 'fool' who sits in the pew.

Additional Rationale #3
SPIRITUAL GROWTH

Jesus told the disciples to pray: "...pray therefore the Lord of the harvest to send out laborers into His harvest" (Luke 10:2B/RSV). Prayer is a strategic Kingdom activity in which all children of God are called to take part. Not only does such prayer exhibit obedience to the Lord, it is also strategic in the sense that the mission in which we participate is ultimately God's mission (*MISSION DEI*). If 'the chief end of man is to glorify God and enjoy Him forever,'[29] then those Christian disciplines which draw believers closer to the heart of God are to be encouraged and actively pursued with vigor and tenacity. In light of the importance of prayer, and the fact short-term mission goer-guests have been found to grow significantly in mission-focused prayer,[30] we can appropriately draw the conclusion that short-term mission has a positive impact on the goer-guests' (and on *all* participants') spirituality.

The experiences encountered on-field during a short-term mission often help all participants (including goer-guests) better understand the depth and width of the love of Christ (Ephesians 3:14–19). This, too, is an oft-reported outcome which is clearly rooted in Scripture (the short-termer Paul prayed this same outcome for the Ephesians—cf. Ephesians 3:17–19).

Another prayer Paul prayed at about the same time (while in prison in Rome about 60–62 A.D.) sums up God's desire for spiritual growth as an outcome for goer-guests: "I pray that you may be active in sharing your faith, so that you will have a full understanding of every good thing we have in Christ" (Philemon 6/NIV). Such an understanding (i.e., spiritual growth) comes as a result of obediently sharing our faith, which is often one of the primary intended activities of a given short-term mission.

Additional Rationale #4
ECCLESIASTICAL & WORLDVIEW EXPANSION

The interaction of North American short-term personnel with Christians and non-Christians in other cultures offers a tremendous opportunity to help those from both cultures expand their understanding of the universal nature of the church and of both cultures' myopic worldview paradigms. This is precisely what began taking place in Acts 10 during Peter's second short-term mission, between Peter and his Jewish culture, and Cornelius and his Gentile culture.

The Apostle Paul instructs us, "Do not conform any longer to the pattern of this world, but be transformed by the renewing of your mind" (Romans 12:2/NIV). The stark realities of mission field environments, the blending of cultural perspectives, the working together in oneness (cf. John 17) among various doctrinal persuasions—these are often the very ingredients God uses to begin transforming and renewing a mind, to help goer-guests 'get to the heart of the journey' (cf. Chapter 12—A Post-Script Perspective).

Additional Rationale #5

NEW ENTHUSIASM FOR *MISSIO DEI*

Finally, nothing comes close to renewing and rejuvenating a given church's (or any given group's) passion for God's mission, like short-term goer-guests just back from the field. Their infectious life-change can sweep through an entire congregation and help awaken the stodgiest of souls.

Consider John (the disciple whom Jesus loved). His racist attitude toward the Samaritans, wanting to burn them in God's fire, got a rebuke from Jesus in about 29 A.D. (cf. Luke 9:52–55). Now fast-forward eight years to 37 A.D. John accompanied Peter on Peter's first short-term mission to Samaria. Together, John and Peter laid their hands on the Samaritans and prayed for the gift of the Holy Spirit (which they received—cf. Acts 8:14–17). This short-term visit apparently gave John and Peter the beginning of some new enthusiasm for *MISSIO DEI*. For they chose not to rush back home to Jerusalem, but to begin preaching the Gospel to *many* Samaritan villages on their way back home (cf. Acts 8:25).

The church in Jerusalem began receiving this 'infection' from its returning short-termers. By the time Peter completed his second short-term, the church began "glorifying God" for accepting the Gentiles' "repentance unto life" (cf. Acts 11.18/RSV).

Summary

SHORT-TERM 'MISSION' (as opposed to cross-cultural 'trips') has a strong theological anchoring within the Scriptures. We've cited more than 30 'proof-texts' from the Old and New Testaments in this chapter. But foundational to those proof-texts is the theological basis we unpacked in Chapter 1 (God's Fools): God prefers the 'average-person' strategy, and God is the author and finisher of the 'priesthood of *all* believers.' Finally, the Bible *also* demonstrates that God uses short-term mission for personal gift discovery, training, spiritual growth, ecclesiastical and worldview expansion, and to initiate new enthusiasm for *MISSIO DEI*.

Endnotes
Chapter 10

1. *(p. 198)* **Leslie Pelt**, "What's Behind the Wave of Short-Termers?" (*Evangelical Missions Quarterly*, 28(4), October 1992), pp. 384–388.

2. *(p. 200)* **Donald Kitchen**, *The Impact and Effectiveness of Short-Term Missionaries* (Dallas TX: Dallas Theological Seminary Department of World Missions, 1976), pp. 20–21.

3. *(p. 205)* **Charles F. Pfeiffer and Everett F. Harrison, eds.**, *The Wycliffe Bible Commentary* (Chicago IL: Moody Press, 1983), p. 435.

4. *(p. 206)* **Clarence H. Benson**, *Old Testament Survey—Law and History* (Wheaton IL: Evangelical Teacher Training Association, 1968), pp. 91–92.

5. *(p. 206)* **Pfeiffer and Harrison**, p. 435.

6. *(p. 207)* **Clarence H. Benson**, *Old Testament Survey—Poetry and Prophecy* (Wheaton IL: Evangelical Teacher Training Association, 1972), pp. 77–78.

7. *(p. 208)* Cf. **Henry H. Halley**, *Halley's Bible Handbook* (Grand Rapids MI: Regency Reference Library (Zondervan), 1965), pp. 418–19; and **Pfeiffer and Harrison**, pp. 932–933.

8. *(p. 209)* **Pfeiffer and Harrison**, p. 1080.

9. *(p. 209)* **Halley**, p. 536.

10. *(p. 209)* **T. A. Bryant**, compiler, *Today's Dictionary of the Bible* (Carmel NY: Guideposts (Minneapolis MN: Bethany Publishing), 1982), p. 542.

11. *(p. 210)* **Donald Kitchen**, *The Impact and Effectiveness of Short-Term Missionaries* (Dallas TX: Dallas Theological Seminary Department of World Missions, 1976), p. 24.

12. *(p. 210)* **Lesslie Newbigin**, *The Open Secret* (Grand Rapids MI: William B Eerdmans, 1978), p. 144

13. *(p. 210)* *Ibid.*, p. 144.

14. *(p. 210)* **Charles J. Mellis**, *Committed Communities* (Pasadena CA: William Carey Library, 1976), p. 61.

15. *(p. 210)* **Harold R. Cook**, *Strategy of Missions* (Chicago IL: Moody Press, 1963), p. 109.

16. *(p. 211)* *Ibid.*, pp. 109–110.

17. *(p. 211)* The information in this section concerning Paul's missionary journeys has been compiled by Roger Peterson. In addition to various versions of the Holy Bible and their respective Bible reference maps, and to other sources as cited herein, the reference used for additional information concerning Paul's three 'recognized' missionary trips, and for verification of Peterson's related research, comes from **Andrew E. Hill, compiler**, *Baker's Handbook of Bible Lists* (Grand Rapids MI: Baker Book House, 1981), pp. 231–248. Dates cited have been extracted from two

sources: **Hill** (*Ibid.*), and **Gerrit Verkuyl**, *The Modern Language Bible* (Grand Rapids MI: Zondervan, 1969).

18. *(p. 212)* **Emil G. Kraeling**, *Rand McNally Bible Atlas* (Chicago IL: Rand McNally & Company, 1956), p. 425.

19. *(p. 219)* Because of Paul's reference to the circumcision issue in this Galatians passage, many scholars believe Paul is referring to his mission to the Jerusalem council which occurred in about 49 A.D. (which we identify as the concluding portion of his fourth short-term). And because Galatians is estimated to have been written around 48–53 A.D., this reference does fit with the Jerusalem council (Paul's fourth short-term). However Paul's own introductory statement, "Fourteen years later I went up again to Jerusalem..." (Galatians 2:1/NIV) seems to line up better with his sixth short-term. First of all, "Fourteen years later" appears to be a clear reference to the preceding passage (Galatians 1:11–24) concerning Paul's conversion and his first short-term outreach within Damascus and Arabia, which took place around 37–40 A.D. "Fourteen years later" then places the date at about 54 A.D.—which falls into the range of Paul's sixth short-term outreach which is estimated to have been c. 53–57 A.D. Second, Paul's reference to his private conversations (cf. Galatians 2:2) also line up with his Acts 21:18–19 reference concerning his sixth short-term mission, where he spoke not to an entire large group, but rather to only James and the elders (i.e., a private meeting). Therefore we conclude Titus was on the last leg of Paul's sixth short-term mission.

20. *(p. 222)* Cf. **Kraeling**, p. 462.

21. *(p. 222)* Cf. *Ibid.*, pp. 462–463.

22. *(p. 223)* Cf. *Ibid.*, p. 416.

23. *(p. 226)* **Newbigin**, p. 65.

24. *(p. 226)* *Ibid.*, p. 66.

25. *(p. 227)* Because of Paul's II Corinthians 2:12–13 reference of Troas to Macedonia (which would have been in about 50 A.D. during Paul's fifth short-term), it is logical to assume that his II Corinthians 7:8 reference to Macedonia refers to the same outreach. However, we believe this second reference to Macedonia not to mean Paul's fifth short-term, but rather his sixth, and the second of two visits to Macedonia on that sixth short-term. Paul is downcast and weary (cf. II Corinthians 7:8–9/NIV: "we were harassed at every turn—conflicts on the outside, fears within"), which could fit with his sixth short-term when he left Greece for Macedonia because of the plot the Jews made against him (Acts 20:3). Also, it does not seem likely that Paul would have sent Titus to Corinth before Paul's fifth short-term, but rather after Paul's fifth short-term (after Paul had spent a year and a half with the Corinthians in c. 51–52 A.D.).

26. *(p. 227)* Cf. Endnote #19 above.

27. *(p. 228)* Cf. **Bryant**'s comments on "Dalmatia," p. 160.

28. *(p. 233)* The first four 'additional rationale' have been extracted and re-edited from an earlier STEM*Press* publication, where they were the primary insight of co-author Daniel McDonough [Cf. **Daniel P. McDonough and Roger P. Peterson**, *Can Short-Term Mission Really Create Long-Term Missionaries?* (Minneapolis MN: STEM Ministries, 1999), pp. 28–29.] The fifth 'rationale' came from Kim Hurst.

29. *(p. 235)* **Westminster Assembly**, *The Westminster Shorter Catechism*, 1647, Answer to Question #1 found at: (http://mcgraytx.calvin.edu/gray/westminster_standards/shorter_catechism.html).

30. *(p. 235)* Cf. Endnote #6 of Chapter 5, and the data found on its corresponding page reference.

A CONTEMPORARY HISTORICAL REVIEW

THE GOAL OF THIS CHAPTER IS NOT TO PROVIDE A definitive accounting of all God has been doing in the world of short-term mission the last 50 to 100 years. Rather, the goal is simply to show, in a very simplistic yet accurate way, the history of God moving in our modern time through the avenue of structured short-term mission.

Cataloguing the modern history of short-term mission is an impossible task. Even if there were sufficient time and resource to chase down every lead, interview every person who "remembers when ...", look in every denominational library, or study every book, we'd still have only a small picture of what God has been doing. We sense there are literally thousands of short-term outreaches each year which we will never know about this side of heaven. Individuals, pairs, families, small groups, large groups. Normal, average people going out in obedience, doing what they believed God was commanding. There simply is no human record of their endeavors we can readily access. Many did it for God's glory. Some were sloppy and did a bad job. Others did a great job and actually advanced God's Kingdom here on earth.

Short-term mission is nothing new. But its extent and staggering influence has been exploding through the church at large in just the last 10 years. But for some, it's nothing new. John Kyle wrote in 1987, "Christians need to see that a giant for the cause of Christ is striding among us. It's called the short-term missionary movement."[1] This chapter should give you a helicopter's view of some limbs of that giant.

In November 2002 we did some enlightening non-empirical research. We sent a survey to approximately 700 short-term mission representatives from churches, colleges, and agencies. Our 61 responses of usable data included 17 churches, nine colleges, and 35 mission agencies. Utilizing their responses, and by making other personal contacts beyond the scope of our survey tool, we have compiled the following information.

Pre-1950s

ONE OF the earliest references we found on intentional short-term mission was **1895**. The *Ludhiana Christian Medical College and Hospital* in Northern India began in 1894 by Dr. Edith Brown, who saw a desperate need of medical and nursing care for, and by, women. Dr. Brown began organizing student medical teams to work with these women.[2] We were not able to learn much else about these short-term attempts, other than this college and hospital are still in existence in India today.

Wycliffe Bible Translators began in 1934 with 'Camp Wycliffe,' a linguistics training school. Rita Taubman, Wycliffe's Short-Term Programs Coordinator, reports "Our founder, 'Uncle Cam' (Cameron Townsend) took small groups of businessmen to see Wycliffe's work in the **late 1940s** ... Wayne Huff, Director of Tour Ministries Department of the Southcentral Regional Office, took their first group to Guatemala in February, 1987." Taubman also notes that Wycliffe-USA began their short-term Discovery Program in 1990, and that Wycliffe Associates has been sending construction groups around the world since 1967. This is the earliest example we could find of an agency, formed primarily with career missionaries, that was involved in officially sending short-term mission teams. For 2002 Wycliffe plans to send over 600 individual people on short-term mission outreaches of one kind or another.

Post-1950s

THE PAST five decades is when the contemporary short-term mission movement began to explode (cf. ILLUSTRATION #11.1 below). Unfortunately we are not able to source complete and finalized empirical information to defend our data; it just simply does not exist. However, from scattered estimates that are available, and by applying reasonable extrapolations to these estimates, we do believe that from a globally-sent perspective, the numbers represented by our graph are equitable.

ILLUSTRATION #11.1

GROWTH OF THE CONTEMPORARY SHORT-TERM MISSION MOVEMENT

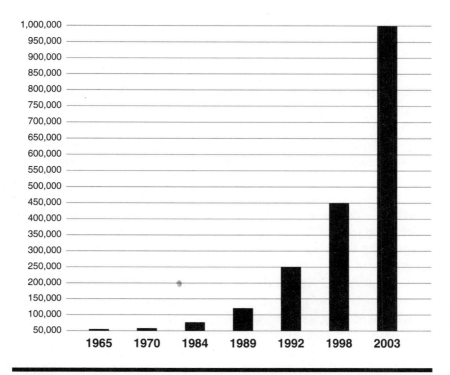

NOTES: (1) Years on the X-axis are not equally scaled. (2) None of this data whatsoever can be empirically defended. (3) Estimates have been derived and extrapolated from several different sources; each source may have used a differing definition of 'short-term mission' when deriving their calculations. (4) Cf. the 'Nebulous Numbers' section and the 'Summary' section of this chapter to reference some of the data used to create this graph.

1950s

Businessman Bill Bright began *Campus Crusade for Christ* on the UCLA campus in **1951**. Campus ministry still remains important, but is now one of 60 different ministries within CCC. James Woelbern, Deputy Director of Communication, informs us that for 2001, CCC had 125,506 short-term volunteers within all 60 of their ministries from across the globe.

Bethany College of Missions was originally established in 1948. Participation in mission outreach is required of all students during their Freshman and Junior years. Rich Tolosi of Bethany tells us, "Most of our short-term outreach was local [within the Midwest United States] since the **early 50s**. Students were sent in pairs or groups. In the 80s, we began sending groups overseas." In 2002 Bethany sent out about 125 short-term workers— Freshman for three weeks, Juniors for nine months.

Leonard Janssen, the Executive Director for *YUGO Ministries* in Baja California reports their organization first started in 1964. But their founder, "Youth Pastor Al Johnson had been taking his groups on outreach trips to the American Indians since **1956**." In 1962 they were invited to take their groups to the Mexicali Valley in Baja California. In 1964 they saw the need for an independent training and sending organization. That is when Youth Unlimited Gospel Outreach (YUGO) was born." The organization has continued to grow since that time, and in 2003 expects to send around 4,500 young people and adults on short-term mission outreaches.

What started as a passion for lost souls in one man has grown into a well-known short-term mission agency. It's founder and leader, George Verwer, is known around the world for his enthusiasm for mission. His organization *Operation Mobilization* (OM) began in **1957** when Verwer and two friends felt God calling them to short-term mission in Mexico. They distributed copies of the Gospel and other Christian literature. As a result, Verwer had a vision about what God wanted to do with an army of short-term volunteers in mission, and OM was born. In 2002, OM launched about 650 'Global Action' short-termers (6-months to 2-years), and somewhere between 1,000 and 10,000 [probably 3,500?] 'Global Challenge' short-termers (up to 6-months).

CBInternational actually began in 1943, but it wasn't until **1958** that they began sending short-termers. Miranda Weigel of CBI reports, "In 1958 one couple went overseas as MAC workers (Missionary Assistance Corps). Their main responsibility was to assist the missionaries." CBI's main focus is reproducing New Testament churches using career missionaries, and they sent 77 short-term workers in 2002 in support of that task.

The history of *Wheaton College* has always been laced with missions, including short-term mission. Wheaton began in 1860, and missions has been an important part of campus life from early on. Some of the most well known missionaries of our country have been Wheaton graduates. But Wheaton College did not officially send out a short-term mission until the year **1958**. Timothy Sisk, Director of the Office of Christian Outreach says Wheaton's "SMP [Student Missionary Project] began forty-five years ago as the vision of Ron Chase (1956). Ron spent the summer of 1957 working at a mission in the jungles of Mexico's Yucatan Peninsula. On campus for a visit in the fall of that year, he challenged a group of students to start an overseas service project. Under the joint sponsorship of the Student Council and the Foreign Missions Fellowship and encouraged by the College, the project began. Out of almost fifty applicants, twelve were selected and sent to Guatemala, Honduras, and Costa Rica." That was the beginning for Wheaton's short-term mission program, and since then they have sent students around the world every year on short-term mission endeavors. (A great book on the subject of Wheaton's involvement in missions is *From Wheaton to the Nations* by David M. Howard[3]). In 2002, Wheaton sent 80 students.

In **1959** the *Seventh-day Adventist Church* sent a junior premedical student to Mexico. This was the beginning of their Student Missionary program that has grown into what is now called 'Adventist Youth Service Volunteers.'[4] Thousands of students have gone out since that time.

1960s

You can't mention short-term mission without pondering Loren Cunningham and *Youth With a Mission*. YWAM began in **1960** as an evangelistic outreach program focused on getting youth into short-term mission. According to their website, "it is now one of the largest interdenominational and international Christian ministries, with about 12,000 volunteer staff based in over 800 locations ... In addition, tens of thousands more people from scores of nations are involved on a short-term basis each year."[5] YWAM has certainly had an impact in thousands of lives during their more than 40 years. For year 2000, YWAM's website lists 10,940 full time staff and 38,608 short-termers in 134 different nations. Yet when speaking off the record with some YWAM leaders, unofficial estimates run as high as 200,000 to 300,000 short-termers per year. YWAM may be the single largest short-term mission agency in the world.

Greater Europe Mission started in 1949. Linda Weber quotes a publication describing GEM: "In the early '60s the summer teams for ministry in Europe was developed. This concept was pioneered by GEM as the first mission agency to seek to enlist college young people for an 8- to 10-week ministry in the summer ... In **1963** the project was first tried at the European Bible Institute in Lamorlaye, France, with nine young people serving that summer, totally at their own expense."[6] Today GEM has short-term programs ranging from 2-weeks, to 6-weeks, to 3-months, to 6-months, to 1-year or longer.

The *Association of Baptists for World Evangelism* (ABWE) had it's original beginnings "in August of 1927. They sensed an urgent need to provide fundamental Baptist churches and individuals with a mission agency that stood true to the Word of God in both doctrine and method."[7] Kay Wharton, current ABWE staffer, says they didn't start any formal short-term mission program until the **early 1960s**. In 2002 ABEW sent more than 300 people to their fields on short-term mission endeavors.

SIM (Serving in Mission) began in 1893 as four separate organizations. Tim Jacobson of SIM Canada reports the first short-term missionaries from SIM went around **1961**. Then SIM staffer Howard Dowdell's proposed short-term mission experiment was unanimously rejected by the West African Field Council, but the West African Director vetoed the rejection, and "insisted we proceed with the plan as an experiment." During 2002, SIM Canada sent about 175 on 2-week to 2-year short-term programs.[8]

VISA Ministries officially launched in **August 1964** as a short-term mission program of the Free Methodist World Missions. That first year they sent four young men on various assignments to Hong Kong and Rhodesia. The following year three teams went out, and since then thousands of individuals and groups have gone. In 2002 VISA Ministries sent 895 short-termers.

Howard Culbertson, Professor of Missions at *Southern Nazarene University*, remembers their first mission team in **1966** very well (he was on that team). Culbertson told us the team was about 20 people who went to Mexico to finish construction on a church building that had already been started. SNU sent 260 people on various short-term mission outreaches in 2002.

In **1969** *Maranatha Volunteers International,* a short-term mission program from the Seventh-day Adventist Church exploded onto the scene. Their first 'flight' was a construction project in Freeport, Bahamas. A group of 28 youth and adults finished construction on a church building. Since then they have sent approximately 45,000 volunteers on short-term mission outreaches in 60 countries. Karen Godfry of Maranatha says in 2003 they will have sent approximately 3,000 on short-term mission endeavors.

1970s

Scott Bessenecker reports *InterVarsity Christian Fellowship*'s first short-term team was a group of students sent to Costa Rica the summer of **1970** to do street evangelism, worship, Bible studies, and learn from the people on the field. During 2002 IVCF sent about 3,300 staff and students (two-thirds international, one-third domestic Urban)—about 1,300 of which were direct IVCF projects. The remaining 2,000 went out through other churches and agencies.

Cedarville University in Cedarville, Ohio, traces their short-term mission program back to **1971** when seven men went with the basketball coach to the Philippines to do sports evangelism. The school has been active since, with Brian Nester reporting they expect almost 300 to participate in their short-term mission programs during 2002.

The *Work and Witness* program of the Nazarene Church began in **1972** at the General NWMS (Nazarene World Mission Society) Convention. The denomination's James Hudson book notes, "It did not originate as a planned, structured program of the church, but was a volunteer effort on the part of the Nazarene laymen sincerely interested in becoming more personally involved in the successful missionary enterprise of their church."[9] Since then hundreds of teams and thousands of men and women have participated in the Nazarene Churches Work and Witness program.

Jenny Collins of *Taylor University* traces Taylor's short-term program to **1972**. She wrote, "It was a practicum experience for students majoring in Christian Education. A team of nine students was selected to present Christian Education workshops for Christian workers in Nassau, Bahamas." That team remained for a month. Collins reports they'll send 200 students in 2002.

Clearly a powerhouse of short-term mission sending is the *International Mission Board of the Southern Baptist Convention*. Bill Cashion told us they expect around 35,000 people to participate in their denominational short-term mission program during 2003. Another employee estimates an additional 30,000 or more Southern Baptist short-termers go out annually without going through denominational headquaters. Originally the IMB began in 1845, but didn't launch their short-term program until **1976** using the name 'Major City Evangelism.' The name has changed twice, and is now 'Volunteers in Mission.'

Russell Blanchard, in his May 1990 Doctoral Thesis gave a short history on the United Methodist Church. "The first effort in *The United Methodist Church* to address directly the call to be in short-term service, in a way that many in the church could be a part of that ministry, was begun in the late **1970s**. It eventually was called 'United Methodist Volunteers in Mission.' In the program, lay and clergy people gave several weeks to several months to travel to a mission field, at their expense, to take part in a mission project."[10]

SEND International traces its roots back to 1945 when "God opened amazing doors during WWII when young military men and women caught a vision to start churches and a Bible school in the Philippines and Japan."[11] Terri Hughes, SEND's coordinator for short-term mission says that in "**1970**, 80 individuals went to Japan, Philippines and then Taiwan ... we started with four to six each year and then we got up to 20 to 25 by around 1980. Around 1990 we started sending out groups and expanded our countries." Hughes projects in 2003 SEND will send 400 people on short-term mission.

Central American Mission (CAM) was founded in 1890 after Dr. C. I. Scofield went on a short-term mission to Costa Rica. CAM began as a sending agency focused on career missionaries. They didn't start any kind of formal short-term program until around **1975**.

According to Kendon Wheeler of *New Life League International*, they began in 1954, but didn't do their first organized short-term mission until **1976**. Wheeler says, "It consisted of some 100 pastors and evangelists and lay leaders who came down to conduct an evangelistic campaign in the large soccer station in Guatemala City. This was organized primarily in response to a massive earthquake that hit Guatemala City in February of that same year."

Hyacinth Urquhart of *Ministries in Action* notes they incorporated in 1961, but sent their first short-term mission team to Haiti in **1978**. Urquhart says, "A prayer cell began under a mango tree and quickly grew into a church, but there was no building to house the group. Funds were raised through Ministries in Action, and its first short-term mission team was recruited from Pennsylvania." The church building was completed within the week that first team arrived. During 2003 they plan to send around 420 individuals on short-term mission outreaches.

Northwest Medical Teams International was established in **1979**, and sent their first short-term medical team that very same year to Thailand. According to Debbie Doty, that team provided medical aid to refugees of the killing fields in Cambodia. And during 2003, they plan to send more than 1,000 people on short-term medical teams.

Angie Seldon, from the short-term department at *Pioneers*, told us they sent their first short-term mission in the same year the organization began. In **1979** they sent a team to Papua New Guinea and Irian Jaya. They taught at a Christian Training Center and did evangelism. Pioneers expects to have sent about 250 on short-term mission in 2002 through their program, 'The Edge.'

Since 1942 *New Tribes Mission* has been involved in missions ministry. But it wasn't until **1979** that they officially sent their first short-term mission team. Lisa Kappeler of NTM describes that first short-term mission this way: "The idea was to take a team into a tribe for eight weeks to handle some physical work and be an aid to the career missionaries in that way. If we did the physical side of it, the missionaries could continue working on language and culture instead of physical stuff." NTM sent about 200 people during 2002.

Brian Heerwagen, Executive Director for *Delta Ministries*, informed us their organization officially began in **1979** when they sent their first mission team. He writes that it was an "all summer long ministry in the Western United States and Northern Mexico. The work included VBS, work projects, concerts and community outreach such as door to door surveys or park programs." Delta has enjoyed continued growth since that first summer, and sent 465 people on short-term mission throughout 2002.

1980s

OC International began ministry in 1951. But David Armstrong notes, "as far as continual short-term mission program, the year would be **1980**; before that there were some individuals who went for one or two years." That first group of 12 did evangelism through ESL (English as a Second Language) in Taiwan. During 2002 OC sent out about 35 people for periods of 2-weeks to 2-years.

The Presbyterian Church of America's mission program is called *Mission to the World*. MTW began in 1973, and their short-term program in **1980** when MTW sent five students on two-year missions to Japan and Mexico. MTW's Joe Brand says they expect to send around 7,500 short-termers in 2003.

Although *Northwestern College* (Orange City, Iowa) began in 1882, their 'Summer of Service' program did not kick off until **1981**. It began with 14 students going to Guatemala, Mexico, Hong Kong, Spain, Papua New Guinea, Kentucky, and Alaska for the summer. Jill Erickson notes they expect about 280 from NWC on short-term mission outreaches in 2002.

Perimeter Church (3,500 members; 5,000 weekly worshippers), Atlanta, began in 1977. Laura Dill reports by 1979 Perimeter held its first mission conference, and in **1982** sent their first short-termer (two-years) to Sudan. Perimeter's first short-term team went in 1986. Working now primarily with national church planting partners, their 'Global Outreach (GO)' mission department sends short-term 'GO Journey' teams to first assist the long-term efforts of their church-planting partners, and second to develop world Christians in goer-guests. In 2002 Perimeter sent 175 people on GO Journey teams.

Jack Isleib, Executive Director of *Christian Outreach International*, says they got started in 1984. Their first team was a group of 11 guys in **1985** who went to the United Kingdom to play basketball as a platform to share the Gospel. Isleib said they anticipate sending 2,500 people in 2002.

STEM Int'l was begun exclusively as a short-term mission sending agency by Roger Peterson in 1984, sending their first short-term mission team in **1985** to Haiti. STEM now works in more than a dozen nations, and anticipates sending more than 400 people on 2-week short-term mission teams during 2003.

World Servants was organized in 1985 and sent their first team in **1986**. That first team was a large group with 250 people going to the Dominican Republic for construction and outreach. Jeff Jones says they expect to send about 3,500 short-termers during 2003.

Rob Carter of *JARON Ministries International* notes they sent their first short-term mission four years before their formal launch in 1990. In **1986**, they sent six to the Philippines to provide pastoral training conferences in a number of cities. In 2003 they expect about 140 people to participate in short-term mission through their efforts.

Randy Schmor, *Gateway Teams,* expects to send about 300 short-termers in 2003. Gateway is the short-term arm of the North American Baptist Conference begun in **1987** when a team went to Cameroon for construction work.

Holly McCleary of *WEC International* (Worldwide Evangelization for Christ) tells us her organization officially started their short-term mission program in **April 1988**. Originally called 'THRUST Ministries,' the now-named WEC Trek was established to serve WEC missionaries on-field. WEC also uses short-term mission as a tool for recruiting career missionaries. According to their website, WEC's short-termers go out for up to 9 months.*[12]*

Sometime during **1987** or **1988**, *Christ Covenant Church* of Matthews, North Carolina, sent their first short-term mission team—an outreach which helped propel the church's overall mission program. In 2003 they will send 18 teams (about 12 or 13 in each team) to work along side their national church planting partners. For the international portion of their mission program, Christ Covenant now raises around $250,000 through Faith Promise every year.

Adam Henry, *Food for the Hungry,* informed us FH started in 1971. He also noted FH's first short-term team was in the **late 1980s**. FH's "short-term department, when first established, desired to take North Americans to our foreign fields to not only experience another culture, but to serve and meet children in our Child Development Program." They have been very active in short-term mission since then, and anticipate sending about 550 people for 2003.

In **1988** *Teen Mania Ministries* was founded in Tulsa, Oklahoma by Ron and Katie Luce. The next summer, 60 teenagers went on the first Teen Mania mission to Guatemala. Teen Mania's short-term cross cultural mission program is called 'Global Expedition.' In a phone interview, Heidi Stevens told us in 2002 they sent 4,031, and in 2003 they expect to send more than 6,000.

In March of **1989**, Don and Gayle Sommerfeld organized a group of 14 people to go to Haiti. They were there to rebuild a church. That outreach led to eight more, and in 1992 *MOST Ministries* was officially incorporated. Since then 89 teams have gone out to do everything from English camps to medical teams. Their website lists 22 more teams scheduled for 2003.[13]

1990s

The 1990s saw such incredible growth in the short-term mission movement (cf. ILLUSTRATION #11.1), that we can't begin to adequately detail the thousands of organized short-term mission programs that began that decade. We note, however, that from our simple observations it is clear that individual church-based short-term mission programs have moved to center stage. Quite a number of churches now develop their own in-house programs, functioning as a short-term sending entity dedicated entirely to the membership of their church (an SE-2.c or SE-2.d sending entity—cf. TABLE #3.7 and TABLE #6.1).

One example is *Southeast Christian Church*, Louisville, Kentucky. SECC began in 1965, growing in less than 40 years to more than 17,000 weekly worshippers. SECC's first short-term mission was a large team of 60 people (too big, says Global Missions Minister Brian Wright) to Jamaica in **1990**. Wright reports for 2002 that SECC sent 57 short-term teams—more than 750 SECC members—to 20 different nations. Their 'Great Adventure' mission outreaches go only to SECC-supported partners, and are planned within three levels: (a) Exploration (closer, easier, less costly, about five days); (b) Excursion (outside the U.S., more cross-culture, about 10 days); and (c) Expedition (culturally and geographically far away, two weeks or longer).

Nebulous (Yet Revealing) Numbers

THIS CHAPTER presents but a sampling of what we could have reported, and of what is actually happening. We believe there may be thousands of other worthy churches and other sending entities that deserve to be listed here and are not. We have only been able to summarize 45 case studies extracted from 61 survey responses and other informal research of our own.

To really understand the scope of the short-term mission movement from the 1990s and into the 2000s and beyond, let's briefly consider *how little we actually know* concerning the total number of short-term mission goer-guests sent by the three largest categories of U.S.-based sending entities:

1. *Churches*

   No one we could find has *empirically* determined the current number of U.S. churches believed to be involved in short-term mission. However, from our anecdotal and other subjective research, we conjecture that 10% of U.S. churches have done, or are currently doing, some form or another of short-term mission.[14] **This means probably 35,000 U.S. churches are doing short-term mission.** If each church sends an average of 12 people every year, U.S. churches would be sending 420,000 short-termers. If it's 40 per church, the annual total would be 1.4 *million* short-termers.

2. *Mission Agencies*

   The *Missions Handbook* (18th Edition 2001–2003) lists 693 U.S.-based mission agencies. During 1999 these agencies reported 106,017 short-termers (6,930 one-year to four-years; 1,815 non-residential missionaries; and 97,272 two-week to one-year), or an average of 130 goer-guests per group. Sensing there were yet other agencies, EFMA president Paul McKaughan had the Network for Strategic Mission search the I.R.S. 501(c)(3) database in 2001 for other groups. By using more than 100 key word searches they determined another possible 3,000 U.S. evangelical nonprofits were involved in international mission efforts. **This means probably 3,700 North American agencies are doing some form of short-term mission.** If each of these 3,700 groups sends the same average of 130 short-termers, U.S. agencies would be sending 481,000 goer-guests each year (note that there would be some overlap between churches and agencies).

3. *Schools*

   The Council for Christian Colleges and Universities lists 103 member institutions of higher learning. We estimate most, if not all, have some kind of program for short-term mission. In addition to the CCCU would be thousands (literally) of Christian grade schools, junior high schools, senior high schools, and home schools—many of which we suspect are involved in some hands-on aspect of short-term mission. *This means probably more than 1,000 North American schools are doing some form of short-term mission.*

John Kyle was right. It is undeniable that a giant lives within our broader community of faith. That giant is the short-term mission movement. In the United States alone, the giant represents 40,000 probable sending entities (primarily the churches, agencies, and schools we summarized above). If each sending entity sends an average of 15 short-termers each year, that's 600,000 goer-guests. If each sends an average of 100 per year, that's 4,000,000.

Modern Influences

FROM such a short sampling, it would be dangerous to try to come to any definite conclusions on influences that 'created' the modern short-term mission movement. A well-known axiom in statistics is this: *correlation does not imply causation*. For example, wherever you find a lot of churches you also find a higher crime rate. But just because there are a lot of churches in a city does not mean they cause crime. In fact, high population rates cause both high crime rates and a high number of churches. But if you just looked at churches and crimes you might wrongly conclude one causes the other.

Similarly, there are some things we believe have had an impact on the growth of short-term mission in the last 50 years. They may not be the only cause of the explosive growth, but they have had an undeniable effect.

Consider the end of World War II in 1945. Many mission societies began soon after the war ended. There was a flood of young, energetic, enthusiastic young people coming home from the war. Many had traveled far and wide. They had seen the world first hand. For the first time in history we saw relatively young people who had experience in world-wide travel and who now had a global perspective. Combine that with a passion for God's Glory among the lost, and it's easy to see why Christian mission exploded after the war.

The importance of affordable air travel is not to be understated. The air transportation industry began in 1914 (St. Petersburg, Florida to Tampa, Florida). However, comfortable pressurized air transports became available in large numbers *after* WWII (1939–1945), when there were fewer than 300 planes in the public's service. The idea of the average citizen flying commercially didn't really take hold until the 1950s when more planes were in the air, air travel was not seen as the exclusive domain of the rich or the military, and the cost of a flight was within the financial reach of more citizens.

It is interesting to note that several mission societies began tinkering with short-term efforts in the 1950s. This is exactly the time young people from the war (now 10 years more mature) would have been exerting increased leadership influence. This is also when commercial air travel opened up to the masses. These two factors may not have been the cause, but they are certainly some dominate influences that need to be noted.

In the 1960s President John Kennedy launched the Peace Corps, which has sent 168,000 Americans to more than 135 countries since 1961. After a day of campaigning, Kennedy

"arrived at the University of Michigan in Ann Arbor on October 14, 1960, at 2:00 a.m., to get some sleep, not to propose the establishment of an international volunteer organization. Members of the press had retired for the night, believing that nothing interesting would happen. But 10,000 students at the University were waiting to hear the presidential candidate speak, and it was there on the steps of the Michigan Union that a bold new experiment in public service was launched. The assembled students heard the future President issue a challenge: how many of them, he asked, would be willing to serve their country and the cause of peace by living and working in the developing world?"[15]

This government-sanctioned 'blessing' to travel abroad, to volunteer time to make a difference in a developing country for a cause greater than one's self—did this have a positive impact on the contemporary Christian short-term mission movement? We think it did.

Also not to be taken lightly is the advent of the internet, e-mail, and other related technological breakthroughs. Now contact with far away places is no longer the domain of the news media or the highly networked socialite. Average people can talk with missionaries in far away places, making the world seem a much smaller place. Before the internet, 'Joe *the missionary*' was someone we heard about from the pulpit on Sunday nights. Now, going 5,000 miles to help 'Joe *my friend*' is revolutionizing Christian mission.

The ever shrinking world after WWII, modern affordable air travel, the Peace Corps, and the internet. All four have had a part in making short-term mission a household word in the evangelical community. But when all other influences are exhausted, we admit that without the Holy Spirit's empowerment, the movement will only sputter and fail. Yet from the brief contemporary history we've researched for this chapter, we do conclude the short-term mission movement is powered by God Himself. (Note we said the short-term *mission* movement, not the cross-cultural *trip* movement—cf. Chapter 8). We believe it's the Spirit of God, breathing through His children—His real fools—who are somehow succeeding in bringing even more Glory to God the Father.

Summary

FOR THE YEAR 1965 student researcher Thomas Chandler noted 'only' 540 individuals from North America involved in short-term mission. In 1989 another estimate put the number at 120,000. Three years later it had more than doubled to 250,00.[16] Today, we estimate at least 1,000,000 short-termers are sent out from a globally-sent perspective every year (cf. ILLUSTRATION #11.1). And considering just the 40,000 U.S. sending entities alone, it is highly probable that our estimate of one million short-termers is actually far too conservative.

Will these numbers continue to increase? Will there even be a need to physically go somewhere to promote the Gospel when digital technology can place your image and voice anywhere in the world at anytime? How will 'electronic relationships' affect evangelism and short-term mission? Time will tell, but we believe relationships still matter. They are key to true knowledge, true change, true Christian mission. *Buildings* don't lead people to Christ, or attend to widows and orphans, or alter the corrupt structures of the greedy world; *people* do. And however human relationship happens in the future, we are confident that God's Kingdom can only be given through real people (real fools) interacting with other real people.

Endnotes
Chapter 11

1. *(p. 242)* **Tim Gibson, Steve Hawthorne, Richard Krekel, Kn Moy, eds.**, *Stepping Out—A Guide to Short Term Missions* (Seattle WA: YWAM Publishing, 1992), p. 5.

2. *(p. 242)* Cf. http://www.friendsofludhiana.org and also **Douglas E. Millham**, *Short-Term Missions: A Model for Mobilizing the Church* (Pasadena CA: Fuller Theological Seminary Doctoral Dissertation, 1988), p. 19, available UM 8816058.

3. *(p. 245)* **David M. Howard**, *From Wheaton to the Nations* (no publisher information listed, © 2001 by David M. Howard, no ISBN).

4. *(p. 245)* **Randal R. Wisbey**, *Collegiate Missions in the Context of Short-Term Mission Experiences*, D. Min. Thesis (Washington DC: Wesley Theological Seminary, 1990), p. 3.

5. *(p. 245)* Cf. http://www.http://ywam.org.

6. *(p. 246)* **Robert J. Cambell**, *Light for the Night in Europe* (Tyndale Publishing Co., 1999), pp. 165–166, no ISBN.

7. *(p. 246)* Cf. http://www.http://abwe.org.

8. *(p. 246)* Some information in this paragraph extracted from: http://www.http://sim.org.

9. *(p. 247)* Cf. **James Hudson**, *Work and Witness—One of the Great Success Stories of Nazarene Missions* (Kansas City MO: Nazarene Publishing House, 1983). 83 pp., ISBN 0-8341-0821-6.

10. *(p. 248)* Cf. **Russell H. Blanchard**, *A Manual for Leaders of Overseas Short-Term Volunteer Work Camps of the Central Pennsylvania Conference of the United Methodist Church* (Philadelphia PA: Eastern Baptist Theological Seminary DMIN Thesis, 1990), available UM 9026395.

11. *(p. 248)* Cf. http://www.http://send.org.

12. *(p. 250)* Cf. http://www.wec-int.org.

13. *(p. 251)* Cf. http://www.mostministries.org.

14. *(p. 252)* ACMC's President Jim Killgore notes that George Barna's research puts the number of U.S. Protestant churches at about 350,000. Killgore's staff also believes that only one out of every seven of these churches, or 14%, have possibly sent at least one cross-cultural worker at one time or another. This means 50,000 churches may have had at least some missionary sending activity. That's why we're comfortable with our 'conservative' estimate of 10%, or 35,000 U.S. churches doing some form or another of short-term mission.

15. *(p. 254)* Cf. http://www.peacecorps.gov/about/history/decades/index.cfm

16. *(p. 255)* For these three estimates, cf. **Thomas W. Chandler**, *A Statistical Study of Short Term Missions*, MA Thesis (Pasadena CA: Fuller Theological Seminary, 1972), p. iii; and **John A. Siewert and John A. Kenyon**, eds., *Mission Handbook: A Guide to*

USA/Canada Christian Ministries Overseas, 15th Edition (Monrovia CA: MARC) 1992, p. 57; and **Gordon Aeschliman and Laurie Berry Clifford**, eds., "Who's Going on Short-Term Missions?," *The Short-Term Missions Handbook* (Evanston IL: Berry Publishing, 1992), p. 16.

A POST-SCRIPT PERSPECTIVE

Getting to the Heart of the Journey

by *GORDON AESCHLIMAN*

NE OF MY FONDEST, PERSONAL MEMORIES OF SHORT-term mission occurred in northern Nicaragua. I was there not long after Hurricane Mitch smashed its way through Central America, leaving close to 20,000 people dead in a period of two weeks. Hundreds of thousands more were stranded—yielded homeless and cropless by that terrible calamity.

On one of the long, hot afternoons there, I came up short on energy from a day of exposure to the cruelties of human poverty and the impotence of my own doctrinal commitments to make sense of all the suffering and destruction. One of mission's ironies was displayed that afternoon on the back of a t-shirt donned by a short-term missionary—"Jesus, the Living Water of Life." A truly strange message for people who had just been demolished by the Creator's water.

I cannot forget the welcome I received that afternoon by a Nicaraguan mother whose own world had been thrown topsy turvy by Mitch. (I only had to deal with doctrinal topsy turvy—she had to live with the whole package). This mother recognized my exhaustion and she invited me under the protection of some palm fronds that served as a ceiling supported on twisted tree limbs. No walls in this home. She had made some tortillas from scratch over an open fire and served me one together with some beans and sweetened water. She may as well have been Jesus and I the beggar invited to the banquet of a gracious host. "The body of Christ broken for you," is what went through my mind when she handed me the tortilla.

I flew all the way to Nicaragua to do good for the poor and instead I found myself the surprised recipient of grace. This mother called my own spirituality to account—not through condemnation or judgment, but through kindness and an attentive spirit. I remember feeling the impoverishment of my own spirituality at that moment—a kind of emptiness in my soul because my doctrine and faith came up wanting. She introduced thirst back into my spirit and I thank Christ for that moment.

In our struggles to see the saving, graceful hand of God at work in the world, we have at times been overwhelmed by the immensity of the need 'out there.' We have faced the age-old philosopher's horns of dilemma: either we believe in a God who is all loving but not powerful enough to save the world from evil, or we believe in a God who is powerful enough to save the whole world from evil but who is not loving enough to do so. My hunch is that a lot of mission work has been based on that second of those two heretical notions.

The uses and functions of short-term mission are myriad—as this book so aptly illustrates. Who could have predicted the explosion in size and form of this industry? Not that a booming industry is of itself a virtue—everything but the economy seems to be growing these days. We build bigger churches, bigger bodies and bigger militaries. But it is clear that churches and colleges throughout the United States and Canada have embraced this enterprise as a central part of their lives. Short-term mission is going to continue its growth curve. The question is, to what end?

There's something at the core of short-term mission that is hard to measure, but it could be the very point of Christian mission. I believe it has to do with our spiritual pilgrimage—a demanding, revolutionary journey that if truly embraced requires much moral courage and high spiritual motivations. I think the key irony of short-term mission is that it turns out not to be merely the journey of thousands of miles to a distant land, but the journey to the center of our own hearts. We can rack up the frequent flyer miles, eat strange foods, share the four spiritual laws, build houses, preach sermons and perform miracles all the while missing the journey of our heart's pathway. Short-term mission at its best will raise both the disturbing and welcoming questions for our souls. It will invite us into a deeper work of transformation. It will come at a great price as we begin to discover that parts of our faith story have become confused with our own national story line, with a political and economic paradigm that don't necessarily line up with the Jesus of Nazareth.

I'm a fan of short-term mission because I believe it is one of our last good hopes as North Americans to get a truer grasp of what it means to live out the life of Jesus in today's world. We live in a day where, in the past 100 years, we have killed more civilians in wars than in all of the previous centuries of human history put together. More than one billion people live on less than a dollar a day. More than two billion people have absolutely no access to clean water. Our natural home, the earth, is being stretched beyond its ability to recover from our excessive plundering of its wealth to support our consumerism. As our nation looks to establish a new sense of its own identity in the wake of September 11, we are sorely tempted to find ourselves defined by strength, military might, and superiority (the leaders of the axis of good). We truly need to be revisited by Jesus of Nazareth in these times. As we humbly engage other cultures—offering them our best gifts of service and our best sense of the Good News, perhaps we will allow our hearts to become students of the gifts from those cultures, of the bounty they have to offer our own impoverished souls and rigid world views. Perhaps we'll discover in the mutual exchange of our humanity that what we have to offer is the tenderness and the welcome of a mother at the side of a road who can make a meal for a stranger out of the leftovers of devastation. There's a kind of purity in here that makes my heart thirsty for Christ and thirsty to love my neighbor as I love myself.

Short-Term Mission Typology in Outlined Definition Format

(see end of Addendum "B" for explanation of abbreviations used in this typology)

1. MISSION—*full definition* (ACTIVE VERB)

Sending messengers (missionaries) away from their 'normal' home culture as soon as possible, and into another culture and people (intended receptors), for the express purpose of proclaiming with word and deed (intended activities) the Good News that sets any person free from anything that binds them.

    1.1.1 Send away

    1.1.2 Into another culture

    1.1.3 A messenger to proclaim the freeing Good News

        1.1.3.1 by announcing in word

        1.1.3.2 by demonstrating with deed

1.1 Mission—*simplified definition* (ACTIVE VERB)

Sending active Gospel messengers into another culture.

1.2 Missionary

A person intentionally sent into another culture to be an active Gospel messenger in both word and deed *(relates to #2.5.1 and #5.2 below)*.

1.3 Short-Term Mission *(defined in paragraph #3 below)*

2. STM DEFINING VARIABLES *(see also Addendum "B")*

The eight primary defining characteristics, containing 69 major sub-categories, of short-term mission.

2.1 *Time*—The length, term, span, or duration of on-field mission service *(corresponds exactly to #3.4 below).*

	69 Sub-Categories
2.1.1 Mini *(measured by days)*	1
2.1.2 Standard *(measured by weeks)*	2
2.1.3 Seasonal *(measured by months)*	3
2.1.4 Extended *(measured by years)*	4

2.2 **Activity**—The goer-guests' intended on-field 'giving/sowing' focus (cf. Chapter 3, variable #2) which consists of the following 16 major task classifications *(corresponds exactly to #6.1.1 below)*.

2.5 ***Participant Demographics***—The five primary identifiers each of the goer-guests, field facilitators, and intended receptor participants *(related to #5.2 and #5.3 below)*.

2.6 ***Sending Entity***—The four primary structures which administer and manage sending-side responsibilities; the sending entity *(corresponds exactly to #5.1.2 below)* is the counterpart and liaison to the field facilitators.

2.7 ***Mission Philosophy***—The mission definition, ministry values, and ministry expectations of the sending entity, goer-guests, field facilitators, and intended receptor participants.

2.8 ***Leadership and Training***—Influencing followers toward God's agenda for the short-term outreach (as mutually determined by the sending entity and field facilitators); and providing effective transfer of knowledge, skill, and attitude to maximize the impact of the short-term outreach.

3. SHORT-TERM MISSION *(STM)*

The God-commanded, repetitive deployment of swift, temporary, non-professional missionaries.

3.1 *God-commanded*

3.2 *Repetitive Deployment*

3.3 *Swift*

3.4 *Temporary* (corresponds exactly to #2.1 above)

3.5 *Non-professional Missionaries*

4. PROCESS TRILOGY

The three periods of consecutive linear time through which any given short-term mission exists as an identifiable commodity.

4.1 *Pre-field*

4.2 *On-field*

4.3 *Post-field*

5. STM PARTICIPANT TRILOGY

The three mega-sets of people always involved in any short-term mission endeavor: Senders, Goer-Guests, and Host Receivers (Senders, Goers, and Receivers are all assumed to be equal participants in any short-term mission endeavor).

5.1 ***Sender Participants***

    5.1.1 Sending Supporters

        5.1.1.1 *SS*—Prayer Supporters

        5.1.1.2 *SS*—Financial Supporters

        5.1.1.3 *SS*—Logistical Supporters

        5.1.1.4 *SS*—Emotional Supporters

        5.1.1.5 *SS*—Communication Supporters

        5.1.1.6 *SS*—Re-Entry Supporters

    5.1.2 Sending Entity (corresponds exactly to #2.6 above)

        5.1.2.1 *SE*—Churches

        5.1.2.2 *SE*—Parachurch Mission Agencies

        5.1.2.3 *SE*—Institutional Non-mission Organizations

        5.1.2.4 *SE*—Self

5.2 ***Goer-Guest Participants***—The 'cultural outsiders' who temporarily enter a given on-field *ETHNOS* to work and serve as missionaries *(relates to #1.2 and #2.5.1 above)*.

    5.2.1 *GL*—Goer-Guest Leaders

    5.2.2 *GL*—Goer-Guest Followers

5.3 ***Host Receiver Participants***—The on-site people and organizations of a short-term mission *(relates to #2.4, #2.5.2, and #2.5.3 above)*

    5.3.1 Field Facilitators

        5.3.1.1 Local/National People and Organizations
- SE-Related
- SE-Contracted

        5.3.1.2 Same-Culture (as GGs) Expatriate People & Organiz'ns
- SE-Related
- SE-Contracted

        5.3.1.3 Other-Culture (than GGs or IRs) Expatriate People and Organizations
- SE-Related
- SE-Contracted

    5.3.2 Intended Receptors

        5.3.2.1 Human Beings

        5.3.2.2 Non-human Elements of God's Creation

        5.3.2.3 Structures and Systems of Man's Creation

6. THE RECIPROCITY OF GIVE 'N TAKE

The two-way on-field serendipity between Goer-Guests and Host Receivers of 'giving/sowing' and of 'getting/reaping.'

6.1 ***Giving/Sowing***

    6.1.1 by the Goers, *to* the Receivers *(corresponds exactly to the "Activity" Defining Variable of #2.2 above)*

    6.1.2 by the Receivers, *to* the Goers

6.2 ***Receiving/Reaping***

    6.2.1 by the Goers, *from* the Receivers

    6.2.2 by the Receivers, *from* the Goers

Short-Term Mission Defining Variables in Horizontal Relational Format

The eight primary defining characteristics of short-term mission and how they relate to their 69 major sub-categories.

(NOTE: all left-side numbers correlate directly to the outline of Addendum "A")

(see end of Addendum "B" for explanation of abbreviations used)

69 Sub-Categories

2.1 Time
- 2.1.1 Mini — *1*
- 2.1.2 Standard — *2*
- 2.1.3 Seasonal — *3*
- 2.1.4 Extended — *4*

2.2 Activity

2.2.1 Evangelism
- 2.2.1.1 *1*—Proclamation — *5*
- 2.2.1.2 *2*—Church Planting — *6*
- 2.2.1.3 *3*—Spiritual Warfare — *7*
- 2.2.1.4 *4*—Bible Translation — *8*

2.2.2 Witnessing
- 2.2.2.1 *5*—Social Ministry — *9*
- 2.2.2.2 *6*—The Arts — *10*
- 2.2.2.3 *7*—Sports Outreach — *11*
- 2.2.2.4 *8*—Manifestational Gifts — *12*
- 2.2.2.5 *9*—Multiple Activities With Given IR Grp — *13*

2.2.3 Discipleship
- 2.2.3.1 *10*—Disciple Making — *14*
- 2.2.3.2 *11*—Education-Giving (Teaching) — *15*
- 2.2.3.3 *12*—Education-Receiving (Info Acq'n) — *16*

2.2.4 Helps
- 2.2.4.1 *13*—Construction Work & Physical Labor — *17*
- 2.2.4.2 *14*—Blue Collar Program Spprt Services — *18*
- 2.2.4.3 *15*—White Collar Program Spprt Services — *19*
- 2.2.4.4 *16*—Hospitality — *20*

2.7 Mission Philosophy

2.7.1 the Sending Entity
- 2.7.1.1 *SE*—Mission Definition — *50*
- 2.7.1.2 *SE*—Ministry Values — *51*
- 2.7.1.2 *SE*—Ministry Expectations — *52*

2.7.2 the Goer-Guest Participants
- 2.7.2.1 *GG*—Mission Definition — *53*
- 2.7.2.2 *GG*—Ministry Values — *54*
- 2.7.2.2 *GG*—Ministry Expectations — *55*

2.7.3 the HR Field Facilitator Participants
- 2.7.3.1 *FF*—Mission Definition — *56*
- 2.7.3.2 *FF*—Ministry Values — *57*
- 2.7.3.2 *FF*—Ministry Expectations — *58*

2.7.4 the HR Intended Receptor Participants
- 2.7.3.1 *FF*—Mission Definition — *59*
- 2.7.3.2 *FF*—Ministry Values — *60*
- 2.7.3.2 *FF*—Ministry Expectations — *61*

2.8 Leadership and Training

2.8.1 Leadership Effectiveness upon the Goer Guests
- 2.8.1.1 *LE-GG*—pre-field — *62*
- 2.8.1.2 *LE-GG*—on-field — *63*
- 2.8.1.3 *LE-GG*—post-field — *64*

2.8.1 Training Effectiveness upon the Goer Guests
- 2.8.1.1 *TE-GG*—pre-field — *65*
- 2.8.1.2 *TE-GG*—on-field — *66*
- 2.8.1.3 *TE-GG*—post-field — *67*

2.8.3 Training Effectiveness upon the Host Receivers
- 2.8.3.1 *TE-HR*—Field Facilitators — *68*
- 2.8.3.2 *TE-HR*—Intended Receptors — *69*

Abbreviations Used in Addenda "A" and "B"

FF	Field Facilitator	*LE*	Leadership Effectiveness
GF	Goer-Guest Follower	*SE*	Sending Entity
GL	Goer-Guest Leader	*SS*	Sending Supporter
GG	Goer-Guest	*STM*	Short-Term Mission
HR	Host Receiver	*TE*	Training Effectiveness
IR	Intended Receptor		

The Code of Best Practice for Short-Term Mission

EFC—The Evangelical Fellowship of Canada
www.globalmission.org

(reprinted by permission from the EFC)

The EFC Code of Best Practice in Short-Term Mission is designed to apply to all visits, experiences, teams, and placements of up to two years duration, organized by Canadian mission agencies, churches and other organizations. Though formed initially with cross-cultural contexts in mind, it can apply to both same-culture and cross-cultural situations, in Canada and overseas. It is a Code of Best Practice. Our motivation is based on our desire that God be glorified in all that we do. We also recognize our responsibility toward all participants and partners in our programs, that we serve them to the highest standards possible. The Code does not necessarily indicate current achievement, but rather our aspirations towards high standards in short-term mission practice. Nonetheless some minimum accomplishments are implied in the Code. The Code is not intended to establish legal standards or liability.

Adopting the Code should therefore be seen as a step in a process rather than an end in itself. It is recognized that not every situation permits a literal application of every element of the Code. For example, a sending local church involvement on rare occasions is not always a reality. Nevertheless it is desirable, and so must be included in a Code of Best Practice. In every case where literal application is impossible, consideration must be given to the question of who may have equivalent responsibilities.

In addition, this Code has some underlying core values, which include:
1. *A commitment to culturally appropriate expressions of lifestyle and ministry activities.*
2. *A commitment to all the stakeholders in short-term mission, the participants, sending local church, mission agency, and host church and/or ministry.*
3. *A commitment to partnership and co-operation.*
4. *A commitment, wherever possible, to communicate as early and as fully as possible.*

SECTION 1: AIMS AND OBJECTIVES

1.1   A Short-Term Mission program will have a defined purpose within Christian mission.

1.2   A Short-Term Mission program will have clear and realistic aims and objectives, which include viability, expectations of outcomes, and consideration of how the program serves the long-term objectives of all those involved.

1.3   The benefits to, and responsibilities of, the participant, the sending organization, the sending local church, the host organization and the host local church will be clearly defined and communicated.

1.4   Partnerships will be established, as far as possible, with host local churches and communities. These relationships, in the context of unity love, will be defined in terms of agreed-upon priorities, ownership, and expectations.

1.5   Appropriate sending local church involvement will be sought. A partnership will be developed, as far as is feasible, between the agency, participant and sending local church.

1.6   There will be a commitment to the participant to provide opportunities for personal and spiritual development throughout the experience.

SECTION 2: PUBLICITY, SELECTION AND ORIENTATION

2.1   Publicity materials will be accurate, truthful, and used with integrity.

2.2   Publicity will clearly represent the ethos and vision of the sending organization. It will not reflect negatively on the host culture or ministry. It will also define the purpose of the program in the terms of service, discipleship and vocation.

2.3   The application process, including timeline, all financial obligations and use of funds, will be clear and thorough.

2.4   A suitable selection process will be established, including selection criteria and screening. A pastoral care element will be included, regardless of whether or not the individual is accepted as a short-term participant.

2.5   It is essential that there is disclosure of the relevant details concerning the short-term participant between the church, agency and field.

2.6   Appropriate orientation and training will be given prior to departure, and/or after arrival on the field. Team leaders will be briefed on the orientation and training provided.

2.7   Preparatory information will be provided as early and as fully as possible.

2.8   Placement decisions and changes will be made with integrity and communicated clearly to all involved.

SECTION 3: FIELD MANAGEMENT AND PASTORAL CARE

3.1   Clear task aims, objectives, and job descriptions will be developed jointly by the sending and hosting leadership.

3.2   Home and field-based communication and reporting guidelines will be identified, implemented, and reviewed.

3.3 Mutually-defined lines of authority, supervision, communication, responsibility, and accountability will be established and implemented through regular reporting and/or meetings.

3.4 Pastoral Care and support structures will be provided, and respective responsibilities clarified with all parties.

3.5 Opportunities for spiritual, personal, and character development will be provided, promoted, and pursued.

3.6 Participants will agree to follow guidelines on behaviour, relationships, and financial management that are appropriate to the host culture.

3.7 Policies and procedures covering finances, healthcare and insurance, medical contingencies, security and evacuation, acts of terrorism or political violence, stress management and conflict resolution, misconduct, discipline, and grievances, will be established, communicated, and implemented as is appropriate.

3.8 Where and when requested, necessary equipping and training of hosts will be provided.

SECTION 4: RE-ENTRY SUPPORT, EVALUATION AND PROGRAM DEVELOPMENT
4.1 Re-entry debriefing and support will be seen as an integral part of the short-term package.

4.2 Re-entry preparation, including field evaluation, will begin prior to return.

4.3 The mission agency and sending local church will assist the participant through re-entry, including facing unresolved personal issues, and future opportunities and direction in discipleship and service.

4.4 Evaluation of the mission agency's procedures and performance will be filled out by the participant. (The agency's procedures will also be evaluated by local sending churches).

4.5 On the request of the host organization, an assessment of the host organization will be carried out in an appropriate way by the participant.

4.6 The results of evaluations will be communicated to relevant managers, for the improvement of future projects and the keeping of permanent records. Confidentiality, integrity, and accuracy are required.

in 3

Proposed

U.S. *Standards of Excellence in Short-Term Mission*

(Draft #3.1—February 2003)

www.STMstandards.org *and* www.FSTML.org

(reprinted by permission from the FSTML)

The proposed U.S. 'Standards of Excellence in Short-Term Mission' are being facilitated by FSTML (the Fellowship of Short-Term Mission Leaders)—a U.S. 501(c)(3) nonprofit fellowship of churches, agencies, and schools. FSTML's mission is "Bringing God's Glory to the Nations by Promoting Increasingly Effective Short-Term Mission." Like the Canadian Code, The U.S. 'Standards' are not intended to establish legal standards or liability.

The following 'draft #3.1' document is only reprinted in part. Each of the seven proposed 'Standards' will have an entire supplemental page to fully describe each 'Standard.' This draft has been reprinted as of February 2003. FSTML anticipates finalization in October of 2003; wording, concepts, or even the number of 'Standards' could change by that time.

Introduction:

WE ACKNOWLEDGE that many people are affected by our involvement in short-term mission—some positively, some negatively, some whom we may never meet. We further acknowledge that short-term mission "participants" include not merely those who go, but those who send (III John 5–8) and those who receive (Matthew 10:40–42).

WE ALSO ACKNOWLEDGE that short-term mission is not an isolated event—but rather an integrated process over time affecting all participants. This process consists of pre-field, on-field, and post-field.

AS U.S-RELATED SHORT-TERM MISSION PRACTITIONERS,[†] we therefore desire to strengthen our overall effectiveness worldwide, by adopting and voluntarily committing ourselves to the following seven Standards of Excellence in our short-term mission efforts.

[†] *U.S.-related short-term mission practitioners include, but are not limited to:*
- *U.S.-based Sending Entities (churches, agencies, schools, other Christian sending groups)*
- *U.S.-related Field Facilitators (field-based churches, agencies, and other Christian receiving groups)*
- *non-profit organizations which provide support services to U.S.-related short-term mission efforts (STM conferences, STM trainers, STM affiliates, etc.)*

An Excellent Short-Term Mission:

1. *releases...* God-centered Kingdom Growth
Expressed in the lives of All Participants by:
- Sound Biblical Doctrine
- Persistent Prayer
- Integrity

2. *is based on...* Partnership between Sending and Receiving Sides
Expressed by:
- Primary Focus on Intended Receptors
- Planned Outcomes Which Benefit All Participants
- Mutual Accountability

3. *delivers a program which has been...* Mutually Designed by Sending and Receiving Sides
Expressed by:
- Common Philosophical Base and Alignment to Long-term Strategies/Mission
- Goer-Guests' Ability to Deliver (and Receive)
- Host Receivers' Ability to Deliver (and Receive)

4. *provides...* Reliable Set-up & Thorough Administration for All Participants
Expressed by:
- Sound Financial Practices
- Appropriate Risk Management
- Program Delivery and Support Logistics

5. *screens, trains, and provides...* Qualified Leadership for All Participants
Expressed:
- Pre-field Through Training and Equipping Leadership
- On-field Through Program Delivery and Support Leadership
- Post-field Through Debriefing and Follow-up Leadership

o r :   *Expressed by:*
- Spiritually Mature Servant Leadership
- Competent, Interculturally Experienced Leadership
- Empowering and Equipping Leadership
- Prepared, Organized and Accountable Leadership

6. *is evidenced by …* Participants Trained & Equipped to Deliver the Mutually Designed Program

Expressed by:

- Biblical, Appropriate, and Timely Training for All Participants
- Commitment to Continuous Training (Pre-field, On-field, Post-field)
- Qualified Trainers

7. *is committed to …* Thorough Debriefing & Follow-up for all Participants

Expressed by:

- Debriefing Throughout Entire Process (Pre-field, On-field, Post-field)
- Re-entry Preparation for Goer-Guests Prior to Leaving the Field
- Post-field Follow-up & Evaluations

Boarding Pass (used)
and Complementary Drink Voucher (unused)

TWA Flight #841, April 4, 1979

(from story on pages 173–175)

(technical details of the flight on next two pages)

Other Technical Details of
TWA Flight #841, April 4, 1979

As Reported by Roger Peterson

(from story on pages 173–175)

I SAT in window seat 21A (the smoking section back then) of TWA flight #841 from New York to Minneapolis, one of 82 passengers and seven crew members that night. We were cruising at 39,000 feet on a rather smooth flight; seat belt signs had been turned off. Flight attendants had cleared the evening meal. At about 9:30 that evening while in the vicinity over Saginaw, Michigan, the plane, a 14-year old Boeing 727-100, barrel-rolled one and a half times (a wing over wing right-hand roll).

Midway through the second roll (in the belly-up position), our airplane nosed down 60 degrees and began accelerating toward the earth at an average decent of about 45,000 feet per minute (the decent rate in the final moments apparently reached 76,000 feet per minute). At speeds believed to exceed 650 miles per hour, the aircraft broke the sound barrier—the first time in history a commercial airliner (other than the Concorde) had done so. Nothing the three-man cockpit crew frantically tried to do was working; they simply couldn't slow us down or get the nose up to regain the tri-jet's flight characteristics. In a last-ditch effort, Captain Hoot Gibson noticed First Officer Scott Kennedy's left hand on the landing gear lever and shouted something like, "yes, drop the gear!" to see whether that action would create enough drag to help slow down the still-diving, accelerating plane. Somewhere between 5,000 to 6,000 feet above ground, the welcomed rush of turbulence and drag created by the opening gear finally allowed the airplane's elevator to push the tail down, pitching the nose up. Flight recording instruments later revealed we pulled 5.5 g's (gravity forces) coming out of the dive. One report claimed we were just two seconds away from impact (the math actually works out to around four seconds). Except for the grace and mercies of Almighty God that night, it would have been an imbedding explosion, a fiery, life-instantly-ending-as-I-knew-it crash. It was, instead, 44 seconds of going down, straight down, in an airplane. And now the plane was flying again, with badly damaged landing gear and a constant pull to keep rolling over. (The mechanical culprit eventually proved to be the number seven leading edge slat—a two-foot by eight-foot flap-like device which is the third slat on the right wing. It somehow became (or remained) extended during midflight. One slat out of sync with the remaining seven caused slat asymmetry between the wings, and therefore the roll).

All 89 of us had just survived the longest recorded dive by a commercial jetliner in history in which the plane didn't hit the ground. But it wasn't over yet. Twenty pensive minutes later we were circling the Detroit airport. Other airplane traffic had already been cleared. Only the fire trucks and ambulances sat waiting for us, the eerie blood-colored glow of their heart-thumping emergency lights beckoning us to the grave yet one more time that night. "Upon impact..." were the very words a crew member used to begin training us for our emergency 'landing' in Detroit (how does 'impact' correlate to a 'landing'?).

The culprit number seven slat had torn off at some point during our dive or recovery. Now the airplane (without that slat) was trying to roll to the left. To keep us from a left-hand roll on his runway approach, Captain Gibson strained hard with full right aileron and rudder, and with full right trim. To maintain the airplane's lift in those same final few seconds (without the use of flaps), he touched down at a ground speed 40% faster than normal—on landing gear only the cockpit and ground crews didn't know whether it would hold.

A slightly harder bump, a little extra thump, some of the man-made bird's wounded metal skin scrapping the runway—but nothing too dramatic. A few passengers reported injuries. We walked away, everyone of us. *Praise the Lord!*

Author Information

Roger Peterson, Minneapolis, Minnesota, went on his first short-term mission with his home church to Haiti in 1980. He is one of five people who founded STEM Int'l (STEM Ministries) in 1984, serving as Executive Director. STEM specializes in training, sending, and leading 2-week short-term mission teams in partnership with churches, schools, and other organizations; and in training churches and other sending entities to do their own short-term mission; and in publishing and distributing quality short-term mission books and literature. As of December 2002, Roger has trained, led, or overseen 284 short-term mission teams (4,914 goer-guests) to more than a dozen nations, including 10/40 Window nations. He also serves as Chairman of the Board of Directors for FSTML (Fellowship of Short-Term Mission Leaders), the organization facilitating U.S. "Standards of Excellence in Short-Term Mission." Roger is the co-author of two other STEM*PRESS* publications (*Is Short-Term Mission Really Worth the Time and Money?*, and *Can Short-Term Mission Really Create Long-Term Career Missionaries?*), and a popular nationally-recognized speaker on short-term mission. He has been married to Melanie since 1993, and they have two children—Rachel age three, and Matthew age one. Roger is also a semi-professional musician.

For more information on STEM short-term teams, or other quality short-term mission publications: Teams@STEMmin.org *or* www.STEMmin.org
For more information on FSTML: www.FSTML.org
To schedule a speaking or training engagement: rpeterson@STEMmin.org

Wayne Sneed, Memphis, Tennessee, lived with his family in Iran during 1976–1977 where his dad was employed in a secular job. Wayne began his missions career in 1981 when he went with his home church on a short-term outreach to Mexico. He has been President of Orphanos Foundation since its inception in 1997. OF's three-fold strategy is to Give/Go/Pray for children in orphanage settings primarily in Latin America. OF provides grants for orphanage capital improvements. OF's 'Adventures in Love' short-term mission teams provide hands-on assistance. And OF's monthly prayer bulletin highlights specific orphans needing intercessory prayer. Wayne has participated in more than 50 short-term outreaches in 17 different nations during the past 20+ years. He, too, serves on the Board of Directors for FSTML (Treasurer). Wayne and his wife Angela have been married four years and now have their first child—Audrey Joy born just as this book went to press (March 2003). Wayne is a musician and worship leader.

For more information on OF's Adventures in Love short-term teams: www.orphanos.org
To schedule a speaking or training engagement: wsneed@orphanos.org

Gordon Aeschliman, Villanova, Pennsylvania, is a citizen of South Africa, born to missionary parents in Zululand. Gordon lived in South Africa until age 18, and has been an anti-apartheid activist ever since he witnessed first hand the ugly systemic racist treatment of South Africa's original citizens. Gordon created 'Potter's Clay' in 1977, a student service program that since annually hosts 500+ students from Southern California in Mexico. He also created 'World Christian Teams' from 1997–1990, an international cross-cultural exchange program that involved 3,700 students in 42 nations (six continents). Gordon was the founder and editor of *World Christian Magazine* from 1979–1990. He created *PRISM* magazine in 1993, a religious publication of culture and social justice. He created *Green Cross* magazine in 1994 for the Christian Society of the Green Cross. Gordon is the author of 12 books including *Global Trends* (IVP), *Apartheid: Tragedy in Black and White* (Regal), *Cages of Pain: Healing for Disillusioned Christians* (WORD), *The Hidden Half* (MARC), *Romancing the Globe* (IVP), *50 Ways You Can Help Save the Planet* (IVP), *and 101 Ways Your Church Can Reach the World* (Regal). Since 1993, Gordon has been President of Target Earth. Target Earth's mission (Serving the Earth, Serving the Poor) focuses on communities which live on less than a dollar a day where developmental issues result from an interaction of human poverty and destruction of the earth. Target Earth is committed to a global stewardship view that integrates justice, peace-building, and sustainable development. Gordon also serves as Director of the South Africa Community Fund he established in 1999 to address peace-building, earth-keeping, and faith in the post-Apartheid era. SACF has hosted hundreds of U.S. and Canadian students (from 25 Universities) in South Africa for an 8-week summer intensive. SACF also offers a semester-long program in Cape Town for students who want to study Peace Building. Gordon is also a musician and artist.

For more information on Target Earth: www.targetearth.org
For more information on the South Africa Community Fund: www.southafricacommunityfund.org
To schedule a speaking or training engagement: GordonAeschliman@aol.com

Ordering Information

Additional copies of *Maximum Impact Short-Term Mission* can be ordered from distributors of Christian mission books such as:
- William Carey Library (Pasadena CA)
- World Vision Publications/MARC (Monrovia CA)
- ACMC (Atlanta GA)
- YWAM's World Christian News & Books (Colorado Spring CO)
- International Resource Network (Christchurch, New Zealand)
- other re-sellers

Single or multiple copies can also be ordered directly from the publisher STEM*Press* (using check or major credit card) at:
- www.STEMmin.org (24/7)
- by calling toll-free within the United States: 1-877-STEM-min (M–F, 8:00AM–5:00PM U.S. Central Time)
- by e-mailing: STEMPress@STEMmin.org (24/7)
- by faxing: 952-996-1384 (24/7)
- by postal mail: STEMPress, Box 386001, Minneapolis MN 55438

Re-Sellers and Other Distributors:
Contact MISTMbook@STEMmin.org for case lot discounts and STEM*Press* re-sell/return policies.

Churches, Agencies, Schools, and Other Sending Entity Organizations:
If you will be using *Maximum Impact Short-Term Mission* to train your staff and team leaders (your 'goer-guest leaders'), contact MISTMbook@STEMmin.org for case lot discounts. (You must agree not to re-sell the books for a profit.)

Mission Professors and Instructors/Teachers in other Training Institutions:
If you will be using *Maximum Impact Short-Term Mission* as a classroom text, contact MISTMbook@STEMmin.org for case lot discounts.

For other short-term mission resources
("how-to" manuals, other publisher's books, training videos, etc.)
visit:

www.STEMmin.org

and click on the "STEMPress: Order Mission Resources" button.

This secure website offers discounts
and accepts most major credit cards.